Jewish Responses to Modernity

REAPPRAISALS IN JEWISH SOCIAL
AND INTELLECTUAL HISTORY

General Editor: Robert M. Seltzer

*Martin Buber's Social and Religious Thought:
Alienation and the Quest for Meaning*
LAURENCE J. SILBERSTEIN

The American Judaism of Mordecai M. Kaplan
EDITED BY EMANUEL S. GOLDSMITH, MEL SCULT,
AND ROBERT M. SELTZER

On Socialists and "the Jewish Question" after Marx
JACK JACOBS

Easter in Kishinev: Anatomy of a Pogrom
EDWARD H. JUDGE

*Jewish Responses to Modernity:
New Voices in America and Eastern Europe*
ELI LEDERHENDLER

ELI LEDERHENDLER

JEWISH RESPONSES TO MODERNITY

New Voices in America and Eastern Europe

NEW YORK UNIVERSITY PRESS

NEW YORK & LONDON

"Guides for the Perplexed" was first published in MODERN JUDAISM 11 (3): 321–41, 1991. Reprinted by permission of The Johns Hopkins University Press.

"Against the Tide" was first published in the AJS REVIEW XVII, no. 1 (Spring 1992): 51–82. Reprinted with the permission of the Association for Jewish Studies.

"Interpreting Messianic Rhetoric in the Russian *Haskalah* and Early Zionism" was first published in STUDIES IN CONTEMPORARY JEWRY: AN ANNUAL, Vol. VII: JEWS AND MESSIANISM IN THE MODERN ERA: METAPHOR AND MEANING, edited by Jonathan Frankel, 14–33. Copyright © 1991 by Oxford University Press, Inc. Reprinted by permission.

NEW YORK UNIVERSITY PRESS
New York and London

Library of Congress Cataloging-in-Publication Data
Lederhendler, Eli.
Jewish response to modernity : new voices in America and Eastern
Europe / Eli Lederhendler.
p.   cm.
Includes bibliographical references and index.
ISBN 0-8147-5084-2 (alk. paper)
1. Jews—Europe, Eastern—Civilization.   2. Jews—Europe, Eastern—
Politics and government.   3. Europe, Eastern—Ethnic relations.
4. Jews—United States—Civilization.   5. Jews—United States—
Politics and government.   6. United States—Ethnic relations.
7. Immigrants—United States—Intellectual life.   8. Immigrants—
United States—Political activitiy.   9. Judaism—History—Modern
period, 1750–   I. Title.
DS135.E83L33 1994   94-2486
947'.004924—dc20   CIP

New York University Press books are printed on acid-free paper,
and their binding materials are chosen for strength and durability.

Manufactured in the United States of America

10 9 8 7 6 5 4 3 2 1

ספר זה מוקדש

לזכר אבי-מורי אהוב נפשי משה לדרהנדלר ז״ל

Contents

Jewish Responses to Modernity

Introduction

The texts and studies in this book deal with Jewish responses to modernity, both in America and Eastern Europe. They explore a realm that exists in the interstices between social, cultural, and political history. Having devoted a monographic study to the analysis of Jewish political development in Eastern Europe up to 1881, I was persuaded that a semiotics of Jewish politics existed that merited further exploration, and that the culture and rhetoric of the Jewish adjustment to modernity were profoundly linked to political issues.

This book does not present an integrated narrative account of Jewish society and culture in the nineteenth and twentieth centuries. Rather, I think of the essays and texts included here as "pictures at an exhibition," whose thematic unity and overall statement to the viewer is cumulative, as one moves from chapter to chapter. That statement, put into simple form, runs as follows: there is a *culture of modernity* to which social, political, literary, and linguistic issues are all related. Moreover, the nexus between culture and politics, as it may be seen in the Eastern European context, was relevant to the Jewish experience in America as well. Here, the key motif is the ripple effect, or afterlife, if you will, of the Haskalah, the Jewish Enlightenment (late eighteenth to nineteenth century), which is discernible in all the texts and topics addressed in this book. That continuity exists even where the impact of Haskalah was negative—that is, where it elicited mainly an opposing reaction or counter-ripple.

Culture and politics may, of course, be studied separately. In real life, however, such laboratory conditions do not obtain; compartmentalization is, therefore, necessarily arbitrary. Politics and culture are both aspects of social interaction and they are experienced in tandem, like space and time.

The substantive categories of politics (power, control, conflict) and the categories of culture (language, community, the possibility of art) are certainly *distinct* from one another; but they represent *intersecting* dimensions of human experience. The common spheres of discourse include gender, class, religion, and nation. We are also familiar with such hybrid concepts as ideology, civil religion, political culture, public opinion, and "the media." The study of history, myth and folklore, linguistics, jurisprudence, and philosophy have been bound up (to one extent or another) with political structures and attitudes, ever since the rise of the nation-state. The geographic boundaries that demarcate political units also unite, combine, or divide cultural units.

As a corollary, it may be said that all minority (or colonized) cultures are inherently politicized, and majority (or imperial) cultures enjoy the patronage and other structural advantages afforded by the state. When members of a minority culture adjust to the dominant culture of a state, the process inevitably has a political aspect, whether the minority blends into the majority or whether it emphasizes its own group boundaries and loyalties even while acculturating.

Migration across national boundaries is another factor, one that introduces flux and destabilization, in the relationship between politics and culture: As newcomers confront and mix with an established population, the lives of all of them may change.

If politics pervades the cultural life of social groups, culture may also be said to be a profound influence on politics. Attachments to a religious worldview and traditions, to a mother tongue, or to a particular lifestyle predispose people to react in particular ways to government, political parties, or proposals for concerted action in matters related to public policy. Religious skepticism may undermine the normative structures of an entire society or a part thereof. Attitudes of a conservative nature in matters related to family, education, and sexual behavior have their political correlates, as do their opposite counterparts. "Advanced" technological societies interact with "underdeveloped" ones, affecting the self-image and

the aspirations of people on both sides, and producing unantici-
pated, long-term effects on both cultural and political structures.

The value of addressing such issues in the round lies in the
fact that one may better be able to understand complex social
phenomena. Just such phenomena are what we find in the modern
history of the Jewish people: normative religious patterns and institutions alongside reformation and "freethinking" rebellion; immigration from agrarian, underdeveloped lands to highly developed,
urban industrial societies; minority cultural survival, adaptation,
and acculturation; and various ideological formulations, including
forms of nationalism and socialism.

Naturally, no one can hope to deal with all of these aspects
adequately (or even one of them) in a single book. But in more
modest terms, specific case studies may offer insight into some of
these dynamic processes. Out of the diversity of particular settings,
personalities, and issues, certain commonalities might be discerned.

The first chapter, "Language, Culture, and Politics," presents a
general thesis regarding the historical interconnection between
these three elements in the modern Jewish experience. It also introduces the subject of migration as a problem in cultural transmission
and the subject of language as a central axis in Jewish cultural
politics and political culture. The succeeding chapters take up these
themes by presenting a series of texts, each of which constitutes
one type of response to modernity within Jewish society.

Traditionalism and modernism (or preservation and innovation)
are antithetical strategies adopted vis-à-vis modernity, and they are
expressed in distinct cultural idioms. The words and languages used
in the pursuit of either the one or the other strategy are keys to
understanding political-ideological choices, methods of adaptation
and legitimation (or subversion), and the limitation or expansion
of options in the life of a collective community. The case studies
and texts presented in the rest of the volume deal in some way with
the relationship between the rhetorical medium and the cultural-
political message.

The second chapter, on the use of messianic rhetoric in early
Jewish nationalism in Eastern Europe, illustrates the overall concept of rhetoric as a political and cultural code. The chapter deals
with the problem of cultural legitimation that faced a modern,

secularized nationalist intelligentsia which sought a broader constituency. They needed to persuade their readers that nationalist
ideology was a natural extension of traditional Judaism, while at
the same time they were asserting that traditional Judaism could
no longer provide sufficient answers to the sociopolitical needs of
the Jewish people. The study, therefore, reveals the rhetorical re-
formulation of traditional concepts in the service of a modern political worldview.

The next chapter presents an autobiographical text from the late
nineteenth century. The excerpts from this unpublished manuscript
illustrate one young man's odyssey in search of a proper understanding of the modern world and of his place in it as a Jew. The acquisition of languages looms large in this account of youthful rebellion.
Moreover, the memoir illustrates—on the individual level—a process of social and cultural differentiation that lies at the heart of
the Jewish response to modernity. In concrete terms, it provides an
insight into the crisis of authority that affected traditional Jewish
society at the time, the proliferation of ideological options, and
the personal factors that led some Jews to a positive espousal of
sociocultural change. In short, it contributes to our understanding
of secularization in its Jewish habitat.

The fourth chapter delves into the question of how the culture
of traditionalism was intertwined with a political posture and a
rudimentary political opinion in Poland and Russia in the pre-1914
period. The texts and documents presented describe the predicament of Orthodox communal leaders, who faced critical social and
political issues on almost every front: in their relations with the
Russian authorities, in confrontation with religious deviance and
political dissidence within the Jewish population, and even inter-
nally, in the relations between different subgroups among the Orthodox traditionalists. These were Jews who assessed all novelty
and innovation negatively, but did not simply withdraw from the
fray. Theirs was, in fact, an alternative response to modernity.

It is noteworthy, too, that the theme of emigration is alluded to
in the three sets of texts taken from the East European milieu. The
nationalists wrestled with the idea of mass settlement of Jews in
Palestine as a social program for modernization; the memoir speaks
of the departure of young men for the West; and the rabbinical

letters address aspects of social dislocation and communal turmoil that were both causes and effects of mass Jewish emigration. The references to emigration provide the historical "bridge" to the American case studies in the chapters that follow.

The three selections concerning the New World all relate in different ways to the problem of Americanization: the adaptation of an immigrant minority to a majority culture and social system. The transformation involved not merely linguistic acculturation, but a wider range of value-adaptations. It was a process that was heavily influenced both by the American political culture and by East European Jewish ideologies. The key concept involved in Americanization—the redefinition of national affiliation—entailed issues of self-definition for those who chose to maintain their minority-group distinctiveness while making the most of opportunities for integration. The cultivation of that delicate balance was charged with political implications not only for the Jews themselves, but also for American society, which (then as now) was grappling with fundamental questions of national identity, immigration policy, and multiculturalism. Jewish techniques of Americanization that evolved in the era of mass immigration (1881–1924), and strategies of minority-culture persistence that were deployed in the interwar period, were worked out in creative tension with the majority culture and with the European culture of origin.

The earlier, European stratum of the Haskalah—Enlightenment—and its offshoots (Hebraism, Yiddishism, nationalism, religious reform) may be discerned throughout, because the Haskalah and its rhetoric were a venture in self-transformation in response to modernity. Herein lies the hard core of continuity between nineteenth-century Eastern Europe and early to mid-twentieth-century America.

Something else is involved, however, in coupling East European subjects with American ones. A continuum is created that raises substantive historiographical issues. The history of American Jewry can be legitimately studied with reference to two different contexts: first American society (in which the Jews figure as one among many ethnic or religious groups), and second the interface between the immigrant community and its "mother" society in Europe. Implicit in the progression of topics chosen for this volume is the adoption of the latter option. The interplay of language, culture, migration, and ideology within one, integrated Euro-American conceptual framework is what forms the overarching scheme or "agenda" of the book.

What is implied, therefore, is a phenomenological unity (or at least an overlap) of the significant cultural-political confrontations in East European and American Jewry. These are the confrontations between traditionalism and secularization, parochialism and cosmopolitanism, rebellion and accommodation, alienation and the search for new reintegrative formulas. These confrontations are not, in fact, limited to the East European or American historical settings, and they do have wider cross-cultural implications. But in the cases before us, comparisons are relatively simple, given the similar base population. Only the venue and the time frame are somewhat shifted.

That does not diminish the considerable and obvious disparities between the East European context and the American one. But I would argue that the comparison remains valid, as long as the significant distinctions are never disregarded. The key concept is comparability, not complete equatability. The types of issues raised by the encounter with modernity—bearing upon ethnic or national affiliation, language choice, and the relative merits of religious continuity and change—seem to be common to the "new" and the "old" worlds.

The experiences of Hebrew writers confronting American language and culture in the 1930s and 1940s may, for example, seem far removed from the experience of a Jewish teenager in fin-de-siècle Poland, confronting Russian and German as well as modern Hebrew literature and nationalist ideology. Both are, nonetheless, related to common issues of cultural and political identification, the elaboration of rationales for minority-group survival, "coming of age" amid the confusion of new social and ideological options, and individual versus collective concerns.

Moreover, the juxtaposition of East European and American Jewish examples of "responses to modernity" is intended to underscore the idea that "old world" culture was *a conduit for modernity*, not merely a repository of premodern values and preurban structures in what nostalgia-seekers might think of as a simpler time. Such a simplistic view is quite out of keeping with historical realities. East European paradigms—and especially, the creative utilization of those paradigms and resources by American Jews—were not only relevant to the American Jewish experience in the immigration period, but also, I would argue, retain lasting validity for any serious project in ethnocultural survival in the present.

A word about the *New Voices* in the title. The "new" quality refers to the newness of modernity, against the backdrop of the historical past. As for "voices," with the exception of chapter 1's overview on "Language, Culture, and Politics," the material gathered here includes a great deal of directly quoted text or actual primary sources. These speak in the authentic "voices" of participants and contemporaries. Because language, rhetoric, and culture form the thematic backbone of this volume, the "voices" and texts are centrally important, not merely illustrative.

Finally, I wish to express my thanks to a number of people. My grateful appreciation, first of all, to Robert M. Seltzer, editor of the Reappraisals series, and to Niko Pfund, editor-in-chief at New York University Press, as well as to Despina Papazoglou Gimbel and Jennifer Hammer, for their professional and expeditious handling of the publication process.

Parts of this book were read in manuscript by Sidra Dekoven Ezrahi, Jonathan Frankel, David G. Roskies, and Steven J. Zipperstein, all of whom I want to thank for their comments and suggestions. (Naturally, all flaws and errors in the essays remain solely my own responsibility.)

My mother, Bluma, remains, as ever, the one who inspired me to be a Jewish educator. There are no adequate means of thanking her for that, but there is the knowledge of the kinds of satisfactions that we share.

This book is dedicated to the memory of my late father, Moyshe, who was in so many ways a living example to me of the modern East European Jewish heritage, both cultural and political. His recent passing has left a void in my life, but throughout this difficult period I was able to count upon the moral support and love offered by close friends and family. My heartfelt gratitude, therefore, is due to my children, Adina and Aryeh; my wife, Amy, and her family—who have been my family for twenty years—Roz and Mel Levin, Eric Levin, Gladys and Alan Schwartz; my brother-in-law, Alex Sela; and to Mark and Ora Kiel, Terry Toll, David Roskies, and other friends, both near and far.

CHAPTER I

Language, Culture, and Politics

> But the most noble and profitable invention of all other, was that of SPEECH, consisting of *Names* or *Appellations*, and their Connexion; whereby men register their Thoughts; recall them when they are past; and also declare them one to another for mutuall utility and conversation; without which, there had been amongst men, neither Common-wealth, nor Society, nor Contract, nor Peace.
> —Thomas Hobbes, *Leviathan*, Part I, chap. 4

The political life of Jewish communities in modern times was woven from various threads: the collapse of old regimes and the rise of new ones; the demands of inclusion and exclusion posed by modern nation-states; processes of adaptation to developing and industrial economies; migration and the encounter of East and West—all of which prompted Jews to choose between competing survival strategies. Among the chief preoccupations in modern Jewish politics have been the invention of social and political models to replace the premodern Jewish *kehilla*, and the renegotiation of the terms of interaction between Jews and non-Jews.

Precisely for those reasons, a cluster of related issues arose regarding the cultural orientation of particular Jewries, language choice, and religious reform. The birth of modern Jewish politics is intertwined with the great cultural and intellectual ferment that stirred Western Jewries from the seventeenth and eighteenth centuries onward, and East European and American Jewry from the nineteenth. In modern Jewish history we encounter a politics of language and culture that has profoundly affected modern Judaism.

The politicization of Jewish education—the refashioning of the

9

Jewish school as a tool of socialization for the modern state or, alternatively, for Jewish political groups—is a case in point. Issues of curriculum and language of instruction in primary schools were not the only bones of political contention in this sphere. Professional education (such as rabbinical training) and the academic study of Judaism were similarly inseparable from political considerations, because governments or power elites frequently imposed standards of licensing and control over clergy and restricted Jews' access to some academic professions.

It is no accident that figures like Moses Mendelssohn, Naftali Herz Wessely, and Joseph Perl stand at the dawn of both Jewish Enlightenment culture and Jewish Enlightenment politics. Leadership in one area went hand in hand with leadership in the other. The history of our great political clashes—such as that between Ahad Ha'am and Herzl, or between Brandeis and Weizmann—can be written as the story of a *Kulturkampf.* Just as easily, we can take major cultural figures—such as Peretz, Sholem Aleichem, Bialik, and Dubnov—and read them as political spokesmen.

Language choice, as a Jewish issue, also clearly demonstrates the nexus between the "Jewish question," in all its diverse forms, and questions of cultural orientation. Partisans of Hebrew, Yiddish, Polish, Russian, or German, respectively, were apt to find themselves on opposing sides of the barricades. In choosing a language, one chose also a political program, a constituency, allies and opponents. Criteria of political correctness were applied to language, and (in true Romantic spirit) languages became powerful mythic symbols. Socialists and Zionists, nationalists and integrationists all concurred that it was imperative to choose one language over all others.

This peculiarly modern compulsion arose from the need to take an unequivocal *political* position: for or against the "masses"; for or against national self-determination; for or against accommodation with and assimilation to the majority society; for or against regional separatism, and so on. While it is conceivable to maintain a bilingual or multilingual culture, it is much more problematic to maintain two opposing political philosophies. Thus, when language and culture became entangled with politics, choices became necessary.

In this way, fundamentally extrinsic criteria were used to invest language with quasi-metaphysical attributes, determining that one language was ostensibly "obscurantist," while another was "progressive"; one, cosmopolitan and civilized, while others were parochial; one classical and national in spirit, while others were alien; one aesthetically perfect, while its rival was a "mongrel tongue."

Rather than dismiss such ideas as simplistic, specious, and downright silly, we ought to see them as manifestations of serious political concerns.[1] Language and culture could provide a basis for political legitimation: the outstanding example is the Bund, which in its early years relied on Yiddish to provide its raison d'être as a separate party within Russian Social Democracy. At the same time, political correctness could determine linguistic orientation. Indeed, there were writers who changed their medium as their politics shifted: Abramovitch (from Hebrew to Yiddish) and Peretz (from Polish to Yiddish) come easily to mind.

The engagé intellectual or writer is a well-known phenomenon of modern culture, whether in Europe or in what used to be called the "Third World." The Jews are, in this respect as in so many others, "just like everyone else, only more so." That is because Jewish intellectual and political development has taken place in such varied settings: both in nation-states and in multinational empires; both in long-established, native-born communities and in migrant populations; both outside and inside a territorial homeland. As a result, cultural and linguistic choices, as well as political-ideological choices, were multiplied, and the nexus between language, culture, and politics has been that much "thicker" or multilayered, where the Jews are concerned.

Whereas intellectual and political elites of many countries have wrestled with the dilemmas of secularization versus traditionalism, with left versus right, with religious and racial bias, with colonialism versus independence or reunification, with local-language-loyalty[2] versus a national, imperial, or cosmopolitan lingua franca, modern Jewish elites wrestled simultaneously with more of the above, and over a longer period of time, than most others. It is now two hundred years and more since the onset of the great Jewish language wars, first associated with the Haskalah in Central Europe.

For much of that period, the politicians, diplomats, and states-men of the Jewish people were challenged by a rising class of writ-ers, scholars, journalists, rabbis, and philosophers who made poli-tics their avocation. The Jewish nationalist movements, in particular, were led by such figures, and their politics were essen-tially the politics of a counterculture. Language, education, litera-ture, modes of dress, religious behavior, women's participation in public and cultural affairs—these became the characteristic weap-ons of strife between political camps in the Jewish community, even when other means (power, money, influence) continued to be primary in external relations. Indeed, in a wry comment on the Jewish penchant for focusing on rhetoric and argumentation in so many circumstances, including political affairs, one historian has called the Jews "drunk with the use of language," and jibed that "Jewish power is usually the power of words rather than of ac-tion."[3] While this may be something of a deliberate exaggeration, it correctly underscores the linkage between political culture and the whole realm of language and culture as such.

That language choice should have become so vexed an issue becomes understandable within this broader context. Clearly, the politics of culture dictated the seriousness with which this topic was invested, not the other way around: that is, it was not normally language preference that determined one's politics, for language was subordinate to political concerns, just as the symbolic values attached to language, as noted, usually derived from political no-tions.

In order to better assess this language-politics nexus, I would like to propose a set of typological categories. These categories fall into two sets of distinctions: first, the distinction between language loy-alty, language expediency, and language chauvinism, all of which we encounter as Jewish language policies; second, the distinction between two types of sociolinguistic settings: migrant communities, on the one hand, and second-generation or native-born communi-ties, on the other.

"Language loyalty" covers those instances in which a given lan-guage is thought to retain ideological significance, at least for some social functions, despite adverse conditions for its development. ("Loyalty" implies a conscious commitment, one that is necessary only when language cannot be taken for granted as part of the social landscape.) Within a given sociopolitical program, this kind of language policy can become an article of faith. Language loyalty itself is felt to be conducive to or necessary for the fulfillment of ideological goals. Into this category I would place the following historical examples:

- Zionist settlers in early twentieth-century Palestine, whose insistence on Hebrew as the language of daily commerce and education was based on an a priori ideological commitment to cultural modernization and to nation-building, not on objective social needs;
- Hebrew writers in America, of whom there were over a hundred in the 1930s,[4] who staffed so many positions in the field of Jewish education in the United States and Canada, and who continued to write and publish Hebrew essays, poems, and fiction in their own cultural-Zionist periodicals, despite the lack of a significant readership;
- postwar Yiddishists and refugee enclaves in North America since the 1940s who, like their Hebraist counterparts earlier, made a point of language loyalty in the face of the cultural dominance of English, whether for political, religious, or other ideological reasons;
- Yiddish writers, cultural figures and educators under the Soviet regime who continued to work in and to promote the use, development, and study of Yiddish despite a gradual but overwhelming drift in favor of Russian as the spoken language of much of the Jewish population, and despite repressive manipulation by the regime. (To be sure, it was the regime itself that officially sponsored the non-Russian nationalities' linguistic and cultural media and activities, often reducing nationality culture to language-use as such, and to that extent gave limited and strictly supervised license to the maintenance of Yiddish.)[5]
- Orthodox and Conservative rabbinical and lay leaderships in the United States (and, to some extent, the Reform rabbinate in more recent decades), who have maintained the ritual and liturgical use of Hebrew texts, and therefore also championed Hebrew-language education, in otherwise non-Hebrew-speaking settings.[6]

Though verbalized in terms of preserving traditional religious values, the choice made in favor of particularism and, by extension, in favor of some degree of self-marginalization, has significant social ramifications. I will return to this example later, when dealing with the question of language policy in second-generation or native-born Jewish communities.

All of these examples reflect programmatic loyalty to a language and its use in at least some social contexts, growing out of a particular social, religious, or political worldview. Indeed, such language loyalty forms a significant part of the substance of those worldviews. It is not a policy that exists in isolation, but rather is correlated with other behaviors, preferences, and objective factors—such as religious practices, intensive investment of the self in an ethnic-subcommunity, country of immigration, governmental or other external pressures—that render language choice ideologically meaningful and consistent. Take, for example, one of the ideologues of the Yiddishist nationalist trend, Chaim Zhitlowsky, who situated his Yiddishism squarely within a broadly conceived program for national-cultural particularism, in a multicultural America:

> We contend that our national cultural existence [in America] will be built on the foundation of the Yiddish language. Through Yiddish we will preserve all the significant cultural treasures of universal culture as well as our own rich Hebrew heritage. We will educate our children in this language. . . . [W]e need a power capable of binding all Jews into one entity while allowing each the freedom of decisions, beliefs, hopes and actions. . . . Such a spiritual power can only be the Yiddish language.[7]

While this was clearly a holistic political-cultural faith, in fact language loyalists need not necessarily use the particular language in all circumstances; but one *must* use it whenever *not* to do so would violate ideological norms.

The obverse of this type of language policy is what we may call "language expediency." This refers to a policy that places other ideological or tactical goals first, and language-choice goals a distant second, if at all. This linguistic pragmatism will foster an adaptation to existing conditions and norms in a given target population, rather than sacrifice political influence.

One classic example is the decision by Russian Jewish radical intellectuals in the 1880s and early 1890s, first in New York and then in Vilna, to use Yiddish rather than Russian in order to reach Jewish workers with the socialist message. In the history of the Bund, this shift was associated with the move from intensive training of small Marxist cells—an activity known as "propaganda"— to a broader-based popular appeal, with the emphasis on a few key ideas broadcast to a mass audience—an approach called "agitation."[8] The new political tactics dictated a new type of communication, tailored to the needs of the majority of Jewish workers rather than to the Russian-educated elite: hence, the expediency of choosing Yiddish as the main language of activity. In later years, of course, the Bund would use both Russian and Polish extensively in its activities and publications whenever it addressed itself to non-Yiddish-speaking sympathizers, thus exhibiting once again the kind of flexibility that its tactics required.

Strikingly similar is the example of the Zionist movement in diaspora countries. Throughout the Diaspora, the World Zionist Organization and its affiliates ran their congresses, administration, press, and other activities in every major language spoken by their constituencies. The choice of German, Yiddish, Polish, Russian, English, and so on, was made for good objective reasons that set aside any ideological commitments to Hebrew.[9] Imagine the dramatic difference in the history of Zionism had the movement not opted for Yiddish in dealing with its East European Jewish backers, whether in Europe or America,[10] and had it not used the local language of each country as well, with a view toward winning sympathy from non-Jews and from the growing population of non-Yiddish-speaking Jews!

Sometimes, however, the line between language expediency and language loyalty was blurred. Dyed-in-the-wool Hebraists, Yiddishists, or proponents of any other monolingual cultural agenda could (and often did) find a niche within an ideological group that was, on the whole, more pragmatic. Those active on the education front, for example, were often more committed to purist cultural positions than those engaged in political activity per se. Largely through their efforts, particular movements came to be identified with certain cultural profiles—each with a characteristic linguistic trademark:

Yiddish, for the Bund, and Hebrew, for the Zionist movements in Palestine.

When language loyalty gave way to language chauvinism, the politics of language seemed to take on a life of its own. In extreme cases, aggressive campaigns were waged against the rival language: the anti-Hebrew crusade of pro-Yiddish communist officials in the Soviet Union in the 1920s, for instance, or anti-Yiddish and anti-German manifestations in interwar Palestine. Nevertheless, it was not the intrinsic qualities of the linguistic medium as a means of communication that explain this sort of militant behavior; rather, it was the extrinsic political-programmatic principle involved. To the anti-Hebraists of the Evsektsiia, for example, Hebrew represented "obscurantist," clericalist, Zionist, and bourgeois values, all of which were considered counterrevolutionary and, as such, to be combatted.[11]

Moving on to the other major distinction regarding the politics of language—namely, the distinction in context between migrant and settled communities—it is possible to further subdivide the experience of migrant communities between two phases. "Phase one" communities, formed by recent immigrants, maintain their native language; in "phase two," immigrant communities use both their native tongue and the language of the new country.

Thus, in the mass Jewish migration to the West, the entire spectrum of East European immigrant Jewish politics was represented by a range of newspapers, journals, schools, trade unions, mass rallies, and other activities and institutions in a single language—Yiddish. That was true for the labor-oriented, radical, anarchist, Zionist, and Orthodox alike. Language expediency was dictated by the social context of immigrant society, where the universal medium of communication was the immigrants' native tongue.[12] Moreover, in terms of twentieth-century Jewish politics, the universal use of Yiddish helped to preserve organizational links to analogous groups in other countries: throughout Eastern Europe, first of all, and elsewhere in the East European Jewish archipelago. As David Roskies puts it, "In the absence of a state or a single geographical base, [Yiddish] encompassed the whole of the modern Jewish dispersion. For a time, even Berlin and Paris were Yiddish cultural centers."[13]

Yet, in retrospect this was clearly a transitional phase. In the second phase, as Roskies himself points out: "As a bridge to modernity and to the New World, Yiddish was rendered superfluous. Who needed the bridge once they had arrived?"[14] The processes of acculturation that affected Jewish immigrant communities in the West—noticeable even by the turn of the twentieth century in some quarters, and hastened by the coming of age of a second generation—necessitated a bilingual policy, based on the very same criteria of language expediency that were at work earlier in favor of Yiddish.

The growing use of English, French, and Spanish by transplanted East European Jews in North America, England, France, and Latin America, respectively, enhanced several elements in their political life: First, it helped foster cooperation with like-minded groups belonging to other immigrant nationalities. This was of vital importance to the labor movement, in particular. Second, it allowed immigrant Jews to emphasize their commitment and patriotic attachment to their adopted country—a definite plus in the era just preceding, during, and after the First World War, characterized as it was by racism, suspicion of aliens, antiradical and anti-immigration sentiment. Not only the overtly political groups, but also the large immigrant-aid organizations, such as HIAS (Hebrew Immigrant Aid Society), found it necessary to engage in intensive public relations activities of this sort.[15] Third, the use of the new language made it easier for members of the immigrant Jewish community to participate in local and national politics, to win elective office, and to contend with the established, native-born Jewish leadership for power and influence on a more equal footing. Finally, it allowed for some "crossover" to occur when native-born figures assumed leadership roles in organizations and institutions whose rank and file were composed largely of immigrants—one thinks of Louis Brandeis, Stephen Wise, and Judah Magnes in connection with labor relations in the New York garment industry, the American Zionist movement, the New York Kehillah, the campaigns for an American Jewish Congress, and the anti-German boycott.[16]

The political implications and uses of language played out somewhat differently when the social context was that of a settled, native-born population. In such communities, whether in Eastern Europe or the West, the issue of language choice arose within the broader question of how Jews should interact with the non-Jewish majorities around them. Opting for the language of the majority implied a host of other social and political considerations that, in the nineteenth and early twentieth centuries, were linked with the politics of emancipation.

All modern cases of adoption by Jews of the local majority language were conditioned on the peculiarly modern political situation of emancipation or pre-emancipation. That is what distinguishes this pattern of language adoption from the more typical medieval Jewish pattern of Hebraization and Judaization—that is, the creation of a specifically *Jewish* version of the local language, usually using the Hebrew alphabet—which gave us Judeo-Arabic, Yiddish, and Ladino, among others. These languages gave the Jews a linguistic bridge to the majority culture, but also made sense only where Jewish society existed as a separate entity. The logic of emancipation politics, however, rendered this pattern obsolete by eliminating the legal, and some sociocultural, barriers between Jews and non-Jews.[17]

The politically conditioned background of language choice is especially clear for areas where rival or antagonistic political elites and ethnic cultures confronted one another, with the Jews caught in the middle. For Jews, the choice of Polish over Russian, or German over Polish, or Hungarian over German made sense only in terms of the extrinsic criteria of political interests and political loyalties. The classic case in this regard is that of Bohemian Jewry, which first adopted German but later, under the impact of Czech nationalist politics, switched their linguistic allegiance to Czech.[18]

In these instances, much more was involved than language expediency; for, where the choice of language was merely pragmatic, one did not attach positive cultural value to the medium so much as to the message: the primacy of getting the point across outweighed ideological considerations of language loyalty. But where the adoption of a non-Jewish majority language resulted in a major shift in cultural orientation, language choice represented a complex stance vis-à-vis the majority society, so that the medium *was* the message: it indicated a desire for change in civil and class status, for political and cultural participation, and for social interaction.

This, then, was programmatic language loyalty of a different sort: it involved a process of internalizing the cultural norms of the majority, to such an extent that those norms became vital to the functioning of Jewish society and culture, too. This is what lay behind the maintenance of German even in overseas German Jewish synagogues and religious schools—for example, in nineteenth-century America—sometimes long after expediency dictated a switch to English. I would cite here the case of Rabbi David Einhorn, who immigrated to America but wrote and preached exclusively in German. In his valedictory sermon, he declared:

> Germany is my home. I am an *ivri*, a wanderer, and I journeyed with thousands of my brethren from there to this God blessed republic! As proud as I am of my adopted citizenship . . . I will never forget that the old home is the land of thinkers, presently the foremost land of culture, and above all the land of Mendelssohn, the birthplace of Reform Judaism. . . . If you sever from Reform the German spirit or— what amounts to the same thing—the German language, you will have torn it from its native soil and the lovely flower must wilt.[19]

The internalization process in the mother country had gone so deep that it was transportable, and the linguistic *Geist* thus internalized could become virtually synonymous with Jewishness itself.

This case and others clearly show that to label the adoption of majority languages as "assimilationist" is simplistic. Hungarian-speaking Satmar hasidim patently do not fall under the "assimilationist" rubric; neither do German-speaking neo-Orthodox Jews; nor do a host of other Jewish subgroups in modern history that were French-, English-, Polish-, Hungarian-, Italian-, or Arabic-speaking. Adoption of a majority language *may* be assimilationist in either intent or effect—where language choice is parleyed into far-reaching social integration; but, alternatively, it may signify a preference for mutual understanding and, hopefully, tolerance, without at the same time prompting a break with group attachments; and, finally, it may simply be situational, rather than political: a function, not of ideology, but of the degree to which Jewish-gentile interaction is or is not a pervasive aspect of daily life.

The other option for a settled, native Jewry is to adopt the language of the majority only minimally and simultaneously to maintain its own minority language. One may say that this was the solution that characterized East European Jewry up to and right through the transition from a traditional to a post-traditional society. This is the reality that confronted such political groups as the socialist Jewish intelligentsia and the nascent Zionist groups at the end of the nineteenth century, forcing them to adopt policies of language expediency in favor of Yiddish.

Quite different, however, are the cases in which the majority language is adopted for most social purposes, while the minority language is maintained solely for specified—usually religious—functions. I would return, here, to the instance of American Orthodox and, to an extent, Conservative and also some Reform Jews, who prefer some degree of language loyalty, with respect to Hebrew, over the wholesale translation of liturgy and ritual into English. This is a phenomenon that characterizes a population heavily made up of second- and third-generation Americans and, therefore, is not quite in the same category with immigrant populations, either socially or politically. What, then, explains this language policy and what does it imply in terms of the politics of culture?

I suggested earlier that this option involves an ideological preference for some degree of marginality. It is of a piece with other such preferences, such as the preference for endogamy or conversionary marriage over intermarriage—still upheld in principle, even if less adhered to in practice than in generations past.

Self-marginalization is a social statement about the right to be not just different—after all, there are many differences that divide us without significant social consequences—but the right to go out of one's way not to conform to the majority. That is a difference with a distinction. By extension, it is also a political statement about the kind of social order required in order to make it possible to exercise this right at minimal cost in terms of physical security, economic opportunity, and participation in the political system.[20]

Self-marginalization through minority cultural and language maintenance may even be cost-effective from the political point of view. Here, I have in mind the way in which American Jews have created an enviable network of political action and support groups. Mobilization into such organized networks and PACs (political action committees) may be, as some have contended, a sign of thorough integration into the American political system—indicating that Jews feel completely at home in asking their representatives to be responsive and accountable to their constituents.[21] Alternatively, it may be an example of the fact that ethnic political mobilization as such is now more an accepted part of the American political system.

Be that as it may, a minority that voluntarily affirms its particularist *cultural* agenda may be better able to identify with a particularist *political* agenda and—when conditions are otherwise favorable—may be more willing to go out on a limb in defense of its interests.

Of course, with the exception of a tiny percentage of the whole, most of American Jewry limits its cultural self-marginalization to certain spheres, making sure that in most walks of life Jews are able to reap all the benefits of integration. Though retention of their own minority language may be a useful tool for group preservation, it is the majority language that pervades Jewish social, cultural, and intellectual life. The minority language is therefore not a vernacular, but assigned a very specific and limited role. The political logic of emancipation and integration continues to impose cultural and linguistic choices.[22]

The nexus between politics, language, and culture is as much a part of Jewish life today as it has been throughout modern Jewish history. You have only to scratch the surface of the politics of Jewish culture, in any language, to discover the Jewish political culture. Jewish politics is *not* just about the power of words— there is action, too—but words represent the meanings we wish our actions to convey. Politics and culture are both social constructions through which people define and regulate their interaction with others, and through which they create a normative interpretation of their environment. Politics and culture are, thus, both creative enterprises, and they intersect wherever people refuse to take the human condition for granted.

In the next chapter, we will look more directly at a specific historical example of how political meaning is conveyed through the encoded normative culture of a society. The example chosen derives from the second half of the nineteenth century, when Russian Jewish intellectuals were seeking to establish a new political rhetoric to suit their cultural and ideological sensibilities, but were at pains, nevertheless, to anchor their new message in a historically and religiously sanctioned older vocabulary. The subject, thus, is really the *levels of meaning* that exist within language (words that mean different things to different people or that change their meaning in changed contexts), and the ability of a new cultural elite to maneuver among those levels of meaning and to manipulate language for its own ends.

CHAPTER 2

Interpreting Messianic Rhetoric in the Russian Haskalah and Early Zionism

The Semantic Conundrum: When Is Messianism Not Messianic?

What constitutes a genuine messianic movement in postmishnaic Judaism? This seemingly simple question is difficult to answer because messianism is a paradoxical idea that contains its own negation. Given the fact that all such movements occur in history—that is, in the unredeemed "present"—they are, in theological terms, "false," and have, indeed, been referred to as "antimessianic." They are "false" in the sense that they fail, by definition, to actualize their redemptive vision. And they are antimessianic insofar as they challenge and reject the classical, "passive," theurgic approach to Redemption as it appears in the rabbinic tradition. Hence, they are often related to antinomian impulses and may be fairly described as heretical in and of themselves.

Indeed, messianic movements in Judaism may be characterized as unorthodox attempts to choose one component of Jewish eschatology—or set of components—over another, and thus undermine or override a delicate dialectical balance that classical rabbinic Judaism has left unresolved. These components may be expressed as pairs of antitheses, all of which are, paradoxically, included in the Jewish messianic tradition. Thus, there is, first of all, the tension between universalism and particularism. Redemption embraces all humanity but it pertains primarily to the Redemption of Israel: the people of Israel become, as it were, God's agents for salvation in this world. Second, apocalypticism coexists with restorationism:

23

there is no definitive answer to the question of whether the messianic era is essentially beyond human experience, human history as we know and live it, and human comprehension, or is, rather, a theocratic restoration within the natural, human realm.

Finally, there is the question of divine control as against human responsibility. The Redemption is variously understood as having to be accomplished through God's direct and miraculous intervention in the course of history according to a predestined plan, whose existence is predicated on the implausibility of an unredeemed, tragically flawed universe created by a perfect and omnipotent God; while at the same time, Redemption can also be contingent on human deeds and religious integrity, of the Jews in particular, so that its timing, its inception, and even its very substance depend on human acts.[1]

Millenarian movements in Jewish history typically reduced these polarities to a simpler conception of the End of Days. They departed from and rejected the rabbinic-Judaic norm in that they adopted a unidimensional understanding of Redemption to a greater extent than was sanctioned in the classical tradition as such. The impulse to "force the End" is a revolutionary one, roundly condemned throughout history by most Jewish spiritual and civic authorities as an essentially erroneous approach, the product of false consciousness, a doctrine gone awry.

If it is difficult to decide whether such bona fide millenarian movements as that of Shabbetai Zvi are messianic or antimessianic, the semantic-conceptual thicket becomes virtually impenetrable when we attempt to categorize a modern social and political movement such as Zionism in relation to messianism. Zionism resembled the radical messianic movements in Jewish history in the sense that it, too, was reductionist in its definition of Redemption. Taking our three sets of antitheses, Zionism—though it incorporated elements of a universal vision—was committed, first of all, to a particularist program. It took restorationism to be the real meaning of Jewish messianism through the ages, firmly rejecting apocalypticism. And, in its secular forms as well as in mainstream religious Zionism, it unequivocally opted for human responsibility and human action over passive expectations of miraculous divine intervention. In fact, it may be considered a rebellion against the quietist approach.

Jacob Neusner has written about the analogous, if different, characteristics of the seventeenth-century Sabbatean movement and Herzlian Zionism:

> The contrast between the two is instructive. Sabbateanism phrased its message in strictly theological, Kabbalistic terms. Shabbatai Zvi was not merely "the Messiah," but rather played a central role in the metaphysical drama created by tensions within the Godhead itself. Zionism spoke in political and thoroughly worldly terms, identifying the Jewish problem with sociological, economic and cultural matters. Herzl was never "the Messiah," though Zionism unhesitatingly utilized the ancient Messianic scriptures and images of Jewish messianism. The contrast is, therefore, between theological and ideological messianism, and it is rendered significant by the fact that *the spiritual experience, apart from the verbal explanations associated with it, in each case exhibits similar features: an emotional millenarian upheaval, dividing friend from friend, leading some to despair and others to unworldly hope, and leading a great many to act in new ways.*[2]

Yet, how far can we press this functional resemblance of Zionism to messianic (ideological or theological) heresies without ourselves being reductionist to the point of the absurd? May one speak at all of messianism where there is no guiding Messiah-ideology (to say nothing of a messianic figure as such) and little eschatological content other than the very loosely defined goal of national redemption and the pursuit of a radical solution to the Jewish question?

Both early Jewish nationalists and Zionist historians indulged in a form of anachronistic analysis when they identified the Jewish messianic tradition with nationalist consciousness and political restorationism. Modern nationalists certainly made this identification and, perhaps understandably, attributed the same underlying motives to premodern Jews. But seen within the religious context of its time, traditional messianism was not so much a political or nationalist-restorationist ideology as a theodicy.[3] It was a consoling mechanism that, on the one hand, played a key role for premodern Jews in their ongoing polemic with, and defense against, Christian conversionism and, on the other hand, served the internal purpose of countering and restraining the more radical and heretical beliefs promoted by Jewish messianic movements. It was not intended to be a realistic program for reshaping the Jewish political condition.

"Next year in Jerusalem" is not a statement of geographical intent, but of spiritual aspiration.

The issue is clouded by the messianic rhetoric or allusions to Redemption employed by Jewish nationalists, and it is further complicated by the accusation of false messianism leveled at the Zionists by their early Orthodox detractors:

> [We cry out] against the delusions of the new false messiah that appears in somewhat different garb than [the] messianic pretenders of the past, and that calls itself "Zionism."
>
> Activity faithfully undertaken for the public welfare has always been respected and held sacred among our people. . . . But public service and public servants have always stayed within strict limits. First, such activities have only been directed toward achieving the modicum of improvement in the material and religious life of the Jews that would permit them to live according to their faith. And they retained their faith in an everlasting salvation that would come only in the End of Days. [Jewish leaders] never violated those limits by seeking complete and perfect Redemption, which is the proper task of the Messiah. . . . And now the Zionists have come and have broken the age-old rules. They have replaced the efforts to win improvement in the material and spiritual status and conditions of our lives with an effort to achieve a complete and perfect Redemption. . . . They intoxicate the masses with the heady wine of eternal salvation and thereby deflect their attention from daily needs . . . and mislead them with . . . the lie that Redemption is here at hand.[4]

Translated into historical terms, this charge (voiced, in this instance, in 1900) amounts to a perception—by some contemporaries, at least—that the Zionists were would-be, although grossly misguided, messianists of the first order. Thus, the charge of antimessianism or false messianism makes for a complex, almost insoluble, semantic problem.

Some scholars, who do not wholeheartedly subscribe to the thesis (most closely associated with Ben-Zion Dinur or Josef Klausner)[5] that ties Zionism directly to the age-old Jewish yearning for Redemption and for the return to the Land, nevertheless often speak of Zionism as a modern sequel to religious messianism that transformed, adapted, or otherwise derived from the messianic heritage. Jacob Katz, for example, maintains:

> [The Zionists] were inspired by the conviction that a Jewish society, rebuilt in its ancient land, would somehow reestablish a direct link

with its pristine past. This was an obvious and conscious adaptation of a basic feature of Jewish messianism, and was reflected in particular in the symbolic vocabulary employed by the Zionist movement. . . . Zionism's deep involvement with the messianic expectations of the Jewish people served as its driving force . . . given the obvious historical link between the two. For without the messianic hopes of restoration to its ancient homeland, why should the Jewish people have chosen this spot of all places on which to reconstruct a national state?[6]

[Zionism was] Jewish messianic belief. . . purged of its miraculous elements.[7]

Yet, others have argued—none better than Gershom Scholem—that messianism is actually an escape into myth, an antipolitical and ahistorical impulse that inevitably remains unfulfilled: "a life lived in deferment [in which] nothing can be done definitively, nothing can be irrevocably accomplished . . . nothing concrete . . . can be accomplished by the unredeemed."[8] In that sense, Zionism was profoundly antimessianic. To Scholem, a messianism shorn of miraculous elements is no longer messianism at all. The politicization of Redemption in Zionism created the precise antithesis of the messianic idea, a conscious rejection of its mythic worldview and, therefore, something quite unidentifiable with Sabbateanism.

Dinur and Scholem operated with diametrically opposed definitions of religious messianism and, not surprisingly, held opposite convictions regarding the relationship between Zionism and the messianic tradition. Thus, any attempt to come to grips with these questions must first seek to reach some understanding of the relationship between traditional messianism and political action. Beyond that, there is the issue of the rhetoric or symbols used by the Zionists in stating their case. Why did they do this? And what did it mean to them?

Finally, there is the problem of subliminal messianism: the possibility that a movement such as Zionism elicited support or aroused opposition in Jewish society because it struck a familiar chord or resonated with older traditions and yearnings, even if the movement as such was not explicitly messianic in either form or content. Whether or not this perception was sound and whether or not allusive rhetoric that conjured with prophetic promises was just that and nothing more, the "messianic" or "false messianic" label itself had social consequences that are significant historical data. Some Jews probably did determine their attitude to Zionism on the basis of their ideas about messianism. Thus, Stephen Sharot argues, "While Zionism in Eastern Europe was not a direct product of religious millenarianism, part of its appeal was that it presented a secular solution that had similarities to millenarianism."[9] Yet how sound, historically, is the contention that Zionism, regardless of its stated positions, was able to tap a subterranean source of messianic inspiration in the popular Jewish imagination?

It is quite possible that there are no conclusive answers to any of these questions. The present examination of a small group of pre-Herzlian nationalists is insufficient as a basis for comprehensive conclusions. Nevertheless, I will try to suggest why an examination of early Jewish nationalism in nineteenth-century Russia tends to weaken the case for a strong nexus between Zionism and messianism.

Early Jewish Nationalism: Haskalah as Context

In trying to understand why early Jewish nationalists said what they did, I proceed from the assumption that it is more fruitful to see them not primarily as proto-Zionists, but as part of a certain social group and as products of a certain intellectual tradition. Their social position helped to determine how they expressed their convictions, and rhetorical norms that were prevalent in mid-nineteenth-century Jewish intellectual discourse certainly affected the way certain words were employed in the 1870s and 1880s.

In analyzing the processes of political modernization and secularization within the Russian Haskalah (one of whose products was Zionism), a key question relates to legitimation. Secular political ideologies were first articulated and developed within limited circles of the Jewish intelligentsia (primarily *maskilim* [modernists] and students). Unlike the politics practiced by Jewish spokesmen and notables in premodern times, the new politics of the middle and late nineteenth century did not command widespread assent and authority. Lacking the legitimacy of an age-old political tradition, such new political creeds as nationalism and socialism, when

applied to the Jewish situation, required explanation and justification. Their adherents, a minority within the preponderantly traditionalist Jewish population, were inevitably defensive. They ver-
bally assaulted their opponents with the kind of polemics that
attested, deep down, to their relatively weak position. Rhetorical
aggressiveness hid apologetic motives.

The search for legitimacy led the *maskilim* to appeal to a new
source of authority—the will of the people.[10] Appeals to public
opinion and the people's interests served the modern intellectuals
as effective surrogates for the more traditional underpinnings of
Jewish politics: the authority of rabbis and other leading figures and
the cultivation of stable relations with the organs of state government.

Yet, the immanent and inchoate historical force represented by
the people's will could not so easily provide the transcendent, fixed
purpose that in traditional politics was played by God's guidance,
by Providence. In traditional society, political activity was undertaken by Jews to sustain the well-being, security, or integrity of
their communities, and it was invested with religious legitimacy
and purpose. In theological terms, survival in Exile—maintained
through the efforts of Jewish political and spiritual leaders—both
reflected and justified God's continuing Covenant with Israel. The
belief that the surviving remnant would someday be redeemed by a
messiah-king lent consolation, purpose, and confidence to the life
of an embattled minority. Politics in this system expressed on the
temporal plane the Jews' conviction that their existence retained
ultimate meaning, not only for themselves, but also for humankind,
for the cosmos, and for God. Along with the performance of *mitsvot*
(religious ordinances), politics made the Jews partners with God in
the unfolding drama of their own salvation.[11]

The sense of purposiveness in the march of time and the sense of
the Jews' unique place in history with which the redemptionist
faith endowed traditionalist Jews could not be adequately replaced
by "the people" as the basis of the new Jewish politics. Populist
or nationalist ideas tended toward a reconciliation between "the
masses" and the intellectual elite and reflected a fundamental reorientation in Jewish politics—a new democratic consciousness and
a desire to reconstruct a Jewish political community.[12] But, by

themselves, such propositions indicated no direction, purpose, or agenda that transcended short-term goals. In order to express transcendent values and fixed purpose, the adherents of the new cultural and political trends pressed into service another myth—in addition to the myth of "the people"—namely, the national "destiny" of the Jews, their historical singularity, and their "prophetic" mission.[13] Recourse to terms laden with messianic symbolism allowed the expression, in Hebrew, of contemporary romantic and utopian ideas.

True, the linguistic difficulty faced by *maskilim*, who found few apt Hebrew equivalents for modern social and political concepts, was surely another and an important factor in their use of traditional terms. In and of itself, however, the lexicographic problem does not exhaust the issue. (One might point to the way in which Polish romantic nationalism was also expressed in messianic terminology.)

Jewish nationalism, in particular, has so often been linked by historians to the Jewish messianic tradition, in part because of the rhetoric and symbolism that accompanied the early development of the Ḥibbat Zion (pre-1897 Palestinophile groups) and Zionist movements.[14] I suggest that messianic rhetoric had no specific eschatological referents for late nineteenth-century Russian Jewish intellectuals and that such rhetoric embodied a code—that is, a vocabulary that made it possible for nationalists to enhance their effectiveness and legitimacy by hitching their star to a transcendent purpose—in order to pose both a romantic challenge to the liberal rationalism of the Enlightenment and to explain to *themselves* (even more than to others) that they were heirs, in a new form, to an older tradition.

In their struggle to gain recognition and support, they brandished certain evocative words—*geulah* (Redemption), *yeshu'ah* (salvation), *ye'ud* (destiny), *kibbuẓ galuyot* (the Ingathering of the Exiles), *ḥazon* (prophetic vision), *ẓiyon* (Zion), and *ereẓ avoteinu* (the Land of our Fathers)—that they knew were central to religious meaning in Judaism. By using such terms they were declaring their intention to decipher and proclaim their contemporary significance. Previously the sign and scepter of rabbinic dominance, the invocation of such consecrated words was intended to carry political weight in Jewish society. The nationalists used them to assert their claim to be a new national priesthood who could read the Urim and Thummim of history.

The Rhetoric of National Salvation

David Gordon's programmatic essay of 1863, "In Peace and Tranquility Shall Ye Be Redeemed," lamented the fact that some Jews and "self-anointed scholars" (those, primarily, of the Reform movement in Judaism) had abandoned the traditional belief "that the time would come for [Jews] to return to the land of their fathers." Those who denied Israel's future hopes were lacking in

> Jewish national pride [but] thank God, most of our brethren still yearn for their ancestral land, their holy city, their sacred Temple. . . . This hope is an axiom of our faith [that] has no parallel in any other nation. . . . The mission [te'udah] of the Jew is and always has been to be a full participant in all civic affairs and especially in the search for wisdom and knowledge, and to demand the rights that he deserves as a human being, without slavishly subordinating himself to others, but rather standing up for his holy Torah. He should not sell his birthright for a mess of pottage.[15]

Modern history had shown (he argued) that nations could attain marvelous achievements and could restore their ancient glory. In the light of such developments, "Redemption for Israel, too, is awaiting its fulfillment in our time."[16] Thus, the progress and direction of history itself pointed the way to a Jewish national renaissance and possible restoration (with the help of an enlightened Europe).

Although such hopes proved premature, the nationalist Hebrew press continued to emphasize the essential identity between the Jewish people, their religious faith, their national spirit (Volksgeist), and their national destiny, particularly in the wake of the Reform rabbinic conferences of 1868–69 (in Kassel and Leipzig). Responding to the decision of the Reform rabbis to de-emphasize the messianic theme in the prayer book, Gordon contended:

> The ultimate destiny of the Jews never was and never can be this life of Exile. [It can never mean] that the Jews will remain dispersed and simply melt away among the nations of the world.[17]

With all our love for knowledge, for science and for the lands of
our birth, the Jews should also be entitled to raise their eyes to the
holy mountain—that is, to Zion—and to recall the holiness of their
people in days of old, to take courage from the beautiful hope for an
Ingathering of the Exiles.[18]

Mordechai Ben-Hillel Hacohen, warning of the dangers of assimilation facing young, Russian-educated Jews, emphasized the su-
preme importance of national unity:

[The leading Jewish thinkers] do not mourn simply the rejection of
ritual practices by the youth, or their abandonment of certain customs . . . but, rather, the progressive weakening of the *spirit* of Israel. . . . What fate awaits Israel when the new generation will no
longer understand the tongue of their ancestors, no longer cleave to
the Torah, and no longer recall that they are scions of an ancient
stock? . . . The language and Torah of our ancestors were what kept
Israel united until now.[19]

Dr. Yitzhak Kaminer, of Kiev, wrote in his poem, "The Nationhood of Israel":

> Our breath of life, God's Messiah,
> the spirit that animates all our history,
> the faith in Israel's Redemption . . .
> This is the positive touchstone,
> the elixir of light and life
> for those who bear the bitterness of the Exile.

Shorn of this faith, the poet warned, Jewish survival itself would be
endangered in an age of waning religious observance.[20]

But perhaps the most systematic exposition of romantic nationalist ideas and their presentation in terms of the Jewish traditions of
messianism was that of Peretz Smolenskin. In his essay of 1872–73,
"A Time for Deeds," Smolenskin marveled at the Jewish people's
ability to survive while more powerful nations rose and fell. The
Jews owed their survival neither to physical power nor to bravery
as such. "Rather, God's angel was always leading [them] to pave
the way. . . . That angel is the destiny [of the Jews], for which
[they] were created and which has been [their] constant aim."[21]

All these writers couched their appeal for national pride and
national unity in terms that defined Jewish peoplehood as a powerful organic bond (to use the romantic terminology) in which reli-

gion, generally, and the messianic-redemptive vision, specifically, had once performed a cementing and guiding function. For "religion" the nationalists read "national spirit," clearly subordinating theology to national ideology. Under the impact of modernity, the cement of religion was crumbling, threatening to bring down the entire edifice unless it could be shored up by a modern appreciation of peoplehood and destiny. In short, their argument represented a post-traditional celebration of tradition, not so much as a way of life for the contemporary Jew but as a national asset that ought not to be heedlessly squandered.

Smolenskin expanded on this thesis at great length in his rather long-winded manifesto, 'Am 'olam (The Eternal People), in which the nationalist polemic was explicitly aimed against the Reform rabbis of the West and the trends toward assimilation.[22]

The prophecies of eventual salvation, he averred, had "struck deep roots in the heart of the people and had given it something to live for during times of trouble and persecution." And he continued:

> This faith—the faith in a Messiah or future Redemption—became the cornerstone of all [Jewish] thought and practice. . . . A nation cannot live without such hope to raise its spirits . . . and forge its collective existence. But if a nation [believes that it] has achieved all it can possibly hope to accomplish, and disavows all further ambition for its people and its land [the way the Reformers have done], then the customs of the nation will cease to unite it. Each individual will live for his own sake alone, and the collective life of the nation will, without intention, diminish to the point of complete disintegration. . . . As each of them goes about his own business, the life of the nation will end, and a generation will arise that has no knowledge of that life, for the nation will have died, its severed limbs will have been grafted onto other nations.[23]

Without collective ideals, there is no collective consciousness, Smolenskin maintained. On the other hand, a people that retains a healthy spirit of hope is safeguarded from the perils of complacency amid plenty and against the grievous wounds that history can visit on nations. Even under the worst conditions, a guiding hope has the capacity to galvanize a nation. Some nations had indeed succumbed and disappeared, but Israel had survived because of what he termed its "life-spirit." The Torah and its message of hope, he continued, had therefore been the Jews' "salvation and comfort

. . . , a shelter and a fortress that united them as much as country and statehood [did for others]."[24] The two (Torah and salvationist hope) were intertwined; the waning of one or the other had always led to a period of stagnation, disintegration, or assimilation.

Given the hope of integration into European society raised by the emancipation, the Jews of the West were denying the national hope of Redemption and editing it out of their Judaism. Were the Reformers to succeed in snuffing out the messianic belief ("that keeps Israel's spirit alive . . . and still today has the power to unite them"),[25] this would threaten the very existence of the Jewish people. Hope for a future Redemption was all the more necessary because religious observance was lax and Torah study no longer widespread. Without the messianic hope nothing at all would be left to stand in the way of the Jews' complete disappearance.[26]

Moreover, Smolenskin maintained, everyone understood that this hope was just that: a creed, a point of subjective consciousness that in no way interfered with the Jews' ability to function at every level of civic life in the Diaspora. "Our obligation is, nonetheless, to preserve that faith [in the Messiah], because for us it is a bond of unity," even more than religion as such; for the religion practiced by a Jew in Vilna was quite unlike the Judaism practiced in Berlin.[27]

For Smolenskin, then, it was the gravitational weight of the messianic idea that counted most. It was a distillation of the historical consciousness of Jewry, the emblematic basis for a community of *fate* even when a community of *faith* was no longer possible. Neither the exact content of messianism (with its attendant eschatological features) nor the expectation of its actual fulfillment explained its true force and value. Rather, its affirmation alone was enough to create unity out of diversity and to prevent the egoistic, materialistic, and perhaps transitory successes of individual Jews from sapping the vigor of the collective. When Smolenskin evoked the messianic idea, then, he did so in order to reassert nationalist values in his debate with the Reform movement and with Berlin Haskalah generally.[28]

Just how the nationalist-Zionist idea might be promoted—and a more activist dimension added—was illustrated in nationalist texts of the late 1870s and early 1880s that employed rhetorical catchphrases lifted directly from the messianic tradition.

Thus, the Society for Redeeming [!] the Land, established in Palestine in 1876 to purchase land for Jewish settlement, declared in its statement of purpose:

By this we hope to bring closer the ultimate and true Redemption that will surely come . . . ; for, despite the dark and troubled times [we live in] . . . and the poverty we see around us here . . . we, nonetheless, can perceive the glimmerings of a new day that is slowly dawning and the signs of a salvation that is drawing nigh.[29]

David Gordon, writing in the early winter of 1880, declared:

The sacred and noble idea of settling the land of Israel is bound up with our national destiny and the hopes we harbor for the future. . . . [Assimilated Jewish notables] and the Reformers would have us believe that Israel's destiny is only to be dispersed among the nations! . . . [Their error] can only smother in the hearts of our youth any feeling for our national destiny and the sacred hope of Jeshurun, the hope for the future that will see an end to our dispersion.[30]

The political situation in the Orient [has afforded us the opportunity] to establish a sizeable area for Jews to till the land of our ancestors. That would mark, God willing, a first step toward our future hope [*tikvateinu ha'atidah*], toward the ultimate hope of Israel for salvation [*mikveh yisrael*].[31]

In *Hashaḥar* of 1883, one writer expressed the nationalist impulse with the following fantasy, filled with messianic motifs:

Were Ezra and Rabbi Akiba alive today, their joy over our unprecedented national self-awareness would be boundless. . . . Were Nehemiah and Bar Kochba to be brought before the people, they would proclaim: Behold your gods, O Israel, who will go forth before you to take you up to the land that God swore to your fathers![32]

Or, to take another striking example from the same year:

For the sake of the Torah and their hope of Redemption, Jews were prepared to suffer death at the hands of their oppressors. . . . Survival is an instinct of every living thing and is implanted in every person. The people of Israel sensed that the Torah and the memory of their [lost] homeland were the foundation of their very existence, on which their lives [as a people] depended. Just as other nations go to war to defend their country against its foes, so, too, did the Jews battle for their spiritual homeland—that is, the Torah and the hope for Redemption—as in a war for survival. . . . [The people] sensed that they themselves, their Torah and their hope for Redemption were indivisible, and they have made that [perception] a principle of life and death.[33]

Yet, references to the organic and spiritual bonds of nationhood (i.e., the indissoluble union of martyrs' blood and the symbolic soil of the cherished homeland) and messianist terminology were tempered by an important disclaimer, one that indicated to the reader the essential distinction between myth and reality, metaphor and meaning.

Thus, David Gordon argued that Jewish settlements in Palestine would serve the limited, nonmessianic, and perfectly legitimate purpose (in the theological sense) of providing a haven ("cities of refuge") to be available to the Jewish people should their enemies attempt to disturb their peace and security in Europe.[34]

Alexander Zederbaum (publisher of *Hameliz*) stated his support for Jewish agricultural colonies in Palestine by invoking the prophetic-messianic visions of Daniel, but he preceded his statement with this caveat:

> It does not enter our minds at all today to involve ourselves in calculations of the End of Days [in the manner of Daniel]. . . . But we should bear in mind what Daniel heard in his vision [about the return to Jerusalem] as the word of God in heaven that has guided Israel throughout its history, and we should pay close attention to the significance of the events of our time.[35]

Smolenskin, too, pointed out the essential distinction between messianists of the past and nationalists of his own day. The latter, in looking forward to a time when the Jews might take their place among the nations of the world, were not in the least bit interested in calculating the time of the *eschaton*; neither were any of them hoping to rebuild the Temple and restore the sacrificial cult.[36]

And Mordechai Ben-Hillel Hacohen spoke of the general nonmessianic tenor of the times, even as he issued a stirring biblical call to "Rise up and go unto Zion":

> Among the present generation there are many who do not believe in all those miraculous events that are supposed to accompany the Ingathering of the Exiles. And yet, their gaze is still fixed on Zion and on a Redemption there in time to come, and they retain their hope for a rebirth of our nation on the holy mountain in Jerusa-

lem. . . . Those among the new generation of Jews who love their people and look to its future embrace the hope that if Jewry will accurately read the portents of what lies ahead, then the hope of Redemption can serve as its beacon, just as this country [Russia] has brought salvation to the Greeks and to the peoples of the Balkans. . . . There are many today who believe that the salvation of Israel, too, lies this way [i.e., in movements for political independence]. *To the extent that such believers increase—and those who wish to witness [salvation by means of] miracles and wonders decrease—the day of our national Redemption will draw ever closer. . . . My people, your salvation lies within you. . . .* Our own eyes should tell us that the present moment calls to us from out of the whirlwind: Rise up and go unto Zion![37]

The distinction here is explicit: messianism is of instrumental value only insofar as it can be transcended.

The drive to establish Jewish settlements in Palestine and to organize Ḥibbat Zion societies throughout the Pale of Settlement (and abroad) received added impetus after 1881. Romantic nationalist ideology—and the rhetoric that it inspired—became an important aspect of Jewish modernism in Eastern Europe at the end of the nineteenth century. Nationalist ranks swelled in reaction to the wave of anti-Semitism that hit Central and Eastern European Jews during those years—the pogroms in Russia, in particular.

Most of the nationalist positions, however, had been adumbrated by Jewish intellectuals during the 1860s and 1870s. Indeed, although such men as Moshe Leib Lilienblum and Leon Pinsker were profoundly shaken by the pogroms, others, such as David Gordon, Mordechai Ben-Hillel Hacohen, and Eliezer Ben-Yehuda, did not perceptibly alter their basic convictions because of the pogroms. (Smolenskin, previously opposed to a territorial definition of Jewish nationalism, was more disposed after 1881 to accept a Palestinocentric point of view. Despite this new operative conclusion, his basic nationalist ethos remained largely as before.) Instead, the Palestinophile movement they had helped to create merely took on added urgency and greater organizational coherence as efforts were turned to mobilizing supporters and funds.

Eclipse of the Messiah

I have argued that the employment of rhetoric possessing metahistorical and even messianic overtones in the service of Jewish nationalism ought to be understood, within the context of the Russian Haskalah, as a code—a kind of developed metaphor—that was meant to suggest a link between romantic ideals of nationhood and a higher purpose, or to establish a living tradition retrospectively.[38] The manipulation of significant passwords was also a way to suggest that the moral claim to national leadership advanced by the nationalists was more than mere chutzpah or hubris.

What sort of support could they hope to rally, what sort of legitimacy could they hope to gain on this basis? Was it an appeal to a messianically attuned audience, and therefore clothed in messianic rhetoric? Is this, then, an indirect form of proof that Zionism tapped into a reservoir of messianic yearnings or was fueled by an undercurrent of messianic tension?

To explore these questions we will have to consider briefly some background issues in East European Jewish society in the course of the nineteenth century. I will contend, first, that the level of messianic tension in that society was remarkably low; second, that the rhetorical conventions of the Russian Haskalah had already paved the way for the use of messianic vocabulary emptied of all eschatological meaning; and, third, that the fact of the massive Jewish emigration westward from all parts of Southern and Eastern Europe, during the very years in which nationalist writers appealed for the Jewish resettlement of Palestine, tends to undermine claims that most Jews had been primed in an operative sense to prepare for a redemptive return to Zion.

This is not to say that there was a total absence of messianic consciousness in East European Jewish society in the nineteenth century; only that, in the post-Sabbatean period, messianic language was often used in ways that tended to mute or obscure tensions with the gentile world, rather than express such tensions openly and radically. More explicit messianist positions, when they did surface, did not elicit a widespread response, either positive or negative.

In the first instance, this thesis is applicable to Hasidism, a religious lifestyle that embraced or influenced perhaps a majority of East European Jewry in the nineteenth century. In the formulation proposed by Gershom Scholem, Hasidism "neutralized" the messianic-apocalyptic element in the Lurianic kabbalistic tradition, replacing it with an accent on the inner spiritual life of the individual and his particular group.[39] Scholem argued:

> Redemption of the soul without redemption of the social body, i.e., of the nation from its historical exile . . . has never had a messianic meaning in Judaism. . . . Hasidism, with the destructive consequences of [Sabbateanism] before its eyes, renounced the idea of messianic revolt and made its peace with exile.[40]

The acute messianic tension was removed by altering the redemptive timetable: the process of *tikkun*, the restoration of holiness in the universe, which in Lurianic kabbalah was considered to be all-but-complete, was seen in Hasidic thought as only just having begun. The end was far indeed from imminent realization.[41] The essence of early Hasidism, Scholem asserted, concurring with Hillel Zeitlin, was that "every individual is the Redeemer, the Messiah, of his own little world."[42]

Scholem further observed that Hasidic homiletic literature took to its logical extreme the device of spiritualizing and allegorizing such terms as "Zion," "*galut*," and "*geulah*," thus revaluing such concepts in terms of the inner life of the soul.[43]

Another observer has put the case somewhat differently, namely, that Hasidism sought to revive the faith and the willingness of the Jews to await the Messiah's coming without the excessive impatience of the discredited Sabbateans.[44]

From a sociological point of view, the most important element in this neutralization of millenarian potential is probably to be found in the multicentered or fragmented and "routine" nature of the charismatic leadership that emerged within Hasidism and that prevented messianic expectations in one Hasidic court from spilling over into others.[45]

The most sustained counterargument against this trend of thought is advanced by Dinur, to whom Hasidism represented a messianic movement par excellence. He maintained that Hasidism consciously set out to pave the way for Redemption by replacing the rabbinic-bureaucratic communal elite, which had failed to meet the challenges of the time and the expectations of the rank and file. Hasidism brought to the fore a renewed "prophetic" leadership.[46]

And yet, for all the messianic consciousness that pervaded Hasidic thought, it would seem clear that Hasidism did not turn into a sectarian heresy, but remained within the parameters of Orthodoxy, precisely because of its sublimation of millenarian impulses.

As for the non-Hasidic, "Lithuanian," wing of East European Jewry, it has been suggested that it gave birth to a truly millenarian movement in the first four decades of the nineteenth century.[47] According to this (rather controversial) thesis, advanced by Aryeh Morgenstern, the disciples of the Vilna Gaon carried on a living tradition—derived from the oral teachings of their master—that enjoined them to spearhead a collective return to, and colonization of, the land of Israel. This was to be an active, this-worldly preparation for the Final Redemption, based on the contention that the time had come to abrogate the time-honored "three oaths," the rabbinic formula proscribing rebellion against gentile rule or "forcing the End" through mass resettlement in Palestine.[48]

The circle of disciples (five leading rabbinic figures), their students, and their families brought 511 settlers to Palestine by 1812; other organized groups followed in 1819 and 1826.[49] They constituted a distinctive stream within a larger wave of immigrants, many if not most of whom were apparently inspired by the belief that the Messiah's advent would occur in the year 5600 (1840)—a belief shared by other Jews in various parts of the world and by Christian millenarians.[50]

The disciples of the Vilna Gaon, Morgenstern argues, coupled this belief with a messianic doctrine of specific content, including the assignment of responsibility for initiating the Redemption to the Jews themselves. Settlement of the Holy Land was one aspect of this activist approach; another was an attempt to restore the line of rabbinic ordination, suspended in antiquity, and thus permit the development of a new Sanhedrin. They also introduced liturgical innovations in accord with their sense of living in the "Sabbath eve of time" (i.e., the eve of Redemption). Finally, the failure of the

Messiah to arrive on schedule led to what Morgenstern calls a crisis of faith, an ideological retrenchment, and even two cases of conversion to Christianity—all expressions of an authentic millenarian trauma.[51]

The validity of the evidence has been contested by those who question the messianic nature of the Lithuanian movement and find that Morgenstern has read the sources tendentiously. At any rate, it seems clear that this group had relatively little impact outside its own limited ranks. It appears to have acted with a certain degree of circumspection and, thus, no more than a flurry of attention was attracted by the events in Jerusalem in 1840, which were considerably overshadowed by the much-publicized Damascus ritual-murder affair of that year.[52]

A similarly feeble response greeted the proto-Zionist messianic ideas propagated by rabbis Zvi-Hirsh Kalischer and Yehuda Alkalai who, independently of one another, reached similar conclusions concerning Jewish settlement of the Holy Land as a precondition for God's final deliverance of Israel. Both men were more or less ignored insofar as their messianic message was concerned. Kalischer developed his theories connecting the emancipation of Western Jewry with a providential scheme of Redemption, unfolding by stages, during the 1830s and 1840s.[53] As Yosef Salmon has suggested, however, some of Kalischer's messianic rhetoric had more to do with Orthodox opposition to religious reform in Central Europe than with millenarian restoration.[54]

Both Kalischer and his Southern European counterpart, Alkalai, were active on behalf of their ideas until the 1870s, but neither one succeeded in establishing a following in traditional circles (although David Gordon, as well as Moses Hess, seem to have been influenced by them).[55]

The atrophy of radical messianism—its reduction from a historical force of some potency to the preserve of isolated groups and individuals, as well as the shrouding of the idea of the Messiah in layers of spiritual metaphor—can also be illustrated by the way in which the Russian *maskilim* used the term *mashiah* (messiah/anointed one) to designate the Russian tsar as a divine-right monarch.[56] This unconventional usage combined elements of *maskilic melizah* (flowery and hyperbolic rhetoric), Russian political theory, and an implied dismissal of more traditional ideas about a messiah-redeemer.[57]

A similar device appears in some poems of Avraham Ber Gottlober, who depicted the coronation in heaven of Alexander II as performed by none other than King Solomon (hence, bestowing Davidic/messianic symbolism). He also had God address Nicholas I as "my dear son."[58] Adam Hacohen Levenson, in his *Kelil yofi*, wrote that the tsar must have unlimited power on earth just as God is the "autocrat" of heaven. The tsar is "the heavenly king on earth."[59] Such rhetoric matched the political agenda of the Russian Jewish intelligentsia that, at mid-century, made much of the benevolence of the enlightened absolutist state.

Maskilim of the late 1850s and early 1860s also heaped scorn and derision on any attempt to calculate messianic years. Shortly before the new Hebrew year of 5620 (September 1859), one such writer pilloried those who suggested that the new year was numerologically auspicious. He reminded his readers that such dabbling in eschatological guesswork had had only deleterious results in the past.[60]

Others proposed that the messianic era was to be reinterpreted as the coming of a liberal age and identified with the emancipation of Jewish communities from their medieval disabilities. Basing himself on both the Babylonian sage, Samuel, and on the teachings of Maimonides, a *maskil* from Ekaterinoslav wrote:

> In the messianic age, nothing of the natural order that we know today will change. Only the yoke of oppression will be removed from us. All the words of the prophets [about the miraculous End of Days] are meant only metaphorically. . . . [Samuel did not mean that the Jews would no longer be ruled by gentile kings, but rather that] in the fullness of time, the burden of oppression and persecution that Israel suffered in his day will be lifted, . . . the reign of the wicked will cease . . . , those who hate Judah will be cut off and all men will call on the name of the Lord, Creator of the universe, and they will offer the gift of brotherly love on the altar of peace, without distinction of religion or faith: those will be the days of the Messiah. . . . Our era is truly [like the messianic age] a time of liberation [from oppression] because of the spirit of truth and peace that pervades all peoples of the world. The exulting voice of brotherhood and fellowship resounds all around us. Anyone with human sentiment [observing all this] must have a sense of holiness, a sense of the Divine, and

will want to say: O Lord, Your name is great, for You have passed Your arm of holiness in blessing over all mankind, bringing peace and showing us all the great goodness that You promised us in Isaiah's vision of the End of Days.[61]

Another contemporary *maskil*, urging the Jews to love Russia, the land of their birth, counseled them against taking messianic promises too literally to heart. Even Jeremiah, he reminded his readers, had encouraged the Jews to build homes in their land of Exile and to pray for the welfare of that country, even though he also prophesied that the Exile would end after seventy years. We do not (he continued) live in the hope of returning and regaining our land by force; we merely pray for God's salvation. Moreover, "the concept of the advent of the Messiah is, in essence, meant only to raise the morale of the Jews, lest they lose heart under the burden of their sorrows."[62]

In an article entitled, "A Word for Our Time: Footsteps of the Messiah," a *maskil* from Warsaw argued that the messianic salvation promised by Scripture was not a matter of restoring the Jewish people to the land of Israel, but of elevating their status. The saviors of the nation are those who act to achieve this, including the men of the Alliance Israélite Universelle and "all the Jewish newspapers and their writers and supporters, writing in Hebrew and the various languages of the other nations," as well as "the men of wise heart and courage who wage God's [i.e., the Jews'] battles against their enemies [and] who are our protectors, those in high positions and wise in matters of state."[63]

Finally, we have the example of Judah Leib Gordon, one of the foremost figures of the Russian Haskalah, whose own conceptualization of the messianic Redemption was couched in rationalistic terms of progress, enlightened reform, and the victory of civilization. As Michael Stanislawski has pointed out, Gordon demythologized the concept of Redemption and gave it a new meaning when he asserted that the Jews, through their entry into modern European society, could determine their own fate.[64] He admitted that his references to a messianic future were a "polemical device," part of a critique of Orthodox obscurantism, and he insisted that modern "right-thinking" Jews hope only for "redemption by means of the universal recognition of their human rights."[65]

Gordon's recasting of the messianic doctrine in the service of the Haskalah was undoubtedly an important step in the effort of East European Jewish intellectuals to invoke for their emerging new strategies for redemption the most profound and evocative chords in Jewish consciousness, while at the same time subverting traditional Judaism, its politics, and its culture.[66]

The sublimation of messianic activism within Hasidic spirituality, the lack of popular enthusiasm for messianic speculations, and the emergence of a group of Europeanized rationalists who were willing to use messianic language as a political symbol are each very distinct phenomena, occurring in their own, rather unrelated, sociocultural contexts. Yet, each would appear to be related, if not to one another, then to a common perception of the Dispersion that did not include its imminent demise. By and large, Russian Jewry did not succumb to the temptation to narrow the gap between "this world" and the "days of the Messiah." *Maskilim* who did so had first to empty messianic terminology of its supernatural content and eschatological substance. Their metaphorical use of messianic terminology was in reality a way of fostering a this-worldly consciousness, not a way to preach Redemptionist theology.[67]

Last, but not least, there is the matter of the mass emigration of East European Jews to the West, conventionally dated from 1881 (though it had its beginnings in the 1870s). Here we have sociological evidence that may help us to identify the position of the inarticulate masses of Jews with regard to the issue of messianism. Over a forty-year period, two and half million Jews literally turned their backs on Palestine as they uprooted themselves to improve their lot abroad, causing the greatest mass migration in Jewish history.

This circumstance casts doubt on any assumption that most Jews were imbued with a messianic yearning for a Jewish national rebirth and that the Zionist appeal was overtly or subliminally directed to stimulate those yearnings. Granted, some of the immigrants were undoubtedly Orthodox in their beliefs, including beliefs about the Messiah, and their rejection of the Zionist program possibly rested on traditional messianic teachings. Thus, their choice of destination does not imply any negation of religious messianic faith. By the same token, however, it hardly attests to deep stirrings of an intensely messianic nature. (It would be more accurate to speak of their conventional, low-energy faith in a final Redeemer, expressed in daily prayers.)

It may also be contended that the emigration fever of 1881–82 might well have provoked a much larger stream of Zion-seekers, had it not been for objective political and economic factors in Ottoman-ruled Palestine that blocked a mass immigration at that time. In addition, there were tremendous social forces at work that directed emigrants to the New World (e.g., aid rendered to Russian Jewish emigrants by West European Jewish organizations). Yet, again, we simply have no positive evidence to suggest that the Jewish population as a whole or the emigrants themselves were in the grip of a messianic upheaval. In the absence of any evidence of this nature, the mute facts of the mass emigration to the West must be allowed to speak for themselves.

Nationalist rhetoric that justified Zionism in terms borrowed from the prophetic-messianic tradition was as likely to offend the staunchly Orthodox as appeal to them—if not more so. That consideration, in fact, typically led religious Zionists in Eastern Europe to disavow any messianic intentions, and Yaacov Shavit has cogently argued that the Ḥibbat Zion groups were careful to select symbols and historical analogies (primarily the return to Judea led by Ezra and Nehemiah) that de-emphasized eschatological elements.[68]

What benefit or legitimacy, then, could those early nationalists discussed earlier have hoped to gain by deliberately invoking the messianic heritage? The primary advantage lay in the chance to call on history as witness and support for their arguments. Jewish survival, Jewish unity, the loyalty of the Jews to their unique religious culture, and their continued status as outsiders in European society provided evidence to support nationalist claims—evidence that lent weight, authority, and a teleological conviction to otherwise ad hoc theses based on populism or doctrines of self-determination.

Although this cannot be proved conclusively, I am persuaded, too, that their readers were attuned to the fact that David Gordon, Peretz Smolenskin, and those who followed after them were using messianic rhetoric as a code; that such words as "Redemption" were neither meant nor taken to convey what they had conveyed to earlier generations; and that such writers were (and were understood to be) simply translating into Hebrew terminology and com-

municating in terms of Jewish cultural referents the romantic concepts of nationhood: national pride, national struggle, national
destiny, and national homeland.

They affirmed the messianic tradition but only in a strictly limited sense, construing it as a historical instrument for the preservation of Jewish nationhood. They fostered an intense attachment to
Zion, but only in the same sense that Poles, Greeks, Italians, and
Ukrainians raised "homeland" to a quasi-sacred status. They attracted a following, but not nearly as numerous a constituency as
that of their Orthodox opponents or as broadly based as the mass
emigration. Moreover, there were good reasons—other than any
that might have been connected to messianist passion—for joining
Ḥibbat Zion societies, reasons that had much to do with the social
appeal of such groups.[69]

I, therefore, interpret the use of messianic rhetoric by Jewish
nationalists as evidence not of the *continuity* of messianism within
Judaism, but of *discontinuity*. Allusions to prophetic scriptural passages and liturgical phrases were used because of their recognition
value. Redemption through one's own efforts was a concept that
could be readily transmitted to a constituency who had lost faith in
eschatological visions but who was still firmly embedded in the
Hebraic cultural idiom. References to the constancy of the age-old
messianic faith or to the national "manifest destiny" of the Jews
lent depth to a nationalist conceptualization of Judaism. Such references created a perfect platform from which one might launch
critical barbs at antinationalists of various stripes: against Reformers, assimilationists, and Orthodox messianists alike. Words such as
"Redemption" and "destiny" raised the decibel level of nationalist
propaganda, amplifying the otherwise reedy voice in which early
Jewish nationalists addressed their fellow Jews. They created an
illusion of historical justification for the nationalist position, without which the case of the Zionists would have appeared woefully
out of touch with reality.

In short, messianism was a mythic factor that provided romantic
nationalists with a much richer dimension of oratory and conviction than anything that could be derived (negatively) from the rise
of modern anti-Semitism or (positively) from the fluctuating will of
the people.

CHAPTER 3

The Making of a *Maskil*

Although the Haskalah in Eastern Europe was largely a mid-nine-teenth-century phenomenon, the continued traditionalism that characterized the vast majority of Jewish society contributed to a cycle of constantly renewed struggles between traditional and modern values. Each generation, in its turn, faced the same cultural, social, religious, and political issues; each, in its turn, discovered in the Haskalah a Jewish path toward social and cultural readjustment. With the passage of time, however, the issues were exacerbated: economic deprivation and the rising level of violence that affected Jews in Russia, Poland, and Rumania created human dilemmas of greater and greater urgency.

If this wider context seems to explain the perennial *Kulturkampf* in East European Jewry adequately, we still know relatively little, in concrete detail, of what it was like for the individual Jew to go through the process of inner "retooling." This chapter introduces a document that testifies directly to the personal revolution experienced by a young Jew in the late nineteenth century.

The fragment of a memoir presented here comes from a longer, unpublished Hebrew manuscript that was originally written when its author was nineteen years old, in 1889. Fifty-six years later, the author (then a resident of Toronto, Canada) edited and slightly revised the text. He updated (perhaps polished) the style of the original Hebrew; added a number of brief asides; and made some deletions; but he claimed not to have tampered with the content and flow of the original narrative.[1]

Regardless of how much the retrospective editing has altered the original presentation, the manuscript's authenticity as such is not

in question. The critical reader must make allowances for the bifo-
cal time perspective, but much of the narrative bears unmistakable
linguistic and other traces of proximity to the events described.

The memoir, then, represents a version of the youthful recollec-
tions of someone who was soon to make the arduous and not un-
common transition from traditional small-town Jewish life in late
nineteenth-century Poland to the life of an immigrant in North
America. There he would take up the profession of a Hebrew school
(Talmud Torah) teacher. The memoir captures him in the throes of
self-conscious young manhood, before marriage and before emigration, but not before his inner world was radically altered through
exposure to a different social milieu and new values. Indeed, it is
this radical alteration that explains the writing of the memoir: The
sense of inner crisis is conveyed by the title itself, *Zikhronot shel
na'ar to'eh* (Memoirs of an Errant Young Man), in which the key
word is lifted from Peretz Smolenskin's autobiographical novel, *Ha-
to'eh bedarkei hahayim*, to convey a loss of innocence, a loss of
moorings, and a loss of direction. The autobiographical act, itself,
is related to the discovery of a European language of self.[2]

Harris Pearlstone (Yeshaya Heshl Perelstein) came from a middle-class family whose breadwinner, Pearlstone's father, had been a
successful grain merchant and miller in a small Polish town in
the Lomza district, close to the Prussian border. Having suffered a
complete financial collapse, the family was then forced to relocate
to a dilapidated section of the nearby town of Szczuczyn.
Pearlstone, the eighth of nine surviving children, was entering his
adolescence when the crisis occurred.

It becomes apparent in the course of the memoir that the father—perhaps because of his loss of economic and social status—
was unwilling or unable to effectively curb his intellectually gifted
and inquisitive son's quest to acquire a mastery of Russian and
German (though the father was clearly opposed in principle to such
studies). The reader is given the sense that the son's progressive rise
in social standing, as his reputation as a *maskil* began to produce
economic benefits and useful connections, left the father with no
alternative but to acquiesce—however reluctantly—in the situation.

A confrontation between father and son had already taken place when the young Yeshaya was discovered reading, bareheaded, in his room on a Friday evening. Parental discipline was reimposed, but the contest was ultimately decided in the son's favor when, in a subsequent episode, the son used his earnings from giving Russian lessons to buy himself a decent suit of clothes. The hard-pressed father, who opposed his son's desire to make his livelihood as a mere teacher, simply had no response when challenged:

> "Are you able to provide me the clothes I need so that I needn't be ashamed to show myself in public? . . . In a year or two I'll be called up for military service and it will be necessary to bribe the doctors and the officials. Can you afford that?" That ended Father's complaints. He kept quiet after that.

The impoverishment and humiliations suffered by the parent; the coming of age of a youth (by his own account, never particularly docile)[3] who needed to prove himself; and the opportunities he found in Szczuczyn itself and then in Bialystok to broaden his horizons, all seem interrelated in this particular personal drama. The focal point at which all the factors coincide is the young man's obsession with learning Russian and German.

Taking, first of all, the memoirist's social background, the fact that the father, in his more fortunate years, had maintained a longstanding relationship with the local Polish landowner and had a large clientele among the local peasantry[4] implies that he was able to speak Polish with at least a fair proficiency. As a capable businessman involved with the intricacies of credit arrangements, he also had a local reputation as a man of the world.[5] It was he who instructed his young son in arithmetic and who saw to it that a more thorough grounding than usual in the Hebrew language and in the Bible—classicist subjects considered less necessary than Talmud—would be the basis of his son's education.[6] It was clearly the father's intention to raise Yeshaya as a talmudic scholar, and he arranged for a succession of tutors (in small-group settings), and later on even considered sending him off to a major yeshiva, despite the expense. To a cultural historian, these points are reminiscent of the early lives of other East European *maskilim*—indeed, the components form a kind of recognizable Rorschach pattern.

Also symptomatic is the "erosion" process that affected the

young scholar's Orthodoxy after his initial exposure to European culture. The memoirist himself assumes a causal relationship to exist (and that, indeed, is the conventional wisdom) between broadening intellectual perspective and a crisis of faith. In light of the young man's personal history, however, it is possible to question the assumed sequence, and to posit a reverse causality: that a crisis in parental and, by extension, religious authority (here, the memoirist's self-perception as being the intellectual superior of even the most learned man in the *beit midrash* [study chapel] plays a role) [7] led him to seek other, more reliable authority figures and world outlooks. This he did via the studying of foreign languages that, he may have guessed, held the key to all that was hidden from him. Perhaps secondarily the erosion process set in once the exposure to other cultures undermined his inbred cultural assumptions: "Doubt began to creep into my heart, doubt as to whether the Talmudic sages were really the last word in human wisdom, whether the Talmud was really the acme of knowledge and of Truth." Nevertheless, what is also striking is that such doubts were not allowed (at least at first) to alter his religious observance, and that despite some lapses, religious conformism still held the young man within traditional norms.

Significant personal and intellectual qualities mentioned by the author include a certain rebelliousness, a rationalist aversion to *pilpul* (hypothetical or casuistic argumentation) and to mysticism, [8] and evidently a certain amount of pride in his intellectual capabilities. [9]

Of particular note in the fragments published here are the following elements: the semi-open manner in which young Jews studied Russian in the local *beit midrash*, and the effects of peer pressure among the young; the way in which the urban environment made different Jewish social sets, each with differing standards of social status and cultural values, accessible to one another; the automatic (if naive) equation of Europeanized bourgeois accoutrements with an "advanced" and "refined" mentality (that is, the posh quality of an "enlightened" life style); and the perceived "modernity" of the requirement to have an explicit and pragmatic "goal" in life. The role of the Russian-language *maskilic* press in fostering Jewish national consciousness, and the rather parochial and stunted quality of the early nineteenth-century Hebrew literature available to the author—compared to European classics—are both significant in terms of the history of Jewish nationalist culture in Eastern Europe and the uses and impact of literature.

Finally, and most significantly—from the point of view of the "semiotics of Jewish politics"—it becomes clear that the codes of modern political discourse were all but opaque to one trained mainly in the traditionalist Hebrew idiom. To make the transition to modern, secular, political thought was a quantum leap in vocabulary and terms of reference, no less than in consciousness and ideology.

Memoirs of an Errant Young Man

BY YESHAYA HESHL PERELSTEIN

. . . I had made a point of inquiring about the study chapels in our new town [Szczuczyn] and about those who frequented them. I was told that the spirit of the new Haskalah was dominant there, and that Torah was relatively neglected. There were very few people who devoted themselves to its study. There was a Talmud Society, to be sure, but its influence was barely felt. There was not even one yeshiva *bochur* [student]. The *beys medresh* [study chapel] was filled with the sons of prosperous householders, as usual in Jewish towns; but they went there to socialize and to talk about Haskalah, not to learn Talmud. They all dressed in short coats and affected the style of Westerners [pp. 83–84].

. . . Many young men were seated around the table, and those who found no room to sit were standing at nearby lecterns. . . . They gave me a cold, incredulous look that froze me where I stood and robbed me of the power to commence studying. Even the older ones in the room gazed at me in wonderment. Apparently it was a novelty to see someone so young take his studies so seriously. So, I began my customary sing-song studying. No one disturbed me; they merely kept looking, as if seeing some exotic creature. . . . I was entirely unaware at the time of how strange I looked. I thought my appearance and behavior perfectly normal, for that was how the yeshiva boys looked where I came from [pp. 95–97]. . . .

I decided that they must be *maskilim*, that they felt their worldly discussions were not for the likes of me. But my curiosity impelled me to find out what principles lay behind the thoughts and words of such people.

After studying intensively until my mind could take no more for that day, I edged closer to their table to hear what they were talking about. I heard foreign words that made no sense to me. I could clearly distinguish the words, "Blaustein . . . Paulson," but then heard some half-muttered [Russian] words that I could barely make out: "appellative . . . nominative . . . . " I thought these must be references to vain philosophical stupidities, and for several days I left it at that, not daring to ask them what they meant. Finally, though, I could not help but ask them, and received the answer that these were terms in Russian grammar.

This pricked my ego, and my sense of self-respect got the better of me: "If this is all their Enlightenment amounts to," I thought, "then we'll see if I cannot beat them at their own game in the space of a few months." I made a firm decision that, come what may, I must learn Russian.

I revealed my wish to Father and begged him to buy me Paperna's *Russian Language Primer*. Father agreed, on condition that I spend no more than two hours a day on it. I faithfully kept to that limit, but applied myself during those two hours as zealously as only a Talmud student in a *beys medresh* can. Within the month, I had read and re-read the textbook, mastering the fundamentals of Russian grammar and a small vocabulary.

There is a well-known saying: Give a demon a finger, and he'll take an arm. I had tasted a mere crumb, but my appetite to master Russian perfectly was aroused. How I was to implement this, I had no idea [pp. 97–98]. . . .

The beadle's son, Abba, latched onto me [at the synagogue]. He was my age, a pleasant enough boy. . . . I told him about my thwarted desire to learn Russian. He thought for a bit and then said, "Do you know what? I am not that good in Russian, either. Let's go and get ourselves a tutor."

I considered this a fine suggestion, and for my part I would have agreed right then and there. But what about Father? Would he grant his permission? I knew how strict he was about my time, and he would not be willing to allow me much time off from my Talmud studies. He still entertained the hope that a wonderful rabbinical post awaited me in some great city— so how could I go to him with such a request? I . . . finally decided to win over my sisters first, so that they might plead my case to Father. He would not turn them down.

My sisters readily agreed to this plan and promised to help me. A few days later, Father gave me permission to find a tutor.

There were five Russian teachers in town: Zusmanovich, who also taught at the government school for Jews, charged three rubles a month, which was way beyond Father's purse; Grossman, whose fee was two rubles, which was still too high; and three others whose fee was one ruble. Since Abba would be paying half, that meant an expense of only 50 kopecks, which Father could readily afford. These three teachers were: Moyshe Galatz, a married man with a family; and two single young men, Dunavich and Bishkovich. Father preferred to send me to Galatz, and so, several weeks later, I went with the beadle's son to Galatz's for our first lesson.

Moyshe Galatz, my first Russian teacher, was good-looking and imposing. His eyes were big and brown like potatoes, and his look bespoke an unbridled ego. He dressed in the European fashion and his clothes were immaculately clean, as befitted an educated gentleman. His bearing and his gait proclaimed, "I am an aristocrat," and his speech and manner said, "I am a philosopher." The first time I laid eyes on him I thought, "Now *this* is a *maskil!* This is a fount of wisdom!" He was just the sort of teacher I'd hoped for.

I waited breathlessly for my first lesson and was very excited all the way to his house. I opened the door with moist, trembling hands. I stood, awestruck, in the entranceway. Be-

fore me was a spacious room, the very picture of elegant orderliness, with a high-polished floor. I was certain that I'd come
to some palace. I was afraid to mark up the floor with my
boots.

Then the lady of the house appeared and said to us, "You
must be here for your lesson. If you wait a moment, I'll wake
my husband. He was just taking a little rest, he'll be right
with you."

My stomach started to churn. "Who are you, you ignora-
mus, to be disturbing the rest of such a great man?" I thought.
But before I knew it, he stood before us and took us into his
room. We opened our books and the lesson began. We covered
the first chapter, our teacher translating the words for us into
Yiddish. It was as sweet as honey—just like my old *rebbi* . . .
used to translate the *chumash*, you should pardon the comparison.

When we got to the second chapter, we came across two
words: "jumped" and "hopped." Our teacher translated them
both as "jumped," so I asked him to explain the distinction
between them. Without batting an eye, he said they were
identical in meaning but that one was a masculine form and
the other, feminine.

This was a real shock to me, for I already knew from my
study of the Russian primer how to recognize the masculine
and feminine forms. I thought perhaps that the teacher was
joking, or that I had fallen asleep and a dream-spirit was
speaking to me. I opened my eyes wide and decided that I was
fully awake. I examined the teacher's face and saw that his
expression was quite serious. He was not joking. From that
golden, educated tongue had fallen this pearl of an explanation!

I was greatly disillusioned, and doubly enraged because the
man pretended to be what he was not. He had assumed responsibility for a job for which he was utterly unqualified. . . .
Fortunately, the teacher finally announced that the hour was
up, and we were free to go [pp. 99–102]. . . .

That is how it happened that, with my very first encounter
with this man, whose job it was to bring culture to the young-

sters of Szczuczyn, I was already eager for the month to end so that I might be freed of his haughtiness and his "erudition."

I could not bring myself to quit that very day, as I would not deprive the man of his fee. I thus "benefitted" from a full month of his instruction, including more "gems" of translation, such as: "He stepped in and broke it," instead of "He took the hoe and the pike" [the Russian roots are similar]; or "grown up" instead of "deliberately"; and "a small thief," which should have been "a small blackbird." There were others that I have since forgotten. . . .

Once the month was over I was rid of Galatz, but I faced the old question of choosing a tutor. After several weeks of investigation, I chose Dunavich.

Isser Dunavich, my new tutor, was about eighteen years old. He lacked experience and he had no sense of time. If he was supposed to arrive at four o'clock, he would come sometimes at three, sometimes at five. Once a week he regularly failed to come at all. But he knew his Russian perfectly. For the first few days he supervised me closely as I read, but after that he began bringing a Russian newspaper with him to keep himself occupied. As he was quite nearsighted, he buried his nose in the paper, and I did not see his face at all. Every time I was stumped by a word, I had to break into his reading to ask him its meaning. He would answer right away, then go back to his paper. Father took him to task for this. His defense was—he knew that I would always ask if I had a question.

Father apparently began to realize that his son had no ambition to be a rabbi, and he made his peace with that, somehow. He asked only that I not neglect my Talmud entirely, and I obeyed him in this.

I had secretly come upon some copies of the Bible in the synagogue with a German translation in Hebrew transliteration [probably Moses Mendelssohn's edition]. For about two hours a day I read the Bible in this translation and in this second-hand fashion I learned a smattering of German. I devoted six or seven hours a day to Talmud, thus fulfilling my obligation and satisfying all sides.

I believed that I had finally achieved an inner balance,

when once again I encountered an obstacle in my path. The month of Adar came and my tutor informed me that he was leaving town, having found work in another city. He recommended that I continue my lessons with Grossman, but Grossman had a very busy schedule and could not fit me in. I was therefore forced to take Bishkovich.

Bishkovich, however, was not on Dunavich's level. He would hesitate when I asked a question, and sometimes could not supply a correct answer. I realized that I could not trust him completely. Whenever I had doubts about one of his definitions, I could consult Steinberg's dictionary. There were many such occasions, especially when we read the sections of poetry in my textbooks. But when it came to grammatical questions, I simply had to leave them unanswered.

That is how I spent the month-and-a-half until Pesach. About two weeks before Pesach, Dunavich returned and told me that he was planning to settle down in our town after all. Right after the holiday I went back to my lessons with him. This, I believed, would finally stabilize my situation. . . . But this was not to be. Dunavich fell ill with chicken pox. . . . As the obstacles mounted in my path, my determination grew stronger. I did not take a substitute tutor; I waited for Dunavich to recover, and in the meantime I taught myself with the aid of a dictionary. This was hard work, of course, but hope gave me strength.

Six weeks passed and Dunavich, having recovered from his illness, resumed my lessons. Two months later he informed me that he could not continue taking my money for nothing. He assured me that I no longer required his help, since I knew all the basics and had already acquired a substantial vocabulary. To improve my knowledge of the language all I need do was read a lot, which I could manage on my own. . . . So it happened that after one year—with interruptions—I became my own Russian instructor [pp. 102–5].

Rumor spread among the *maskilim* of Szczuczyn that there was a new recruit to the cause in town, one who had a solid knowledge of Russian, to boot. I denied this, but they chose to take this disclaimer as a sign of my modesty. I smiled at this, for who does not like a measure of recognition? . . .

True, I knew the basics of Russian rather well and I retained a fair-sized vocabulary, but this was hardly sufficient for reading the Russian classics. Easier books for beginners were unavailable in our town. My tutor, Dunavich, had given me two or three such books, but that was all there was. There were no more to be had. I had to read anything that came to hand, and what happened to come to hand at the time was a volume of the weekly journal of the Russian-Jewish monthly, *Voskhod* [*Nedel'naia khronika voskhoda*], for the year 1884.

But the articles remained indecipherable for me, because of both their style and their content. Their style—because they were full of foreign terms that were not in any textbook, nor could I find them in Steinberg's dictionary. And their content—because I was unfamiliar with their sphere of discourse. My world was very far-removed from theirs. I had no conception of worldly affairs, I did not know the people involved or the events referred to, and so I could not really understand what the writers were trying to say.

Instead, I tried reading the letters to the editor, which were written in a simpler style and whose contents were more familiar. At the first attempt, I found even this was a great challenge, but I finally understood what was being said. After reading five or six issues of the paper, I began recognizing terms that cropped up repeatedly, and it became much easier. I read all the letters for the year 1884 and thus killed two birds with one stone: I enriched my vocabulary and I acquired a new awareness of the world around me.

Then I also began to understand the main articles and literary essays. I read almost all the way through the year's issues. My knowledge of the world grew and I broadened my horizons. It was an eye-opener for me: I discovered a whole new world. I found that there were legal rulings apart from those of the Ro"Sh—there were also the rulings of the Imperial Senate, that were causing grief to my brethren. I learned that the Sabbath "limit" [*tekhum shabbat*—the permissible walking distance on the Sabbath] was not the only geographical bound-

ary there was: there was also the "limit" called the Pale of
Settlement [*tekhum hamoshav*]. I read and I learned that there
were questions that offered no solution—known as the "Jewish question." I found that there was an ocean besides the
"ocean of Talmud," and it was called the Atlantic, across
which my unfortunate brethren were fleeing to a strange land,
searching for somewhere they might live like human beings.

I discovered that, apart from the "battle" of Torah, there
was another "battle" to be fought: the war of polemics between our writers and those of the [anti-Semitic Russian news-
papers] *Novoe vremia* and *Grazhdanin*. It appeared that the
words of warning in the Torah had come home to roost in our
time: that we had to be fearful of "leaves" [*'aleh*—leaf, but
also page, as of a newspaper], of falling, rotting leaves.
"Leaves" coming from the provinces, "leaves" that barely had
two hundred subscribers, yet had the power to frighten us, so
our writers had to gird themselves and go forth to wage war
against them.

I realized that here was a scattered and dispersed people,
poverty-stricken and oppressed, a people covered with
wounds, scars, and fresh injuries, almost ready to say die, and
yet clinging to life; on its last legs, perhaps, but surviving, and
determined to go on, despite the schemes of its enemies and
despite the advice of "friends". . . . And I was a son of this
people, my fate was tied to its fate. A warm feeling, a feeling I
had not known before, began to well up inside me and fill me
with emotion. I suddenly felt that I was not an isolated limb,
but a living, organic part of my unhappy people, connected to
it by unbreakable bonds. I felt a brother to my people and
loved them unrestrainedly, I felt their pain and sorrow as well
as their joys, felt comforted when they were comforted, and
was zealous for their honor [pp. 105–8].

As I've mentioned, I divided my time between my religious
and secular studies. Up till then the one never interfered with
the other, and I was able to preserve an equilibrium between
the two. I stood firmly with both feet on the soil of my tradition. Every sacred book, however recent, was an absolute authority for me, never to be questioned. I did not read Haskalah

books, considering them heretical. Even if, for some reason, I neglected my Talmud for a day or two, I always returned with renewed ardor, like a lover who has been parted from his beloved, trying to make up for lost time.

A change came over me—and a recognizable one—after I'd been exposed to classical European literature. My Russian was adequate: I had read Russian literature in the original, and I had read European works in Russian translation. I discovered a new world once again, a world that enchanted me with its novelty, its beauty, its rich colors. I discovered men of letters whose vision soared like eagles, who stimulated one's thinking with their perspective on the world and their critical observations of life. There were writers and books whose engaging style, clarity, and accuracy of description were simply captivating. I realized that there were great thinkers all over the world, even if they had never studied the Talmud.

Doubt began to creep into my heart, doubt as to whether the Talmudic sages were really the last word in human wisdom, whether the Talmud was really the acme of knowledge and of Truth. A pitched battle took shape within me, a conflict between two cultures: my ancient world with its hoary head, to which I felt so strongly attached, and the splendid, exciting, and enchanting new world. I weighed them both in the balance and was terrified to see the new world begin to overcome the old—very slowly, but perceptibly, inevitably! That critical spirit, that healthy logic, that good common sense that had led me to reject the *pilpul* of the Later Sages in favor of the straightforward analysis of the Early Sages—those same factors in my personality now conspired to pick holes in my world, until finally they created a breach that threatened to widen, deepen, and undermine the whole.

Seeking a solution, I went to the new Hebrew literature, hoping to find an answer there. Surely, I thought, some profound thinker among our writers had trod this path before me and charted a course that I might follow between the two worlds, or at least build a bridge between them. Unfortunately, however, such writers were rare in those days and their books were unavailable in my town. The only books I could get hold of, among those of the modern Hebrew writers, were from the early days of the Haskalah. . . . I started reading them but found them awful. I had cut my teeth on the European classics, on talented writers who were experts at their craft, who wrote intelligently and lucidly, and always had something to say. And what did I find in our Hebrew literature? Essays that seemed pointless, stuffed with chopped-up biblical phrases, rhetorical flourishes, and stilted verbiage. They went round and round and said nothing. The authors seemed ill-at-ease or unfamiliar with the subjects they dealt with, revealing an abysmal ignorance.

I decided to bear with it, nonetheless, and I continued reading in the hope that somewhere, amid the dregs, I would come upon one shining light, one spark. Well, I found out something valuable, but not what I'd hoped to find. I found out how rotten literature can be when it is bad, how stupid writers can be. Here you had, for example, a young acolyte of the Enlightenment who had never strayed from his little town, but who waxed eloquent about far-off countries and their inhabitants in the tones of an experienced world traveler. Or else you had an idler of a *melamed* [schoolteacher], with nothing in the world to his name, pretending to be an authority on economics and, with all the seriousness of a renowned professor, giving advice on the new occupations that Jews ought to try.

There were color-blind poets who got the color of the sky wrong, who had to struggle to describe a rainbow. There were timid men who never in their lives so much as glanced at a young lady, who blushed in the company of women and kept their eyes downcast, but who spun love stories in the [erotic] manner of the Song of Songs! Every one of them used pretentious, ethereal expressions culled from Isaiah, Hosea, and Job, words that no one in the world would actually use! And the more of this stuff the better, it would seem. These lame versifiers dared to crown themselves "high priests in the temple of Hebrew literature"! What sheer arrogance! False priests, idiots, with sullied hands, who defiled their people's sacred altar, yet had the gall to glorify themselves and to demand respect!

Idolators like Zimri who claimed the status of the pure priest Pinchas.

As for those among our writers who were truly talented, who had read widely and knew the literature of Europe, and who possessed an aesthetic sensibility—those only used their gift destructively: criticizing, undermining, and causing injury to the beauty of Judaism. No one came to its defense, no one felt the need to insure the survival of our ancestral heritage. I therefore felt very disappointed, both in the new Hebrew literature and its practitioners. [Note: This paragraph may be a later addition to the original text.]

In the meantime, however, the breakdown of my inner world continued, tearing my soul to pieces. True, I continued as before to devote the same number of hours to studying Talmud, but quantity was not the point. Though I'd spend six hours with my texts, I'd not cover nearly as much as I used to do in a third of the time. My former diligence, devotion, and innocent faith were gone. Alien thoughts and ugly ideas stole into my mind when I should have been concentrating on my studies. They froze my desire to learn and prevented me from working conscientiously. Once in a while my old enthusiasm was kindled again, and I was able to devote hours at a time, as before, to my learning. But this upsurge was like the last flicker of a candle before it goes out. It sputtered and turned cold.

I felt a horrible emptiness inside. I longed for the happy days I had known before, in the days of my naive faith when my soul was pure and whole. I wished I could turn back the clock, but I could not. No one can go back to the games of childhood. As Ecclesiastes said, "Man cannot control the spirit."

I decided to try and fill the void within me, no matter with what, and so I began to study German. There was no German tutor in our town, and I was therefore forced to teach myself, using the Ullendorf method. I got to the point where I could read a simple story—but that was as far as I could go. There were no books available in town, and I had no money to buy books. I suddenly felt cramped in that place. I made up my mind to get to a big city, or to someplace where German was spoken and where I might pursue my studies.

Fate chose the place for me. I had two uncles in Bialystok, my mother's brothers, the younger of whom was a German teacher. It was not easy to convince Father to let me go. At first he refused to hear of it. I pleaded with him night and day. Finally, after I promised to continue to set aside my regular time for Talmud study, he reluctantly gave his approval [pp. 108–13]. . . .

My younger uncle, Moyshe-Yehezkel, had run away from home at a young age. Leaving his town, Kolna, he had stolen across the border to Prussia and sent a letter to Rabbi [Esriel] Hildesheimer [in Berlin], asking to be accepted as a student in Hildesheimer's [modern Orthodox] rabbinical seminary. The letter, written in a beautiful Hebrew and attesting to the writer's familiarity with Judaic culture, did the trick. Hildesheimer took him in and made sure he had everything he needed. My uncle was considered one of the best students there, but a year before completing the course of studies things turned sour. He was forced to leave the seminary and Germany, and he came to his brother in Bialystok. There he settled down and became a prominent German teacher. . . . He also studied accounting, and then married his niece. . . . He spent the dowry quickly and lived on what he made teaching German—about a hundred rubles a month. This was a huge sum seventy years ago [note: this is an obvious later insertion]. He lived in cramped quarters in a three-room apartment on the very fashionable Nowo Lippa Street, he dressed like a dandy, and affected a grand style. . . . Upon discovering my intentions, he stood up and delivered a half-hour lecture on the foolhardiness of my mission. How could I have come seeking Enlightenment in such a place as this, a commercial city where people were entirely preoccupied with business and practical affairs, and had neither the time nor the inclination to pursue culture and education? . . . All my dreams and hopes evaporated in an instant. It was like a cold shower. I stood there stunned, abashed, as ashamed as any student who had been given a good thrashing by his teacher.

After several minutes I managed to speak: "Never mind, uncle, don't feel bad. It is not worth worrying about. I see I have made a mistake and I'll just turn around and go back home." "You'll do nothing of the kind," he said. "You are in my house, and I will not have it said that I turned you away from my door." . . . He seemed to forget his irritation and began asking me about my studies. I explained how I'd come to learn Russian, about the writers whose works I'd read, and how I still spent the bulk of my time on Talmud. He asked whether I hoped someday to secure a rabbinical post. I blushed and said nothing, thinking that he must be teasing me. But he repeated the question, in all seriousness, so I told him that I'd never even considered the possibility of earning a living from Torah.

"If that's the case," my uncle went on, why was I spending so much time on Talmud? Of what use was it to me? And the bit of Russian that I'd picked up—how would that benefit me? Were I to learn some German, too, how would that help? "These will not get you a job or fill your stomach," he concluded.

"But I am not looking for work," I said, "I only came so that I might continue my education."

"Why then did you bother coming all this way?" he asked. "Are there no *gemorehs* [Talmuds] in Szczuczyn?" . . .

After a brief pause he went on: "But . . . maybe there is something we can do for you after all. . . . If I could just be sure that you would be able to achieve your goal here, I'd gladly put you up for a whole year. But, you see, such a thing is really beyond reach."

The words, "practical," "job," and "goal" were words I was hearing for the first time in my life, and they utterly confused me. I found it hard to absorb them all at once. At home, when I was studying *gemoreh*, I never considered it in relation to any "goal"; I was only trying to learn so that I might gain wisdom. Now I was hearing this educated person explain the necessity of having an aim in life, that without it one might as well not have been born! . . . [pp. 114–17]

Although I had been a freethinker in spirit even before I'd

left for Bialystok, in practice I had remained as strictly Orthodox as always. I did not violate the least custom or ignore
even latter-day stringent precautions. In my naiveté I thought
that whoever disregarded the slightest Jewish custom or pre-
cept was automatically beyond the pale, that his very Jewishness might be questioned. As I had no wish to remove
myself from the society I lived in, I went on behaving like
everyone else.

In Bialystok I found out that things were quite different.
There I saw people who were undeniably Jewish, but who
behaved like civilized Europeans and who abandoned customs
that stood in their way; yet, they remained loyal to the Jewish
faith and the Jewish people. My younger uncle was not considered exceptional. His home life was conducted in the European manner: people sat down to meals bareheaded, no one
made a fuss over the preliminary ritual of hand-washing, and
no care was taken to recite the blessings either before or after
the meal. Likewise, they paid no heed to the stricter Sabbath
restrictions: they carried handkerchiefs in their pockets, even
money; and they combed their hair and polished their shoes
on the Sabbath. For all that, my uncle was a good Jew, a
frequent guest in the home of Rabbi Shmuel Mohilever [an
early Orthodox supporter of Zionism], a fervent Zionist who
loved his people and honored its language and its literature.
(My uncle published translations from German in such Hebrew papers as *Ha-Yom* and *Knesset*.)

I began to conduct myself as they did, and had no serious
qualms about it. Habit became second nature, and when I
returned to Szczuczyn I found it difficult to go back to the
old, strict regimen. I knew, however, that Szczuczyn was not
Bialystok. Sins that went unnoticed in the big city were cause
for scandal in a small town. I did the best I could to avoid
offending anyone's principles. . . . [pp. 125–27]

The saying goes, "walls have ears" . . . and in due course it
became known that I was giving Russian lessons. I was
swamped with requests to tutor other people's sons and daughters. I turned them down: this was not what I had in mind.

At Pesach-time, however, the son of Urison came and proposed that I teach him and his sister two hours a day, for which he would pay me five rubles a month. This caught me off guard. It was hard to turn down such a sum: thirty rubles for a term would buy me some nice clothes. And it was quite an honor to be welcomed at the Urisons'—the richest family in town. (Urison owned a bank in Warsaw, but his family lived in Szczuczyn.) I also knew that they had a sizable library that I would have access to. . . . By the end of the term I had thirty rubles in my pocket. I spent it all on clothes and had nothing left, but I was very happy. It felt so good to put on clothes bought with my own earnings. For the first time in my life I actually owned something.

Father was surprised, and asked where I had gotten so much money. I told him. I could see in his face his secret satisfaction that I had been invited into such an august home, but his words were harsh. He did not want me to become a teacher, he said.

"But Father," I argued, "in the first place I did not go ahead with this on my own. I asked my brother's advice. In the second place, are you able to provide me the clothes I need so that I needn't be ashamed to show myself in public? In the third place, in a year or two I'll be called up for military service, and it will be necessary to bribe the doctors and the officials. Can you afford that?"

That ended Father's complaints. He kept quiet after that. That next winter I became a tutor openly. The Urisons sang my praises to their friends. I gave lessons in the best homes. I even taught Hebrew at the home of a lawyer, who paid me five rubles a month. By the end of the winter term I had enough for clothes as well as a substantial sum that I "lent" (gave) to Father, so that he might buy wheat before Pesach.

I am welcomed in the homes of our leading families. I have many friends among the young men and women in town, and I have as many books as I might wish. Now I am saving every penny so that I can get out of military service. I sometimes go to the *beys medresh*, to protect my reputation, and so as not to forget Talmud altogether [pp. 128–30]. [Note: The memoir ends at this point—E. L.].

Conclusion

As noted, this memoir reflects a pivotal psychological moment in one young man's transition from the shtetl to the modern city, and from tradition to skepticism. The fact that his odyssey was mediated by the acquisition of new languages is only one point of contact between the memoir and the theme of this book. The other point is the interwoven character of cultural and political "packages."

The memoir also aids us in understanding the phenomenon described in the previous chapter: namely, the use by *maskilim* of rhetoric drawn from traditional vocabulary. After all, most if not all *maskilim* had shared some of the experiences of the young man in this memoir, beginning with the classical-Hebraic and rabbinic education of young boys. It was, therefore, natural for them to hark back to the charged phrases and catchwords of their common heritage, even as they sought to transform it.

The majority of East European Jews were not out to transform their heritage, however. Among most of them, tradition was a given, although it was increasingly beset by new challenges. In the following chapter, we turn to an examination of the politics of tradition as they were played out among leaders of the Orthodox world.

CHAPTER 4

Orthodox Jewish Opinion in Turn-of-the-Century Russia and Poland: A Documentary Study in Culture and Politics

The traditionalist majority of the Jewish population in Eastern Europe seems to have been—politically—a "silent majority" if we apply the standards of political awareness and activity that we use for the secular parties and ideologies that flourished throughout the region from the 1880s to the First World War. Except for the small Mizrachi (Religious Zionist) group within the Zionist movement (founded 1902), a distinctive and significant Orthodox political voice appears to have come on the scene quite late, on the eve of the Great War, to become a force to reckon with in interwar Jewish politics, chiefly in Poland.

Yet, to define political attitudes and political action only in terms of modern, organized, essentially Western modes is to prejudge the issue. As an expression of traditionalism in a posttraditional world, Orthodox Jewry was naturally averse to the idea of adopting the techniques of mobilization and mass communication (let alone explicit ideological programs) that politicization implied.

The very idea of politics as a mass phenomenon was an alien concept, difficult to assimilate for those who continued to view politics as the realm of confidential negotiations and pragmatic

An abbreviated version of this essay, presenting only the first document in the group, appeared previously in Shvut: yahadut brit-hamo'atsot umizrah-eiropah 15 (1992): xxxiii–xl (English section).

arrangements with the gentile powers-that-be. Being privy to these, sometimes dangerous and always sensitive, proceedings, demanded both a highly developed sense of discretion—something that was associated with the type of highly placed "court Jew" or *shtadlan*— plus an instinctive and infallible sense of the Jewish interest— something that no one but the greatest rabbinical sages could be trusted to possess. The public at large could not (and ought not be expected to) deal with such matters.[1]

That does not mean, however, that political action and political awareness as such were foreign to the Orthodox worldview. On the contrary: some of the rabbinical leaders in Eastern Europe in the imperial period were consummate political practitioners, and knew how and when to deploy their political contacts and agents.[2] Similarly, attitudes toward the gentile state and toward fractious dissidents in the Jewish community—who were often branded as violators of Jewish law—formed the basis of a political "opinion" or public consciousness in traditional Jewry, long before the era of partisan politics, and continued to do so into modern times.

Orthodox Jewish culture was never monolithic, and the history of traditional and posttraditional Judaism in Eastern Europe is a complex web of intramural rivalries, ideological rifts, and personality conflicts—all of which was overlaid by the deepening split between traditionalists, on the one hand, and liberal or radical reformers, on the other. The complexity of these relationships infused Jewish cultural and social affairs with a contentious spirit that was openly expressed in public and in private.

The adamant defense of the status quo in religious, cultural, and educational matters led Orthodox figures to band together or look for powerful patrons. By the same token, Orthodox leaders were brought into conflict with anyone—be they Jews or government officials—who sought to introduce change or to challenge established rabbinical authorities. The Orthodox developed their own means of internal communication, mobilization, and persuasion— in effect, a political network and modus operandi of some sophistication and effectiveness. In the nineteenth century these arrangements were largely informal and ad hoc; but under the impact of increasing institutionalization in Jewish political life generally, and especially during the First World War, the Orthodox sector successfully created more formal political pressure groups.[3]

Yet, tracing the history of the Orthodox response to social and political change in Eastern Europe before 1917 remains tricky, precisely because so much of it took place "under wraps" and by word of mouth. Details tend to evade documentation and, therefore, historical scrutiny, even when rough impressions are available.

The documents presented here attest to some of those elusive details. They reflect events and personalities drawn from three corners of the Jewish Pale of Settlement: Vilna (Vil'nius), the southern Ukraine, and Poland (Lomza district and Kielce), and cover the period from 1883 to 1911. They include both public documents and private correspondence. And they provide specific examples of the kinds of rhetoric that were used by those who responded to modernity with a vigorous defense of traditionalism.

With the exception of the Vilna document (a photocopy of which is in the collections of the Jewish National and University Library in Jerusalem),[4] the items are drawn from the papers of the Yerusalimsky family, part of the archival collection of the Schocken Library, Jerusalem (under the auspices of the Jewish Theological Seminary of America). I wish to thank the staff of the Schocken Library for their cooperation and assistance.

The Antisocialist Appeal of the Vilna Rabbis, June 1903

We already know, in general terms, that there was no love lost between the Orthodox rabbinate and radical Jewish socialists. The *kol koyre* (public appeal) of the Vilna rabbis, issued in June 1903,[5] warning loyal Jews to beware of falling into the path of error, illustrates in concrete form some of the problems that faced traditional leaderships, caught between the government authorities, on the one hand, and a restive Jewish population, on the other. Vilna, of course, was a key center of Jewish radical and labor movement activity, and the Vilna rabbis were unable—for various reasons—to simply ignore such disturbing trends.

Wall posters and handbills were a form of communication that obviated the necessity of maintaining a daily press and, when placed in every synagogue and chapel in the city, could be expected to reach the target population immediately and effectively. The appeal of 1903 followed a similar one published in 1901—as is indicated in our document. Fifteen years previously, in 1886, the rabbis of Vilna and the board of the city's central Jewish charity fund—*Hatsedakah hagedolah*—had handled another sensitive political issue in similar fashion. In that case, the problem was a campaign by the provincial administration to enforce long-neglected codes prohibiting conspicuously Jewish attire. The Jewish communal and rabbinical leadership at the time had used a public appeal to urge their constituents to be more circumspect when going about their business on main streets of the city.[6]

The chief clue as to the circumstances surrounding the 1903 document lies in its timing. The most pressing precipitating factor was probably the appearance, at the end of May 1903, of a handbill distributed by the Bund, the underground Jewish social democratic party. Printed in Yiddish and Russian, the Bund leaflet called on the workers of Vilna to strike in commemoration of Hirsh Lekert, the young Jewish martyr of the revolutionary movement, executed in May 1902 for his attempted assassination of the Vilna governor-general, Viktor von Wahl.[7] (It is also not coincidental that all the events in question occurred soon after May 1.)

More generally, strikes and underground socialist activity had been on the upswing since 1902 and Jewish young people were conspicuously active among radical ranks. Jews accounted for a full third of political arrestees in Russia between 1900 and 1905.[8] Chaim Weizmann, writing in June 1903, perceived the situation as follows: "Almost all [Jewish] students belong to the revolutionary camp. . . . It is fearful . . . to observe the major part of our youth— and no one would describe them as the worst part—offering themselves for sacrifice as though seized by a fever."[9] And historian Jonathan Frankel has written, about this period, that "even Orthodox Jews deeply hostile to socialism . . . tended increasingly to sympathize with their young relatives in the revolutionary underground."[10]

By 1900 there were some 1,400 Jewish workers organized in *kassy* or strike funds in Vilna, and these represented only a fraction of those who participated in local strike action in those years.[11]

Whether or not grass-roots sympathy for socialists was growing, even among Orthodox Jews, as Frankel suggests—and the apprehension expressed in our document, if anything, tends to support that thesis—the "clerical" establishment, on the other hand, had little reason to go along with such a trend. Of course, this appeal may have been issued under duress (explicit or implicit) and at the behest of the authorities. In that case it would be difficult to learn anything from this document about Orthodox politics. The possibility of explicit coercion exists because both the local Vilna administration, and key ministers of the tsarist government, believed that the Jewish communal leadership could rein in its radical youth, and insisted on various occasions that it do so.[12]

Yet, it is by no means clear that the rabbis' response was simply pro forma. Some of them had, in the past, willingly complied with requests by the authorities to throw their moral weight against strikers.[13] Socialists were, more often than not, godless renegades who constituted a clear threat to the religious and moral integrity of yeshiva-educated youth, and therefore were regarded with repugnance. They were also apt to place other Jews in danger.

To illustrate, let me mention another document from the same time period, but which cannot be suspected of having been colored by external constraints, and can therefore serve as a "control." The document in this case is a sermon delivered in Chicago, in the fall of 1905, as a eulogy to Jews killed in pogroms in Russia during the revolutionary disturbances. The speaker, an immigrant rabbi from Russia, while he referred to the tsarist government as a *malkhut zadon*—kingdom of wickedness—laid the blame for the victimization of innocent Jews on Jewish radicals, who had gone against age-old Jewish tradition. Note that he uses the same stock proof texts that appear in the 1903 document:

> Day and night I mourn the slain among my people . . . the many victims who have fallen through the fault of our own people: those impetuous and intemperate young boys and girls who went out in the city to sing songs of rebellion. By doing so they provoked the kingdom of wickedness and those evil messengers who do its bidding, and they paid no heed to the words of Scripture (Proverbs 24): "Fear the Lord, my son, and the king, and do not associate with dissenters"; or to the words of the rabbis (B. Ketubot 111 [comment on Song of Songs 3]): "I have adjured you, o daughters of Jerusalem, etc.", by which God

adjured Israel not to rebel against the nations of the world . . . , "If you keep this oath, it will go well with you, but if not, then your lives are forfeit. . . . " And this is the result, that my people have been slain through their own fault.[14]

A second "control," in this case a sermon by the traditionalist Moscow rabbi, Yehuda-Leyb Groybart, after the February Revolution of 1917 (and, thus, no longer subject to the same constraints present under the tsarist regime), points to the paramount religious-cultural concerns of the Orthodox rabbinate. In the quote (cited by Altshuler), Rabbi Groybart assumes that the old regime had, despite obvious negative features, been "good for the Jews" from a spiritual point of view:

> We come [now] to partake of the fruit of freedom, but in our hearts we are apprehensive; for we remember that as of old, in generations past, even though our enemies oppressed us, we nevertheless always remained true to our tradition . . . and no amount of persecution and suffering could sway us from our law. . . . But at the first sign of release, when the gentiles hold out to us a hand of peace and draw us to them with bonds of friendship, we fairly run [toward them]—and we may abandon our stand and assimilate among them.[15]

It is thus almost moot to speculate as to the exact provenance of the Vilna appeal: Although it may have been prompted by official coercion, it also coincided with a political position that can be generically identified with at least part of the Orthodox religious leadership.

Moreover, the gist of the rabbis' appeal was that—in any case—it is in the interest of the Jews to help the government maintain law and order; that civil unrest is dangerous to the Jewish population; and that centuries of Jewish tradition had made this policy virtually sacrosanct, complete with set proof texts from the Bible and the Talmud. In other words, the moral *right* of the authorities to demand that the rabbis take up a position against sedition was not in itself in doubt. And, by the same token, neither was the moral *obligation* of the Jewish community to comply. The argument is instrumentalist and tactical to begin with, which accurately reflects how traditional Jewish politics operated vis-à-vis the gentile state: what may very aptly be called a politics of expediency.[16]

That the Vilna rabbis would feel more than justified in appealing to law and order in the summer of 1903 becomes clear when we consider that only two months had passed since the shocking pogrom in April in Kishinev. In Vilna, despite tensions that sometimes flared between the Jewish community and the provincial administration,[17] the Jews had been spared the mob violence that had wreaked havoc in other communities in the 1880s and 1890s. This good fortune was credited by the Jews themselves largely to the implacable commitment of the local administration to the maintenance of law and order. Since 1901, new directives had reinforced the prohibition against street gatherings.[18] While these regulations may have been directed primarily against radicals and strikers, they also helped to protect Jews against mob violence. (On the role of the local administration in preventing anti-Jewish violence in this period, see below, documents 8–10.)

Thus, when the rabbis of Vilna quoted *Mishna Avot* ("except for the fear of the government, men would swallow each other alive"), their message bore an immediate and ominous relevance for Jews who lived in fear of violent outbreaks. (Early in September 1903, in fact, a new pogrom took place in Gomel.) Vilna rabbis had all the more reason to brook no interference with the authorities on a matter in which their concerns coincided with those of the regime.

As if that were not enough, the governor-general of the Vilna province had, only three months before (March 1903) lifted residence restrictions against Jews in Vilna's suburban district. This gesture preceded a general act by Minister of Internal Affairs von Plehve (in May 1903), canceling regulations enacted in May 1882 that had barred Jews from 101 locations within the Pale of Settlement.[19] The Jewish leadership would have realized how dependent the Jews were on official "largesse" of this kind, and how unwise it might be to forfeit these benefits through failing to take an explicit stand on an issue of common concern.

The Vilna rabbis' appeal of June 1903, therefore, reflects the situation of the local religious authorities in the context of Russian politics. Under the circumstances, they would have considered a denunciation of socialist and revolutionary ideas timely and eminently beneficial for the Jewish population at large. It would distance the loyal majority from the trouble-making minority, hopefully sparing the community from guilt by association with the "transgressors" (compare document 9, below) — a favorite tactic in the arsenal of traditional Jewish politics.

The appeal was printed on one sheet, in three columns (the text in Russian in the center, flanked by the Yiddish text on the left and the Hebrew version on the right). Phrases set off by asterisks and italics are additions or glosses from the Yiddish version that do not appear in the Hebrew text: the Yiddish text tends to be more discursive, with added phrases and extended explanations. The Hebrew text closely approximates the Russian one. The proof text-explication style is, of course, characteristic of traditional rabbinic rhetoric.

Document 1: "Public Appeal by the Rabbis of This City, Vilna"

We have already had occasion, two years ago, to issue a warning against certain misguided and ignorant persons who, to our dismay, have allowed agitators to divert them from the proper path of Torah, *mitsvot*, justice and righteousness [seeking thereby] to destroy the civil peace and our lawful system of government, which is dedicated to implanting justice and morality, *brotherhood and compassion,* in the hearts of the people of our country, that they may walk uprightly before God and man alike. The aim of these agitators is to lead the people astray from the proper path. But we, children of Abraham, Isaac, and Jacob, have been commanded to do only that which is good and right, *and to punctiliously observe the laws and statutes of the government under whose protection we dwell* and to accept the rule of the government willingly and wholeheartedly. As the wise Solomon said in Proverbs 24 [v. 21], "Fear the Lord, my son, and the king, and do not associate with dissenters." Scripture thus equated obedience to the king with obedience to heaven. The reason [why this is so] is that the king, in his gracious wisdom, guides the people toward the proper path and toward piety. He who does not sincerely venerate the king is certain, therefore, to be lacking in his love of God, as well. He who honors the word of God will also honor the king and his ministers with all his heart and soul. We, children of Israel, are solemnly sworn to keep faith with the government and to obey every command of the king, for that is how our sages of old understood the verse [Song of Songs 3:5] in which *when we had been driven into exile* God adjured Israel never to rebel against the nations of the world *under whose protection we dwell*. In Ecclesiastes 8, once again, Solomon cautions us: "Obey the king's commands and do not lightly utter an oath to God." By this he meant to admonish us to honor and observe the law of the king; and as for the "oath to God," this refers to the [aforementioned] oath to which God swore us, namely, never to rebel against the nations of the world. Therefore, as Jews we are solemnly sworn to fulfill that oath. Certainly we must be loyal subjects of the king and faithful to his laws. Our sages of old stated further: "Always let fear [i.e., respect] of the kingdom rest upon you." For example [in his encounter with the Pharoah, Moses said]: "All these, your servants, will come to me," rather than 'You will come to me,' which would have shown lack of respect. And Rabbi Yohanan taught us [that respect for kings should go even further] by citing the verse regarding Elijah [and King Ahab]: "He tied up his skirts and ran in front of Ahab" [I Kings 18:46]. Rabbi Yohanan cited this particular verse because from [the words spoken by Moses] "All your servants, etc.," all we can derive is the duty to *speak* to royalty with proper respect; but this in itself does not illustrate [R. Yohanan's point] that it is actually our duty to *exert ourselves* to demonstrate our respect for the king. That is why Rabbi Yohanan cited [the aforementioned verse] "and he ran in front of Ahab." This illustrates the sacred duty we all must feel to serve and honor the king with all our might. Elijah the prophet, the man of God, exerted himself and ran before the king, out of respect. From this we see that every man must serve the king and venerate him with every fiber of his being. Furthermore, the rabbis taught us in the Mishna, in tractate *Avot*, "Pray for the welfare of the kingdom, for except for fear of the government, men would swallow each other alive." For the king establishes the rule of law throughout the land, that justice might prevail, [so that] "they will not do evil or destroy" [Isaiah 11:9] one another. There are none so blind as those who cannot see how great is God's favor in bestowing majesty upon kings and ministers. *Terrestrial government photographically reproduces or reflects heavenly government.* He who does not appreciate all the good that the ruler performs for all his subjects, every hour of every day, is surely guilty of ingratitude. And ingratitude is so despicable that, of such a person who would repay good with wickedness, King Solomon said, "May misfortune constantly plague his house." It is the wise man who knows how to appreciate and thank the king for his compassionate rule over all his subjects. This applies, above all, to our own monarch, our lord the Emperor, His Majesty NIKOLAI ALEKSANDROVICH, who is a gracious and compassionate ruler who seeks the welfare of all his people.

Therefore, children of Israel, *beloved brethren*, take these words to heart [because] they are true and just, and turn away from the wicked course of deviation from righteousness which some would have you follow. Shun their company, take heed and preserve yourselves and your souls. Let us all remain faithful servants of His Majesty the king, our gracious lord. May God sustain him in life, protect him from harm and save him from injury. May he succeed in all his endeavors. In his lifetime and in ours, may we speedily witness the salvation of Judah, and may Israel forever dwell in peace, Amen.

The Yerusalimsky Papers

The bulk of this family archive is formed by a collection of letters and papers written by Rabbi Moshe Nahum ben Binyamin Yerusalimsky of Tomashpol', Podolia[20] (b. 1855 in Bershad, Podolia); other documents (including his release from military service, in 1876);[21] and letters written by his sons—David-Yona and Yehoshua-Heshl— by his wife, Rivka, and by his brother, Yaakov (Yankl) Yerusalimsky. Most of the items are in Hebrew, with the remainder written in Yiddish. (The official documents, of course, are in Russian.) According to a statement in document 6 (below), Yerusalimsky was a nephew of the Liubavitcher rebbe, R. Sholom Dov-Ber Schneersohn.

Yerusalimsky took up the post of rabbi *(av bet din)* in the small town of Kamenka (Kiev province) in 1880.[22] After an initial period in which he supported the proto-Zionist Hibbat Zion movement, he became an opponent of political Zionism (along with much of the Orthodox rabbinate). In 1895 he passed the state examinations, thus becoming certified as a government-recognized ("crown") rabbi.[23] He moved, in 1898, from the southern Ukraine to Poland, taking up the rabbinical post in the town of Ostrolenka, north of Warsaw,[24] leaving his sons behind to tend the family grain business. His departure from Kamenka was apparently precipitated by the community's failure to pay his salary regularly.[25] Four years later, in 1902, Yerusalimsky (henceforth: MNY) moved yet again to a small Polish community, this time to the south of Warsaw: Kielce.[26] There he served as rabbi of the town and its surrounding district. A letter from David-Yona to his father, dated 1 Adar 5671 (= early spring 1911), indicates that MNY at that time considered becoming a candidate for the post of rabbi in Riga, but there is no further indication of such a development.[27]

According to biographical data, MNY knew both Russian and German and possessed a "fairly rich library of German books." None of the letters I have examined, however, give any indication of how or whether he made use of such volumes. He himself wrote and published several volumes of responsa and a commentary on Maimonides's *Mishneh Torah*.[28]

The documents I have selected pertain to several areas of Jewish cultural and political life at the end of the nineteenth century and the beginning of the twentieth. Documents 2 through 5 relate to both educational and economic affairs: The first, dating from 1883, is an example of Orthodox rabbinical resistance to recurrent efforts by Jewish reformers in Russia to establish a modern rabbinical seminary, where secular studies would be part of the curriculum. Document 3 (1910), a letter addressed to a prominent secular Jewish political spokesman, proposes a collaborative effort to win an exemption for Jews from legislation that would mandate Sabbath rest on Sunday. Documents 4 and 5, from 1911, show an instance of successful lobbying in the interests of *melamdim* (primary-school teachers).

The attempts to establish modern rabbinical seminaries took

place against the background of the earlier closure of the crown seminaries in Warsaw, Vilna, and Zhitomir, a situation that left the *maskilim* and their patrons in Russia without a significant institutional base. Figures associated with the Society for Promoting Enlightenment among Jews (OPE) repeatedly sought opportunities to revive the seminary concept. Plans for a new seminary were discussed between 1881 and 1882, but Orthodox leaders (led by Rabbi Israel Salanter, Yaakov Lifschitz, and Rabbi Isaac Elhanan Spector) orchestrated a massive wave of protests by rabbis in Russia and Poland.[29] The correspondence of MNY demonstrates a clear link between himself and the *misnagdish* leaders in Kovno,[30] and document 2 appears to be a product of the rabbis' efforts to persuade Baron Horace Günzburg, as head of the OPE, to quash the new seminary initiative.

Both this document (a letter to his father in which MNY copied his own letter to Baron Günzburg and a response he received, for his father's benefit) and documents 3–7 demonstrate not only the workings of the internal networks and divisions among the Orthodox rabbinical leadership, but also the rabbis' familiarity with the "who's who" of Jewish politics. In his letter to Baron Günzburg (doc. 2), MNY appears to have followed his mentors' advice on how to approach the subject with tact and respect;[31] and his letter to Sliozberg (doc. 3) again reflects a canny ability to appeal to prominent, non-Orthodox Jewish political spokesmen.[32] In document 15 Jewish nationalists (in the main, non-Orthodox) are mentioned in a favorable context, distinguishing them from "assimilationist" forces in the Jewish community of Warsaw (see below).

The letter to Sliozberg is remarkable in two respects: First, it reveals some of MNY's underlying pessimism with regard to the consequences of modernization ("humanistic progress") for Jewish religiosity. Second, the letter is written in a modern, streamlined Hebrew, stripped of the usual studied archaicism of rabbinic prose. Moreover, in this letter the writer shows that he is able to speak the new political rhetoric of modern nationalism, invoking all the catchphrases of romantic national pride. Possibly, MNY tailored his rhetoric to his reader's susceptibilities.

Documents 6 and 7 deal with preparations for the government-sponsored Rabbinical Commission (held in St. Petersburg in 1910),[33] and also relate to the organization of a more formal Orthodox network, "Knesses Yisroel" (founded 1907). These letters demonstrate the gradual development within Orthodox circles toward more effective political coordination, directed against secularist forces in East European Jewry.

Documents 8 to 10 are letters to MNY from his sons and his brother, each relating to questions of security and the threat of violence, dating from the period 1905–1907. In the first one of the three, Yehoshua-Heshl writes from his home in Teplik to inquire about a "libel" (he does not specify, but probably a case of abduction or rape) involving a young gentile girl in Kielce and the local Jewish community. He also mentions the insecure atmosphere in his own town during the Easter season. In the second letter, David-Yona writes from Khorol', describing the violent repression of socialist activities by the local authorities, and pointing out the special message given to the local Jews. In the third, Yaakov Yerusalimsky, in Tomashpol', tells of the effective action of the local authorities in nipping a pogrom in the bud. All three letters reflect the perilous conditions during and following the upheavals of 1905, in which revolutionary activity was accompanied by other manifestations of violence and persecution. This period also marked the height of Jewish immigration to America, prior to World War I.

It bears noting that most of these letters contain expressions of confidence in the government, some of it *de rigueur*, perhaps, but more likely (especially in view of the private nature of this correspondence) simply a function of the unsettled state of affairs in the country that threatened the security of Jewish communities and caused them to look to the local administration for protection. This is certainly in line with what we find in document 1, above.

New social realities confronted the Orthodox rabbis during this period of upheaval, mass emigration, and large-scale urbanization. Both resistance and adjustment to these conditions are reflected in documents 11 to 14. Document 11 relates to efforts to block the conversion of a traditional, strictly supervised craft—matzo baking—to mass production methods. Here, MNY and his colleagues took a very strict view against innovation, having reached the conclusion that no machine could adequately reproduce the strict ritual conditions of production necessary for Passover matzos. An indication that their objections were not simply a matter of technical legal doctrine, but part of a cultural resistance to modernization, is the extreme language used to describe the matzo-baking machinery as "the devious work of the evil inclination" and the moral equivalent of the "golden calf"—a false idol. That metaphor suggests not only the spiritual threat involved, but also the potentially seductive appeal of the devilish contraption to a modernizing society.

Interestingly, MNY took a more liberal position in a case involving the miracles of modern medicine. In that instance (the case involved urological problems in a male infant that could be corrected by surgical procedures, though risking the child's reproductive capacity), he insisted that the health and welfare of the individual took precedence over biblical injunctions ("Be fruitful and multiply"), even though the child's life was not endangered by the malformation and even though no pain and suffering was yet manifested (and thus the procedure could not be regarded as emergency surgery). He further remarked that one must rely completely upon the medical advice given by the surgeons ("an expert is qualified to render an opinion in his own craft"), and advised the family to seek out the best available medical advice by undertaking a trip to Warsaw for that purpose.[34] The difference between the two cases is not one of sacred versus secular matters (the distinction does not fit the rabbinical-halakhic worldview), but rather that in the first case he was dealing with the spiritual welfare of the public at large, whereas in the second he was asked to rule in a matter of an individual's right to life and health. In the latter case, the law could be bent or disregarded, but in the former, such a course was out of the question.

Items 12 and 13 reflect a growing concern in East European Jewish society at that time: the need to deal with some of the consequences of family breakup that accompanied the great migration of Jews overseas. In document 12 we find a fairly positive attitude toward the mass emigration to America as such, even though MNY expresses concern over some of the dislocation involved. The letter is noteworthy, given the general image we have about the negative stance of the Orthodox rabbinate toward the westward migration, and toward America specifically. Document 14 again relates to the norms of traditional Jewish family life and the challenges they faced under the impact of modern behavioral trends.

The last item (document 15) explores political problems facing the Orthodox leadership due to discriminatory municipal government arrangements and expresses outrage at the political opposition of some non-Orthodox political activists. The document reflects prevailing issues in Warsaw politics in 1911, prior to the elections to the Fourth Duma (1912).

Document 2: Letter Regarding Modern Rabbinical Seminaries

(undated—but apparently written late spring 1883) [35]
[Beloved Father],

. . . as for what you tell me you have read in the newspaper concerning seminaries—this was already known to me. I was involved in confidential discussions about it about four months ago, when I received word from the "higher places" [i.e., the leading rabbis] of Kovno and Moscow. The great rabbis were determined not to rest or remain silent, and their plan was to have letters of protest, petition, and chastisement sent to . . . Baron Günzburg, to let him know that upon [the satisfactory resolution of] this the survival of Judaism itself depended. I myself also composed a letter to Baron Günzburg that, apparently, had an effect, and I had copies of my letter sent—for other rabbis requested this of me—so that they might copy the letter for themselves and send Baron Günzburg similar letters. I corresponded in this matter with all the greatest rabbis. Salvation lies in the hands of God. I will copy the letter here for you . . . :

Wednesday, 7 Shevat 5643 [= 1883], Kamenka.
[I greet you with] many blessings . . . , true friend to all, prince in Israel, [etc.], most esteemed rabbi [title used honorifically] Hirz [Horace] Baron Günzburg [etc.].
I beg your excellency to forgive me for thus intruding upon his noble house, for I do so only out of the love for Torah and our faith that burns in my heart, which mighty waters cannot quench. I make bold to approach your excellency in order to alert him to a thing most precious and most honorable, which touches upon the honor of God and of His Torah, regarding the disturbing rumor we have heard. . . .

The Torah itself cries out bitterly, stretches forth its hands [in supplication] and weeps over the betrayal by those closest to her, who have gathered together only to destroy the stone tablets and to breach the walls defending [the Torah]. Their wish is to uproot the Torah and our faith by asking the government to appoint rabbis from a *seminarium*, from which the law will go forth to all Jews throughout the land; [a rabbinical school] where the students will not begin to study Talmud and codes until after having completed the other [i.e., secular] required studies. It is, however, widely known what kind of rebellious rabbis these are, [such as those] from Germany where this [notion] comes from, which may appear to be attractive, but underneath it is black indeed. The very survival of our religion is at stake because of this threat. This is the cause of the great distress that prompts the shepherds of the flock, the sages of our generation, to raise their voice in sorrow and pain . . . , having heard that there have arisen some men who wish to sow destruction in Israel. The eye that beholds such a thing must weep because of these upsetting rumors. Yet, by our faith in God's mercies that have never failed us, we trust in our great and just government, which, in its grace, compassion and justice has always protected us; for its law has always sought to maintain our religious life as it should be, to preserve the integrity of God's Torah and never to destroy a single foundation of Torah and of our faith. In light of this, how good and pleasant it would be for brothers to dwell together in harmony, where wisdom and knowledge reign, and among them God's chosen, with his wise heart and understanding, his excellency Baron Günzburg, whose name is known far and wide as one who is devoted to God's ways, who loves his people and its Torah, and upon whom we feel we can depend in these times to be for us a tower of strength and a citadel, a mountain on which God's pure Torah can be raised up. All those who are wise of heart, the pillars of Torah, will gladly support his excellency when he stands up for the salvation of the Torah and our faith, for the sake of God and His Torah, and when, from deep within his heart, he speaks words of wisdom to those of his brethren who hearken to his voice and heed his advice: that they may consider this matter as of the utmost importance, and that they should understand that the Jewish faith must be based upon fear of heaven and true wisdom. Only such outstanding scholars whose fear of God and the law precede their learning; only those who have poured out their souls in their childhood years upon the bosom of the Talmud—only they, in time, will reach sufficient wisdom and understanding to teach the proper law in a proper manner. Not so those sons of Germany who in their youth devoted themselves to other studies, long before they even crossed the threshold of the Talmud. Their spirit is different and their heart is alien to true faith in and fear of God. For them Oral Law [Talmud],

which is like a fortification surrounding the Written Law and protecting it, is an object of criticism. Can they ever walk the paths of God's vineyard and achieve understanding of them, sufficient to teach God's ways to the congregation of Israel? Their learning, after all, is built upon foundations of nothingness. The profundity of the ways of piety is hidden from them. They understand not, neither can they learn. What is forbidden they pronounce proper; their marriage and divorce decrees are null and void. I must tell your excellency that I myself beheld, when I was in Bohemia, how one of these seminary rabbis openly and flagrantly desecrated the Sabbath before the entire congregation. Of the Talmud and the codes he knew absolutely nothing. Can such a person be given the title "rabbi" and be appointed to teach God's people the ways of our faith and our Torah? The memory of this [encounter] makes my hair stand on end, it breaks my heart . . . to see how the waters of wickedness have already risen to the waist. . . . I am unable to write more eloquently, for my soul quakes at such an awful sight. Therefore have I come to entreat your excellency—for [I know that] love of Torah and of our faith is still implanted in your heart—to do his utmost to strengthen the Torah once more. To you our eyes are raised in hope that you will stand up for the sake of the Torah, and that you will remove this alien notion from the hearts of those brethren who heed your voice. By doing so you will earn God's blessings [. . . etc.].
Moshe Nahum Yerusalimsky,
Rabbi of the Holy Congregation of Kamenka

That was my letter to Baron Günzburg and, apparently, these heartfelt words penetrated his heart, for even before Purim [i.e., within the month] I received a copy of a letter that Baron Günzburg wrote to the esteemed rabbi of Moscow, to wit:

I have received letters from rabbis from various cities, and from them I have been able to conclude that some wicked gossipmongers and those who would sow dissension are spreading evil rumors throughout the provinces that are distressing to our people Israel. For the reports they spread falsely libel the heads of the Society for Promoting Enlightenment [OPE], accusing them of having decided to establish a school that will be a stumbling block to the Jewish faith, and further alleging that they have already obtained or have asked for a government license for this purpose. Therefore, to set the record straight and to restore peace, I wish to make it known that these are libelous rumors, for there has been no such decision on this matter, and we would not take such a step without first consulting our great rabbis and teachers and the leaders of our people in the provinces. Therefore, you may rest assured that I, for my part, will not agree to anything that might, God forbid, cause damage to our religion or cause the Torah to be forgotten among our people. My late father's life's work, and my own, was always and will continue to be to strengthen our religion and to enhance and glorify the Torah. I will not, God forbid, lend a hand to any plan to wreak havoc upon Israel's sacred faith. We would like to call upon the great rabbis and teachers for their advice regarding this great matter, upon which rests the future and survival of our people. May the Lord in His graciousness bestow His counsel upon us and shine His countenance toward us, and may He give us peace. These words are those of a true lover of his people who desires nothing but its welfare and its benefit. [Signed] H. Günzburg.

However, before the Passover holiday [a month later] I received word from Moscow and Kovno that they suspect that the OPE merely want to deceive the rabbis, to make sure that they do not interfere. As it appears, there may be something to this. But the Compassionate Father will surely have mercy upon the sacred remnant of His possession who are now laid so low in every respect, and He will raise us up again. How good it was to read the words of that great rabbi . . . , Rabbi Gershon-Henokh of Radzin . . . , who wrote me about this matter: "Let not your heart grow weak over the rumor that the wicked have risen up against us, for they have tried many times to do this before, but God will never permit the deeds of the wicked nor will He allow them to carry out their evil intention."

Document 3: Letter from MNY to H. B. Sliozberg (Regarding "Sunday Rest" Law Being Considered in the State Duma)

24 Ellul 5670, 29 August 1910

To my friend, the eminent scholar . . . , righteous spokesman for his downtrodden people, and excellent public servant, Mr. H. B. Sliozberg . . . ![36]

On the fifth of July I sent your honor a letter in which I petitioned him in a matter of public interest, and I had been disappointed in not hearing from you. As I know your honor to be a faithful servant of the community, whose heart is ever alert and warmly inclined to any Jewish matter, I was puzzled at your lack of response, until [I learned that] your honor has only just returned from Hamburg. Therefore, I am writing once again. . . . I myself have just returned from a three-month stay at our summer home and I am overloaded with communal duties. . . .

As your honor knows, the State Duma will resume its work in a few days, and among the items that will come up for a final decision is the question of the "Sunday rest" law. The Duma is supposed to vote on this "humanitarian" law for the last time. A careful look at this matter leads one to believe that this law is deliberately meant to harm our [the Jews'] material condition—which, even so, is very poor; for it is impossible not to realize that our brethren who make a living by selling their wares will be unable to compete with their Christian neighbors, who will be able to sell six days a week, while [the Jews] can do so only five days a week. . . .

Likewise, we ought not to forget that "progress," in the humanistic, coarse, commercial, simplistic, and imitative sense, has poisoned the Hebrew national spirit, has altered those pure sentiments of Old Man Israel, which were always the pride of our people in its exile, since the day we became a nation! . . . Will the "twentieth century" really bring us [again] those sainted heroes whose names we speak with profound reverence, who have so enriched our history? . . . Will there be found among us people who would choose martyrdom on the altar of their love for the holy Sabbath day, so sacred to us for generations? Will love of nation, love for one of the basic principles of our religion and our holy Torah and our national mission, [still] overcome the lust for money, that "foundation stone" of our daily life? The optimists among us will certainly answer that question in the positive, saying: Our people that has endured two thousand years of exile, of wandering from country to country; our people that has lived through such tragic moments—of Inquisitions, persecutions, spiritual and material oppression—and emerged victorious, wearing the crown of national valor, over which hovers an unseen Divine Power; our people, that took such pride and comfort from the verse: "Not only once did an enemy arise to destroy us, but in every generation they have arisen to destroy us, and God has saved us from their hands!"—this people will never be vanquished completely, leaving no remnant. But we also have to consider the less refined among us, those who will not be inspired by the spirit of our people [and who will violate the Sabbath to work on Saturdays]. And, therefore, I think that we must use every means possible to insure that, when the State Duma brings up the Sunday rest law for a final debate— a matter that concerns us vitally—it should know the harm that it would be causing us [by such a law]. Perhaps our sincere and heartfelt words, filled with the pain of all our troubles, will enter the hearts of the lawmakers and cause them to consider our plight in general, and in Poland in particular, where the conditions under which our brethren live compel them to earn their living by petty trade. What is called for, in my opinion and that of my friend, the eminent rabbi, Rabbi Issachar Dov Groybart, is the following: that every community of Jews in Poland that has its own rabbi and communal board should send a petition to the Minister of Internal Affairs, to the chairman of the State Council, or the chairman of the State Duma, in which they should describe our plight and ask that consideration be given to our situation when the Sunday rest law is put into effect. The petition should be drafted by those who are expert and well-versed in such matters, by people who know the travails of their people and who are working to improve its lot, [by people] who know how to frame their arguments according to the laws of our country, and concisely. The petition should echo the people's lament. If such letters will be sent from every town in Poland, there is room to hope that they will find their mark, for as our sages told us: "Words that come from the heart will penetrate the heart."

I, therefore, turn to your honor and ask you to turn your pure heart toward this great matter, upon which depends the lives of tens of thousands of our country's inhabitants. I consider it superfluous to urge your honor any further in this regard, since your heart is alert and warmly disposed to the needs of our people even without such urging. I have also written in this matter to our wise friends, the Baron Günzburg and Mr. Isaac Dov-Ber Morgun. Perhaps you will be disposed to consult with them on this affair, . . . and perhaps it would be worthwhile to take counsel with other public figures in Petersburg. May God be with you and may He guide your actions, so that your work will prosper and bring benefit to our people.

Document 4: Letter from MNY to Rabbi David-Tevele Katzenellenbogen, "Spiritual Rabbi" [Dukhovnyi Ravvin] in St. Petersburg, 1911[37]

. . . I have just seen in the newspaper *Der haynt* that you have sent a petition to the governor in Warsaw regarding the introduction of summer vacation in the *ḥeders* [traditional schools] of the Warsaw province. I am writing to inform you that I myself have already written to the district [officer of the] ministry of education, and received [confirmation] a month ago from the [office of the] Warsaw school inspector— to be precise, the letter is dated 27 January 1911, no. 3247— that *melamdim* [elementary school teachers] are not required to close their *ḥeders* for the summer. Therefore, if the [local] administration attempts to force *melamdim* to to so, they may turn to the provincial school inspector. He will no doubt follow the instructions of his ministry. You may announce this in the Warsaw newspaper so that all *melamdim* will be informed. I have also [informed] Rabbi Shlomo David Kahane of Warsaw, who asked me about the same matter . . . .

Document 5: Draft of Petition to the Governor-General of the Warsaw Province, 1911 (in Russian)[38]

To His Excellency the Governor-General of Warsaw: from supporters of the *ḥeder* schools in the provincial city of Kielce.

PETITION

Carrying out the project of introducing into the Jewish *heder* schools a summer vacation period on a par with the summer vacation that exists in the Jewish crown [public] schools would have disastrous consequences for the *heder* schools and an unfavorable influence on the morals of the children [who study there]. In view of the prevailing special conditions of Jewish life, it has been customary for vacation periods in the *heder* schools to take place approximately in April and September, each one lasting one month. Jewish parents do not send their children to [the same] *heder* for several years, and sometimes not even for an entire year, but [register their children] by the semester; the aforesaid two vacation months mark the beginning and end of the semesters. Consequently, the introduction of a ten-week vacation in the [middle of the] summer term, which lasts not quite four months, would leave only six to seven weeks [of classroom time, part] at the beginning and [part] at the end of the summer. The parents, who mostly belong to the poorer classes, will never agree to pay a full semester's tuition for this period of time. The income of the *melamdim* [teachers] would be cut in half [as a result], and they are already at a disadvantage in that they must rent the premises of the *heder* for an entire year, while [by contrast,] Russian-language teachers are hired on a semester or six-month salary basis. Underlying the idea of introducing a summer vacation in the *heder* schools is a concern for the welfare of the pupils, but we permit ourselves to state that the proposed measure, which, under other circumstances would be beneficial for Jewish children, is unsuitable and might even have reverse, highly negative, results, because it is the responsibility of the *melamdim* to supervise the children in their fulfilment of the obligatory thrice-daily prayers. And if, during the ten weeks the children are left without religious instruction or supervision; and taking into account that the *heder* schools serve primarily the children of poorer parents . . . who are not home all day; then these children, during the vacation period, will remain without any supervision, exposed to the danger of picking up bad habits. . . . In the name of the *mel-amdim*, allow me to ask your Excellency to take into consideration all the foregoing, and the desperate situation that would be created by the new measure for those dependent on the *ḥeder* schools and the harmful consequences that it can bring about with regard to the religious and moral development of the children [through] the introduction of summer vacations. . . .

Document 6: Draft of a Letter from MNY to the Gerer Rebbe (R. Avraham-Mordecai of Gur), Iyar 5669 (= spring 1909) [39]

Long life to . . . our holy rabbi . . . Rabbi Avraham-Mordecai, the venerable *Admor* [hasidic master] of Gur and its environs . . . !

As the letter—*circular*—sent from the Internal Affairs ministry to the rabbis of Poland stated, the government has granted permission to hold preliminary conferences and to submit beneficial proposals on matters touching the Jewish faith, [proposals] which will afterward be vetted by the Rabbinical Commission that is to meet in St. Petersburg at the end of the civil year or, at the latest, the beginning of next year. This certainly comes at an opportune moment, for the Torah and piety have fallen on bad times, [we are plagued with] trouble upon trouble and [Jews have begun] imitating the ways of the gentiles. This is the time for the faithful ones of Israel to join forces and strengthen ourselves for the sake of raising the cause of Torah and faith. Sorely depressed by the plight of my unfortunate people, I was skeptical about the conference until I learned from trustworthy sources the nature of the matters to be discussed at the conference, which rest on the most sacred foundations. Therefore, as time is pressing, a gathering of rabbis from the Kielce district will take place [here] next week, for three days—the 24th, 25th and 26th of Iyar—which, in my humble opinion, will be only a preliminary discussion; for the main idea is to gather in a general conference in Warsaw, God willing, which is to include all the greatest [rabbinical] figures of our day. There they will consider all that has been discussed [at the preliminary meetings] in the various provinces in order to form one unified opinion, to prevent the several provinces from placing varying or conflicting proposals before the government. It will also be a good opportunity to discuss how we ought to join the "Knesses Yisroel" association that was formed, with government permission, in Vilna. This matter [is most important], as my illustrious uncle, the holy rabbi, R. Sholom Dov Schneersohn, the *Admor* of Liubavitch, wrote to me, who is entirely devoted heart and soul to the public welfare. As this is a most exalted and sacred matter, who am I to interfere of my own accord? Therefore, I turn to your holiness with great reverence and ask you to render your considered opinion as to what proposals are worthy of being put forward. Everything you say will guide us in our deliberations next week. I await your early reply and your blessings with eager anticipation. . . . I entreat and beg you to instruct those who are under the aegis of your pure and pious wing, all those who seek to raise the banner of Torah and piety, that they should prepare to join together in the general conference . . . to do the will of our Heavenly Father. . . .

Document 7: Draft of a Letter to Be Sent to the Rabbis of Brest-Litovsk and Vilna Regarding the Rabbinical Commission (Undated) [40]

After the usual greetings; . . . How great is the honor [we feel], and how much all who bear the standard of Torah and piety can appreciate the news, that the holy society "Knesses Yisroel" has been approved, and that it will be led by the greatest rabbis who will raise up the cause of Torah and watch over God's vineyard, to repair the breach with wisdom and piety. It is, therefore, a great puzzlement [to all who love the Torah] that the rabbis of Poland, who are also prepared to do their part . . . have not been included in this great society; although at the end of last year printed circulars were sent to the rabbis of Poland about the founding of a newspaper for Orthodox Jews and about the conference of rabbis in Vilna, asking the rabbis of Poland to endeavor to raise the needed funds [to help defray] the large expenses involved. The strict supervision [by the authorities of such activity] is so terrible in Poland, however, that even the government-approved rabbis could not hope to accomplish what was necessary, or even half of that, before it was decided [by the authorities] to grant permission for the [rabbinical] conferences. (It was especially dangerous to try to collect money, and even now it is difficult to get a permit for that.) Now we see that the law calling for a Rabbinical Commission in St. Petersburg actually applies only to Russia, and not to [the provinces of] Poland; yet the government has not neglected the rabbis of Poland and a circular was sent from the Minister of Internal Affairs to all the provincial governors, "to announce to all rabbis that they will be allowed to express their views on the various matters that will be raised afterward at the Rabbinical Commission in St. Petersburg, to take place at the beginning of the new civil year, and that the rabbis of Poland are to receive permits to hold conferences." The rabbis of every district have begun to prepare energetically for these conferences. It is my intention, as well, to call such a conference of all the rabbis in the Kielce district this month or early next month. But as this matter is so important, we must all work together, for people naturally tend to have their own opinions, [so we should consult] to prevent a situation in which different proposals will be sent to the Commission . . . , God forbid that there should be strife over matters that are of utmost importance to the Jewish world. I, therefore, would urgently request from the great rabbi that, if the "Knesses Yisroel" has for some reason decided not to include Polish rabbis in the conference that is to take place in Vilna, God willing, in the [coming] month of Sivan, at least you should send me immediate word, upon receipt of this letter, of all the discussions that took place and resolutions decided upon in anticipation of the Commission, and any opinions expressed, so that we might use this material for discussion at our conferences, too. . . . Thus, all the conferences that will be held in the ten Polish provinces will all reach a unified position in the interest of upholding the Torah and the faith. I would ask you, also, to let me know if Polish branches can affiliate [with the society] under its legal charter. . . . I await your prompt reply. . . . [L]et there be no division [in this matter] between Russia and Poland, let us all join together as one to repair the breach for the sake of Torah and the faith. . . .

Document 8: Letter from Yehoshua-Heshl Yerusalimsky to His Father, MNY, Spring 1905 (Regarding Anti-Jewish Incident in Kielce and Violence Averted in Teplik) [41]

Teplik, Tuesday 27 Nisan 5665

[Beloved and esteemed Father . . . and Mother],

I received your letters in good time. . . . I am so glad that the holiday [Passover] has passed peacefully for you. But I was greatly upset over the unnatural libel with which the Amalekites [i.e., the anti-Semites] sought to charge the community and you in particular. In this matter you must do everything possible to insure that the investigation is carried out in a thorough, trustworthy fashion, to ascertain whether the household's servant [the servant in MNY's household?] was responsible for the affair, or whether it was some secret society whose purpose is to smear the Jews with false accusations in these troubled times. Therefore, it is most necessary to investigate fully who was responsible. Let the truth be revealed and the perpetrators brought to justice for their wicked deed. For such a thing would, God forbid, have brought down a terrible libel not just on your community alone, but on all Jews. . . . I am certain that the hands of some powerful (powerfully wicked) people are involved in this. And the girl is already seven years old, so she can tell who did it to her. Please let me know how the thing turns out and what the investigation reveals. And when the truth is exposed, a letter should be published, signed by you, Father, and by the community leaders, in the Russian newspapers, to demonstrate the truth about all the things that are being written about our unfortunate brethren. . . . Such a thing would surely have great impact even in very powerful circles. . . .

In our town, too, we had been afraid during the days of [Easter?], but . . . everything turned out alright. An order came down to the priests warning them that they would be held responsible and would pay dearly if any trouble took place. A heavy guard was posted, too. . . .

Document 9: Letter from David-Yona Yerusalimsky to His Father, MNY, Early 1906 (Regarding Police Action against Subversive Activity in the Ukraine) [42]

Khorol', Friday, *parashat Shemot* 5666
During my trip . . . on the 9th of January [I heard] that they are expelling [people] and there is little peace. . . . There was much anxiety over the arrival of the governor-general's official, whose severe reputation is known throughout the area, as I am sure you read in the newspapers. . . . He ordered them all to kneel . . . and surrounded them with Cossacks [and demanded] that they hand over the agitators (who had killed the deputy governor of the district). . . . One old man who was kneeling there sobbed . . . and in answer received blows to the face from that official, which knocked him down. People were killed and many were trampled by the Cossacks' horses. . . . The official called the Jews together, too—I was among the group—and he rebuked us for the fact that four Jews were among the speakers at the "meeting" [i.e., illegal assembly] and told us to dissociate ourselves from them. My father-in-law expressed gratitude [to him], because his actions had prevented violence here. . . . He told us . . . that the old men are paying for the sins of their young sons, compounding their suffering, [and said] that if the government thought well of us we would receive many rights [and live] in peace. The fathers of some of the sinners and wicked ones were there, too, . . . may God have compassion on His people. . . . Please let me know whether the trains have started running again on schedule. . . .

Document 10: Letter from Yaakov Yerusalimsky
to His Brother, MNY (Regarding an Averted
Pogrom in Tomashpol') [43]

Tomashpol' Thursday, *parashat Tavo* 5667, August 16, 1907 [44]
[Beloved brother Moshe . . . and his dear wife, etc.],

I received your letter of last week. . . . May God grant us a
good new year, with every blessing, life and peace. Should you
read in the newspaper that we had a pogrom here in our
town . . . do not be alarmed, for the newspapers have greatly
exaggerated. There was, indeed, great fear and some distur-
bance, but the police and the guards intervened and stopped
them [the perpetrators] in time and did not permit them to
achieve their design. Two of the Christian rioters were killed,
and no Jews were killed at all, thank God. We are safe and the
town is quiet. May God help us in the future, as well, and
insure that nothing bad, God forbid, will happen. . . .

Document 11: Printed Responsum to Rabbi Moshe Pritzker of
Berdichev (Regarding a Machine for the Preparation of
Passover Matzos) [45]

Thursday, 23 Adar 5657 [= spring 1897], Kamenka.
To the honorable . . . Rabbi Moshe Pritzker [etc.],

I received your letter today and I am responding in the
matter of the new *mashinen* [Yiddish] that have been invented
to roll the *matzos*, [and your query] whether it is permissible
to bake Passover *matzos* on these machines: I have in fact
already written about this in my book, *Minḥat Moshe*, where
[you] the esteemed rabbi no doubt also read the words [I cited]
of the great Ramaz of L'vov, of blessed memory—that whoever fears the word of God should never deviate from it, for
His word is forever valid. Even though the *mashina* has been
modified since that time, when all the great rabbinical authorities raised their voices against it . . . , nevertheless, although
the intention of those who modified the machine was to elimi-
nate the problem, in the process they have violated other
prohibitions and raised other doubts, and all of their "correc-

tions" merely undermine the very foundations of our law, for our many sins. [Therefore] it is incumbent upon all the leaders of the generation to step into the breach. I admit that I myself have not looked at the machine itself, but from what I read in the books of the great scholars [I am convinced] that the basic issue is that the machine would lead many people astray unwittingly, because of the chance of leavening in the dough. In 5650 [1890] someone brought the new machine to [demonstrate in] Kremenchug, and showed all the rabbis there the workings of the machine. After an extensive examination we saw that the prohibition remains in force and, moreover, new problems have been added, as was explained in the pamphlet, "An Announcement to the House of Israel." Thank God, our words bore fruit and the one who brought the machine to Kremenchug was unable to realize his designs. He was able, at first, to deceive the great rabbi of Minsk, who wrote a permit for him. But afterward, when I explained to him [the rabbi of Minsk] the substance of the matter and the questions that were raised . . . , he promptly overlooked any false considerations of pride and reputation and he himself joined in a blanket prohibition of *matzos* baked by that *mashin*, ruling that such *matzos* could not be allowed to remain [under Jewish jurisdiction during Passover], and must be sold to a gentile, just like any other leavened bread. It is superfluous at this point to go on adding to what has been said . . . and I can only reiterate what I wrote in my letter to Kremenchug. Although my words contained no new point of law, they were written with great sincerity and found their way to the hearts of those who faithfully keep the law of Israel, so that they all banded together and resolved to banish this [golden] calf [the device] from Kremenchug, . . . for it is a creation of the evil inclination and its infernal machinations. . . .

Document 12: Draft of an Open Letter (Kol-Koyre)
to Rabbis in the West (Undated)[46]

To the honored rabbis who sit in judgment among the holy congregations across the sea, greetings and blessings.

For decades now a constant stream of wandering has taken place from the Jewish communities in our country, and it is not about to end. Many of our brother Jews have been forced, for our many sins, to leave their country of residence and to wander far and wide in search of a livelihood for their families. And the God of Israel has not removed His lovingkindness from His flock: He has sent His angel [along with them] to guard them on their long journey and in foreign lands. Many of our brethren have gone forth and successfully found "a resting place for their foot" [in contradistinction to Noah's dove, who found no resting place—Gen. 8:9], and have brought their wives and children to join them, have treated them as proper Jewish men should, and have established new communities in Israel that are worthy and great.

But, in consequence of this mass departure, many problems have also occurred for many families in Israel, a nation that has from time immemorial excelled in the purity and wholesomeness of its way of life. For our many sins, there are some who have breached the bounds of decency and have cast off the obligation to support their families. When they arrive in a faraway land where no one knows them, and they find a resting place, they find it convenient to forget the wife of their bosom, their parents, and their children of tender years whom they have left behind, destitute, in their old homes. They turn away from the path trodden by their fathers and forefathers throughout history. Among them are men who know no discipline, and who have taken themselves other wives in place of those they betrothed according the law of Moses and Israel. Others of them have been driven, through need, to seek work from city to city, from country to country, and the pressure of hard labor and lack of time has led them into foul paths. An outcry has reached us from many towns and cities from the living widows, left without support from their husbands and without anyone to hear the wailing of their tender children asking for food, when there is none to give: a voice of weeping that pierces the heart!

Who can recount the woe of hundreds of daughters of Israel caught in the chains of abandonment ['igun] with none to comfort them and succour their soul. They extend their hand, asking for aid, and tearfully beseech that we look for the husbands of their youth and restore them to a life of decency. He who hears all prayer will certainly hearken to their bitter lament and bring them salvation. [But] I turn to you, who are called the shepherds of Israel, leaders of the people, upholders of Torah in the lands of the new migration where our brethren are dispersed, wherever you may be, with this request: that you enter into the breach and extend your assistance from afar to the excellent daughters of Zion who weep in bitterness. Have compassion for them and for the lives of their abandoned children, living orphans who have no father and no deliverer. Let there be established, in every city of Jews in the United States, [South] Africa, Canada, and Argentina, a special organization [that], according to the information and particulars that will be sent to it from our country, will seek out the whereabouts of such husbands as have betrayed the wives of their youth and have hardened their hearts to the sound of their lament and that of their offspring.

And you, honored rabbis, in whose hands is the honor of the Torah and the reins of leadership in every holy congregation, speak and win over the renegade husbands with every means at your disposal. Talk to them with reason and persuade them gently, with the help of rabbinical courts, to leave the path that tempts them and to return to the proper path, or else to grant a proper divorce. The children of Abraham our Father are known to be compassionate, and "even the transgressors among us are full of *mitsvot*," etc. He who has compassion for the unfortunate will assist you and will turn the heart of the husband back to his wife, "the hearts of fathers to their sons, and the hearts of sons to their fathers," and may peace be upon all Israel.

Document 13: Letter from MNY to Rabbi Yehoshua Segal, New York, Summer 1908[47]

Monday, *parashat devarim* 5668, Kielce
Greetings and wishes for long life to our friend . . . Rabbi Ye-

hoshua Segal, chief rabbi to the Jews of Russia and Poland in New York, America:

. . . I would ask you to turn aside from your busy schedule and do me this favor, for the sake of an unfortunate deserted wife. The matter is as follows: A person named Shmuel Shperling (whose address is given below) left his wife, Miriam-Devora daughter of Avraham of Kielce, six years ago. He not only betrayed her and failed to send money for her support—not even once, after she asked him at least three times; he also wrote saying that if she would give him 1,000 rubles, he would agree to give her a divorce. . . . How distressed I have been over this unfortunate woman who has been left an 'agunah [abandoned and unable to remarry] for no reason. I have spoken to the woman's father, who is a poor man; still, he told me that, in order to secure her release from the bonds of 'igun [the status of an 'agunah], he would sell everything he has and would give the man 100 rubles. And if that is not enough, he will try to get help from his relatives, perhaps another 200 rubles. I ask you to please do what you can [with] this renegade and appeal to him: for what use is it to him to leave her in this state for no reason and to cause her pain by asking for a ransom that is unrealistic? Let him use his sense and send her a divorce without payment; if he cannot agree to do it for nothing, then he can be sent 100 or 200 rubles. I am sure that if you can do this . . . you can persuade him to set her free, and his reward from heaven will be double. If there will be some costs involved, such as travel expenses for the beadle [of the congregation] and the like, write to me, and the father of the woman will send whatever it is by return mail. I again urge you to do your utmost to persuade this wife deserter to release his wife, Miriam-Devora daughter of Avraham from the bonds of 'igun. . . .

the address of the renegade husband is:

> Mr. S. Szperling 135 More Street
> Broklin [sic] New York Amerika [sic]

On his return address there appears another address, too, and perhaps it is an address of a relative or friend of his, so I include the second address:

Mr. M. Bruchin No. 25 Allen Street New York Amerika
[*sic*]

Document 14: Response to a Query from Rabbi Moshe Shapira of Maglinca, Warsaw Province[48]

Regarding the query about a girl, the daughter of a very wealthy man, about whom it became known that she whored with a non-Jew and then, several months later, ran off by train on a Sabbath with the said non-Jew; and when they searched they found her in Warsaw in the hotel of the said non-Jew, and with great effort brought her back to her father's house, [and then] a match was arranged for her with a Jew who is a *cohen* [of priestly lineage, i.e., someone who must follow a stricter standard in marrying], on the authority of one [rabbi] who granted permission. You do not state your own opinion of the case but ask me to write an opinion on whether she should be permitted to a *cohen* or not.

Now in principle there is voluminous material [on which to base a ruling] and there is no time to go into all the details. I shall merely note briefly all the legal points that are relevant. . . . [A summary of the precedents and relevant rulings: A *cohen* may not marry a woman who has behaved promiscuously by remaining alone for a significant period with a non-Jew—or even with a Jew, as some authorities would have it, though Jews are generally considered to be less suspect in matters of sexual morals—as long as her intent was clearly promiscuous. That that is the case in this instance is beyond question. Therefore, a *cohen* is prohibited, before the fact, from contracting such a marriage. However, once formalized, such a marriage is valid. While some authorities consider it necessary to remove such a wife, by ordering a divorce, most concur that the law does not empower the rabbis to force such a separation.]

In conclusion, . . . if she has not yet been married to him, she is forbidden to the *cohen* and the arrangements for the match should be broken. If, however, the marriage has already taken place, she should remain the *cohen*'s wife.

Document 15: Draft Letter from MNY to a Hasidic Leader (Undated, ca. 1911) [49]

After inquiring after the health of your holiness . . . allow me to address you in writing regarding a matter of great consequence that demands full and serious discussion by the religious leaders, for it portends great danger to all Jews in Poland. Allow me, then, to turn to you out of profound reverence, for I consider you, sir, to be among the greatest sages and saints of our generation, . . . your name is widely respected by tens of thousands of the pious, and you may be able to exert great influence in this affair through your good counsel. . . .

As you know, the State Duma has already debated the matter of [municipal] self-government for the cities of Poland and has decided to remove from the Jews the right to participate fully in this self-government, through instituting for Jewish voters a special electoral section, called a "curia." The Jewish voters will not cast ballots for the [city] council in accordance with their numbers [i.e., on a one-man-one-vote basis], but rather will cast their vote, in such cities where Jews comprise a majority [of voters], on a twenty-percent basis. For example, if in [the city council of] Lublin there will be eighty members, Jews will be allotted a quota of sixteen; and in Warsaw, among 160 councilmen, there will be sixteen Jews. [Note: this figure represents 10 percent, and perhaps the repetition of the number 16 is an error—E. L.] How much influence the Jews [on the council] will have is obvious to anyone with sense. . . . It is well known how the "delegation" of assimilationists sent from Warsaw to St. Petersburg worked to deny the Jews their rights in "self-government."

As a native of Russia, I am well acquainted with the nature of this "self-government," and for that reason my soul grieves silently when I see the harm that is being done to the unfortunate Jews of Poland. Everyone who is versed in the workings of "self-government" must weep over this wickedness done to us. . . . Let me, then, explain what I mean, sir. The municipal government has the authority, by law, to express its view on any matter, even specifically Jewish concerns such as: the rabbinate, ritual slaughterers, cantors, houses of prayer, and charitable and philanthropic institutions. They [sic] can reduce the salary of the one and restrict the funds of the other as they see fit. Even if all the Jewish representatives oppose it unanimously (and this is not very likely, since there would certainly be leftists among the chosen [Jewish] delegates), their voice will not count, as they are but a small minority [on the council]. Already I can give you an example from what has happened in Odessa, where the city government ("duma"), that is composed entirely of "black" [i.e., reactionary] Jew-haters, took away money intended for yeshivas and Talmud-Torah schools—even though the money was given by Jews—and used it instead for the police department, for gas lighting, and the like. Moreover, they are responsible for all local matters, and they are liable to leave those streets where the synagogue, the *beys-medresh* and the *mikveh* are located boggy and full of filth. For all this, and all that is going to descend on us, God forbid, we have the assimilationists, Natanson and Dickstein[50] to thank; for they went and gave the Jews a bad name before the chosen delegates of the Russian nation, the members of the State Duma . . . , that the Jews are not "civilized," that they are "not of the community," and other such lies, out of a shocking maliciousness. Of them it may truly be said, in the words of the divine prophet Elijah, [they are] "ruiners and destroyers . . . "—yet these terrible people stand at the head of the biggest Jewish community in Russia, may the Jewish inhabitants thereof increase: the community of Warsaw. How awful the pain and how terrible the shame. But what is done cannot now be undone. Now that the State Duma has to deal with this important matter, we must set our minds to counter this act somehow. The leading [Jewish] nationalists in Warsaw have learned from reliable sources in Petersburg that if an effort is made to send letters of protest from every city in Poland, from the [Jewish] religious councils and charity boards and so forth, and if there will be a public appeal to our Jewish deputies in the Duma, there is hope that our voice will be heard and our rights will not be denied. The assimilationists went even further by adding another wickedness, proposing that the Christian voters shall have the right to approve the [members chosen from the] Jewish curia. This was done in order to prevent the religious Jews from choosing representatives of their own way of thinking for the city council . . . ; only such assimilated people who walk arrogantly over the heads of our holy people [will be elected]. They know that [otherwise] no one would vote for them; but they look for support from their "brothers," the non-Jews (for these wicked people call the gentiles "brothers"), who will voice their approval of these assimilationists. In doing so they absolutely rob the religious Jews of Poland of their right to vote, even though we constitute the vast majority.

Conclusion

Jewish Orthodoxy, as we know, was a response to modernity, insofar as it was an ideology of conscious traditionalism in a posttraditional age. Militant Orthodoxy, which organized itself to do battle against its foes within Jewry, sometimes found it convenient to pose as the ally of conservative political forces outside Jewish society (the state itself, or other political groups), with whom it shared common interests. On the other hand, Orthodox political figures were prepared to oppose new measures that they felt were inimical to the general Jewish interest (Sunday market-closing laws).

In the foregoing documents, we have seen how this politics of the status quo operated. We have seen, as well, how discontent with modernization in one sphere (rabbinical education, for example) went hand in hand with the defense of traditionalism in all other spheres: rabbinic-controlled traditional crafts (matzo baking), schools, sexual mores and family values, and so forth.

The impact on this culture of traditionalism of major factors of destabilization—violent outbreaks and revolutionary activity, on the one hand, and mass emigration, on the other—was such that the practitioners of traditionalism felt called upon to defend their way of life with renewed fervor. The stakes were higher now. And defection from the ranks (as we saw in the previous chapter) as well as challenges from rival leadership groups (as we saw in chapter 2 on messianic rhetoric in Jewish nationalism) were perceived, more than ever, as dangerous trends. That is what lent political significance to Orthodox militancy: As tradition itself was no longer an adequate warrant for its own legitimacy, techniques of resistance and mobilization had to be developed. In this way, Orthodoxy was functionally transformed and modernized, for it became one ideological camp or party among all the rest.

CHAPTER 5

America: A Vision in a Jewish Mirror

Masses of immigrant Jews were becoming Americans just as the United States was emerging into a new era and the content of what constituted American nationhood was being altered. The closing of the frontier (formally noted by Frederick Jackson Turner in 1893);[1] the passing of the agrarian majority; the changing ethnic and religious composition of the population; the projection of American wealth and power overseas; recurring economic crises and the complex issues of democratization and enfranchisement (relating to the social and political place in society of industrial workers, women, and black people) heralded a process of basic revision and redefinition.

Not coincidentally, the nation also debated the questions of how the privilege of American citizenship ought to be bestowed and who had the right to seek shelter upon American shores. The immigration question was inseparably bound up with the above-named issues of American self-perception, and when immigrants were asked to adapt themselves to "America," that term was laden with a vexing subjectivity.

"Americanism," as a national ideology, and "Americanization," the correlating social process of acquiring an American identity ("becoming an American"), required some elucidation, for they were never self-explanatory or as simply conceived as the concept of citizenship per se, or the concept of naturalization. As a new nation, historically speaking, America's national heritage was perhaps more in need of a process of definition than most (though other modern national identities—the German, the Italian, the Chinese, to mention but a few—were likewise deliberately formed from disparate parts and consciously fostered by political and cultural elites).

The question of American identity was posed as early as 1782, by Hector St. John de Crèvecoeur ("What then is the American, this new man?"), and answered rather perceptively in his oft-quoted formulation, which singled out the three basic components of what Americanization entailed or conferred: *a new mode of life, a new political allegiance,* and *a new rank in society:*

> In this great American asylum, the poor of Europe have by some means met together. . . . Every thing has tended to regenerate them: new laws, a new mode of living, a new social system: here they become men: in Europe they were as so many useless plants, wanting vegetative mould and refreshing showers. . . . Formerly they were not numbered in any civil lists of their country, except those of the poor; here they rank as citizens. . . . He is an American who, leaving behind him all his ancient prejudices and manners, receives new ones from the new mode of life he has embraced, the new government he obeys, and the new rank he holds. He becomes an American by being received in the broad lap of our great *Alma Mater.* Here individuals of all nations are melted into a new race of men.[2]

Above all, the transaction described by the term "Americanization" (the casting off of the old for the sake of the new) was thought of as a net gain for the new citizen. "Every thing has tended to regenerate them. . . . Here they become men." By embracing the new life and by living under liberal institutions, the colonist/immigrant could fulfill his or her destiny and potential as a human being.

The ideological edge apparent in Crèvecoeur's statement is certainly a function of the ideological character of America itself, a new society constituted by a collective act of political will. In that sense, it was unlike most of the European states in which the majority of the world's Jews lived in the nineteenth century. Although a good case could be made that America was no mere rational creation, but, like the states and empires of Europe, was forged through war and conquest and through the triumph of a modern, centralistic regime over local self-rule, a distinction would yet remain. No European state but France—and even France only intermittently—possessed a national ideology equivalent to America's mission of triumphalist "regeneration" vis-à-vis the "old world." Such an ideology is the prerogative of revolutionary regimes and new societies (note the similarities with features of early Soviet and Israeli national cults).

Emancipated Jews in Europe also adapted to modern life in their respective countries under terms of a transaction—leaving the safety of the ghetto's *Gemeinschaft* for the opportunities of the urban *Gesellschaft* of the West European bourgeoisie; but their "civil betterment" did not grant automatic membership in the historical national community. Thus, Jewish emancipation everywhere in Europe required special legislation that was accompanied by acrimonious and sometimes prolonged debate, even occasional violence. In the end, emancipation in Europe simply gave birth to a "Jewish question."

In the American case, equality of status and nationalization were far more closely linked, as Crèvecoeur had noted. The promise of America, he explained, was manifested in the ability of the average "freeman" to acquire property, and thereby to share in the expanding social base of the nation: "Here the rewards of his industry follow with equal steps the progress of his labour. . . . From involuntary idleness, servile dependence, penury and useless labour, he has passed to toils of a very different nature, rewarded by ample subsistence.—This is an American."[3]

Jews in the new republic faced few if any hurdles in this regard. Bourgeois society was virtually synonymous with the national community—resulting in the inclusion of the Jews, even as it excluded those whom color, caste, and class (American blacks or Chinese laborers, for example) defined as second-class citizens. But these precedents of exclusion resurfaced in a new form at the end of the nineteenth century, with direct implications for Jews.

Two separate social processes that first took shape in the 1870s helped to create a Jewish question in America. One of these processes was the emergence of a new, post–Civil War gentry that became a caste of privilege. In a theoretically egalitarian society, this generated a defined interest in highlighting the distinguishing features of patrician, blueblooded, and white-skinned "Americanism."[4] An observation of Hannah Arendt's is pertinent in this regard:

Equality of condition, though it is certainly a basic requirement for justice, is nevertheless among the greatest and most uncertain ventures of modern mankind. The more equal conditions are, the less explanation there is for the differences that actually exist between people; and thus all the more unequal do individuals and groups become. . . . [T]here is one chance in a hundred that it [equality of condition] will be recognized simply as a working principle of a political organization in which otherwise unequal people have equal rights; there are ninety-nine chances that it will be mistaken for an innate quality of every individual, who is "normal" if he is like everybody else and "abnormal" if he happens to be different.[5]

In a society like the American one, she continues, where equality of condition may be taken for granted,

discrimination becomes the only means of distinction, a kind of universal law according to which groups may find themselves outside the sphere of civic, political, and economic equality. . . . It is one of the most promising and dangerous paradoxes of the American Republic that it dared to realize equality on the basis of the most unequal population in the world, physically and historically.[6]

Although American Jews did not find themselves entirely "outside the sphere of civic, political, and economic equality," they were no longer automatically or entirely "inside," either, and the first to feel the cold draft were the most financially secure and the most socially successful among them.

The second process that undermined the old, tacit formulas of Jewish Americanism was, of course, the mass influx of impoverished Jews from Eastern Europe in the forty-year span beginning in the early 1880s. Joining the ranks of the "wretched refuse," the white urban poor in the crowded working-class quarters of the largest cities, the new Jewish immigrant population seemed as unassimilable as any group could be. They seemed bent on preserving, not abandoning, their "ancient prejudices and manners," and they came at a time when the specter of a massive, and possibly dangerous, foreign-born proletariat haunted America.

The question of the Jews' "regeneration" as Americans, once raised, would not easily be put to rest. The identification of immigrant Jews (along with others from Eastern and Southern Europe) as the bearers and breeders of socialism and anarchism—a common stereotype that had a certain basis in reality—added the count of questionable political allegiances to the already damning indictment sheet.

Fed by class differentiation and alienation from newer immigrant elements, a "new nationalism" made itself felt in America, which had a direct impact on Jews and their status in society. Although these currents were to culminate in the years following World War I, they were increasingly articulated, in word and deed, during the decades preceding the Great War.[7] Jews from Eastern Europe were singled out as a particular threat.

In 1920, the Congressional Committee on Immigration, under the chairmanship of Representative Albert Johnson, in recommending a bill for the "temporary suspension of immigration," noted with alarm the swelling stream of postwar immigration from Central and Eastern Europe. "The need for restrictive legislation," the committee reported, "is now apparent. The accommodations at Ellis Island are not sufficient for the avalanche of new arrivals; larger cities have not houses for them; work cannot be found for them; and further, the bulk of the newer arrivals are of the dependent rather than working class." "A large percentage" of these newly arriving men, women, and children, the report went on to state, "were incapable of earning a livelihood." And, according to the committee's findings, some 80 to 90 percent of recent arrivals, coming by way of such major ports as Rotterdam and Danzig, were overwhelmingly of "the Semitic race." (In fact, Jews accounted for no more than 14 percent of all immigrants in any given year prior to 1920, and even when their numbers grew in 1921–22, they still only reached 17 percent of the total.)[8]

Warning that three million more Polish Jews were waiting in the wings, the congressional report claimed that in one month alone (October 1920), at least 50,000 Jews had entered the United States, as compared with the highest *annual* total previously recorded: 153,748 (for the year 1906).[9] Thus, the equation "East European immigrant equals Jew" was explicitly established in the public domain. As if that were insufficient, the committee's report to Congress included, as an appendix, a State Department memorandum (signed by Wilbur J. Carr of the Consular Service), that outlined the reasons why further immigration of East Europeans generally, and Jews in particular, was undesirable. Jews from Poland and Russia (constituting "the great mass of aliens" reported to be passing through European ports) were termed "the usual ghetto type . . . filthy, un-American and often dangerous in their habits." They were physically and mentally "deficient" and economically as well as socially "undesirable."[10] (This report, of course, became the rationale behind the 1921 and 1924 immigration restriction laws.)

On the face of it, the characterization of Russian and Polish Jews as "un-American" is nothing but a tautology. But, of course, the term "un-American" is used here not as a simple statement of fact, but as a pejorative term. It connotes not that Jews in Eastern Europe were *not Americans*, but that they were *primordially unfit to become Americans:* that their physical and mental makeup and social characteristics were *inimical to American values and the American way of life.*

What is reflected here are two ideas that altered the Americanization issue: a social-Darwinist determinism that ran counter to the earlier conviction that free institutions could mold free people (i.e., that Americanization was predicated solely on socioeconomic and political, not psycho-biological, grounds); and a reification of "Americanism" into a fixed pattern of cultural, racial, and other characteristics that were clearly distinguishable from "alien" ones. Martin Marty reminds us that the House of Representatives greeted with applause the following remarks by a congressman (in 1924): "We have admitted the dregs of Europe until America has been orientalized, Europeanized, Africanized and mongrelized to that insidious degree that our genius, stability, greatness, and promise of advancement and achievement are actually menaced." And a second congressman was likewise applauded when he concurred that God had "intended [America] to be the home of a great people: English-speaking—a white race with great ideals, the Christian religion, one race, one country, one destiny."[11]

Formulated in this way, Americanism bore comparison to other contemporary volkish ideologies. Small wonder, then, that a foreign visitor wrote in 1927:

> The essential characteristic of the post-war period in the United States is the nervous reaction of the original American stock against an insidious subjugation by foreign blood. . . . They have a vague,

uneasy fear of being overwhelmed from within, and of suddenly find-
ing one day that they are no longer themselves.[12]

By closing the doors of free immigration, and by doing so in such
a way as to stigmatize particular populations, the American public
and its representatives were, in effect, rejecting the "regeneration"
model as no longer workable. Under the prevailing industrial and
urban conditions, they were saying, "the poor of Europe" could no
longer be so easily transformed into tomorrow's fortunate Americans. A permanent urban proletariat, drawn from Southern and
Eastern Europe, from Asia, and from America's own racial under-
classes might contribute, indeed, to a "degeneration" of America
itself.

Moreover, restrictionist sentiment bore clear implications not
only for the prospective immigrants, but also for those already
settled in the United States, as Oscar Handlin observed:

> As the purport of the deliberations in Congress became clear, the
> foreign-born could not escape the conclusion that it was not only the
> future arrivals who were being judged. . . . The objections to further
> immigration from Italy and Poland reflected the objectors' unfavor-
> able opinions of the Italians and Poles they saw about them. The
> argument that Greeks and Slovaks could not become good Americans
> rested on the premise that the Greeks and Slovaks in the United
> States had not become good Americans. . . . Restriction gave official
> sanction to the assertions that the immigrants were separate from
> and inferior to the native-born, and at the same time gave their
> isolation a decisive and irrevocable quality.[13]

Thus began a prolonged period of unease for Jews in the United
States, during which exclusionary ("restrictive") practices became
common in the corporate and banking sector, in housing and in
higher education, as well as in "polite society." More traumatic, in
the long run, was the refusal of Congress to reconsider its strict
position on immigration, even when it became a matter of admit-
ting refugees, from 1933 through the 1950s.

Ultimately, the period of unease would pass as immigrant Jewish
Americans, and especially their children, took their places (with
remarkable rapidity) in the ranks of the solid middle class. Discrimination against them in jobs, housing, and higher education de-

clined to insignificant levels or disappeared altogether in the decades following the Second World War.[14] Jews were again counted
in the national community, via the "triple melting pot" or via
the "Judeo-Christian ethic," or via the series of realignments in
American society and politics produced by the New Deal, the war
against tyranny abroad, and the cold war.

In the end, then, the formula of regeneration through access
to America's bounty and benevolence did work for them. They
Americanized with a vengeance; and herein lies the subject that I
wish to address specifically.

During the first crucial period, from about 1880 to about 1920,
how did Jews in America conceptualize and formulate their version
of Americanism and Americanization? With the exception of the
privileged minority, they could not adopt the most restrictive of
definitions that were being bandied about, for that would have
been tantamount to self-exclusion. What I want to deal with, then,
is a sort of *Rezeptionsgeschichte* (in brief overview) of Americanist
ideology within the articulate Jewish public. What, in other words,
did "being American" mean to them? How did they seek to overcome the challenges posed by anti-Semitism and the difficulties of
integration? What was the Jewish "take" on Crèvecoeur's formula?
And did the encounter between America and its Jews result in
something specifically American, in terms of Jewish accommodation to modernity, or some specifically Jewish modification to
Americanism?

To Jews, Americanization meant nothing less than full enfranchisement. Crèvecoeur might have been writing specifically about them
when he spoke of those who had counted for nought in European
society, and who "became men" in America. Americanism was a
tremendous, liberating idea that promised to bestow the gift of
human dignity. As such, it should be examined in the same context
as other secular ideas of Jewish liberation (both nationalist and
socialist) that promised to restore dignity and self-respect to an
oppressed people. Americanization belongs in a history of modern
Jewish politics.

The moral force of Americanism as an ideology of liberation is captured in the following lines from the poem, "Statue of Liberty," written in 1897 by the socialist Yiddish immigrant poet Avrohom Liessin (Avrohom Valt, 1872–1938):

> From the dark, medieval night,
> from a world of plunder, a world of war,
> of the oppressive yoke, of rivers of blood,
> of the pious cross and the grievous knout,
> the free set forth courageously
> across the sea to a distant shore. . . .
> Oh come, ye wanderers, ye persecuted:
> from crammed and stifled worlds,
> come here to endless tracts.
> Oh come, ye brave ones, ye free ones:
> Here you'll gather newfound might.
> To you we extend a hearty welcome.
>
> In the New World, beyond the Atlantic,
> lies a wide-open miraculous land,
> where Man, freed from tyranny,
> grows free and proud
> with a spirit that knows no bound
> and a will forged of steel.[15]

But Americanism and Americanization have suffered from poor public relations lately. Other ideologies have fared better, in terms of positive historical assessments. Jewish socialism, crowned with martyrdom in Russia and Poland, and wreathed with the laurels it won in the Jewish labor movements of America and the Yishuv (Jewish community) in Palestine, has enjoyed a full measure of historiographical attention. Jewish nationalism, too, especially as it was shaped and crystallized in the Yishuv and the State of Israel, has claimed a deserved preeminence in Jewish political and social science. Americanism, however, though it was the sociocultural and political creed of several million Jews, has not been treated in the same light.

For one thing, political historians might balk a bit at placing fully fledged political movements (with parties, programs, press organs, and armed underground militias) on a par with a rather amorphous process of social and political integration. Americanism, it will be argued, was more a matter of changing lifestyles than of ideology and organization.

Americanization has also borne the brunt of recent criticism by historians for the heavy-handed ways in which immigrants and their children were programmed to suppress their foreign identities, cultures, and mother tongues. In the recently renewed debate in American society over multiculturalism, the Americanization issue has acquired a mostly negative connotation: the term describes what an immigrant had to *lose* in order to pursue the goals of integration. "Being a good American meant erasing cultural distinctions that had previously set [Jews] apart."[16]

Finally, it may be argued, Americanization was focused on the individual immigrant, or the immigrant family, more than on the larger collective. In that sense, its status as a "liberation movement" may be legitimately questioned.

Yet it is hard to deny that the impact of Americanism was felt across the entire Jewish ideological, religious, and political spectrum in the United States. It was a campaign waged at the grass-roots level, in kitchens and living rooms, in synagogues, public schools, public libraries, and evening classes for adults. But it also had its more public dimension. It was not a Jewish phenomenon per se (for it involved countless other immigrants from many ethnic and geographic backgrounds), and was often directed (if at all) from above more than from below. But it is a common feature in the history of all sectors in the American Jewish population: in the emerging denominational divisions, including the Orthodox; in organized labor; even in American Zionism. When Louis Brandeis equated Zionism with American democracy, he was only saying what those in the Reform movement had already said about *their* principles, and what champions of Diaspora nationalism or ethnic pluralism, in their turn, were claiming for their own programs.

In view of the exclusionary and racist uses to which nativist Americanism was put, both in domestic social relations and in immigration restriction, the embrace of Americanism by Jews, both "uptown" and "downtown" and from every identifiable sector, should be reexamined as a Jewish form of self-defense and legitimation of the Jews' place within the national community. And in light of the multiplicity of Jewish ideological alternatives available around the turn of the century, how remarkable it is to find them all deemed compatible with American ideals!

Something had to happen, both to the Jews and to their concept of Americanism, for this to work. The texts I will cite here ought to elucidate what that "something" was.

1. " . . . *The New Mode of Life He Has Embraced":* *Becoming "Men"*

In asserting that the American model of social and civil equality was consistent with Jewish values, Jewish Americanizers emphasized the importance of group pride, dignity, and self-respect. In the version proffered by Minnie D. Louis (1841–1922), an "uptown" writer and educator active in settlement-house work in New York City, the connection was phrased in terms reminiscent of Crève-coeur:

> *Among the ranks of men to stand*
> full noble with the noblest there;
> To aid the right in every land,
> with mind, with might, with heart, with prayer,
> *This* is the eternal Jew![17]

This "eternal Jew," we note, was no petty shopkeeper or street peddler, but "full noble with the noblest," and (noblesse oblige) he bore responsibility for those less fortunate than he. As a credo of the Jewish elite, this is a fair summation of an ideal American Jewish type: the straight-backed patrician. Group pride is a composite of ancient lineage and high-minded principle, backed up by action. This Jew "stands," he is 'manly,' and true to himself; therefore, he is worthy of the high regard of others. Certainly, this is how the American Jewish elite wished to be thought of.

Whether or not there are specifically American elements in this ideal self-portrait (the positive, expressly male images were common to Western bourgeois cultures generally—and expressed here by a female spokesperson), the message is: You can be a good Jew and an American at the same time. Indeed, attainment of the emancipated American model is a sine qua non for the realization of the essential ("eternal") Jewish ideal. It is false to assume (the

text explains) that authentic Judaism can be found in pre-emanci-
pated "ghetto" Jewry, a Jewry that cannot stand up straight:

> To wear the yellow badge, the locks,
> the caftan-long, *the low-bent head,*
> To pocket unprovoked knocks
> and shamble on in servile dread—
> 'Tis not this to be a Jew.[18]

The argument has two sources. First, as a piece of didactic propaganda, it stems from the poet's desire that immigrant Jews abandon
what she saw as undignified and obsolete forms of behavior, in
order to emerge into the full light of freedom. This, in itself, is a
stock item in the emancipationist arsenal, and represents, in part,
an internalization of non-Jewish criteria. Second, it grows out of a
defense of Americanized Jews as being fully authentic in terms of
both aspects of their identity: as Jews and as Americans. Both theses
lead to the same conclusion: personal and collective dignity.

Defining dignity as the paramount value to champion is itself
indicative of the social context, in which Jewish dignity was under
attack. The theme was reiterated on many occasions, in various
forms. Thus, B'nai B'rith president Julius Bien, speaking in 1889 in
favor of speedy Americanization of the immigrants, told his group
that the newcomers, "trained in the modes and ways of the American citizen, . . . shall be encouraged to identify themselves with
the genius, the spirit, the duties and obligations *of a free man in a
free country*" (emphasis added).[19]

The report of B'nai B'rith's General Convention the following
year explicitly cited the danger of anti-Semitism, which was liable
to spread as the American public came to view the "foreign Jews"
with "apprehension and mistrust." The remedy lay in education
and Americanization of "the foreigner."[20] One prominent leader of
the Order, Moritz Ellinger (1830–1907), added more specific advice,
very close in spirit to the message of "the eternal Jew" (and appro-
priating the language of the Passover liturgy): "Let them [the immi-
grants] be taken out of the house of exclusiveness and clannishness,
which perpetuates the bondage of Russia in this country."[21]

Mores and social or religious forms that were the products of the "house of bondage" had no legitimate place under the warmer sun "in this country." The Jew's honor went hand in hand with an expansive, liberal outlook.

Ellinger's America, like his ideal Jew, was expansive, tolerant, broad-minded, and ready for new challenges. If not the immigrants themselves, then certainly their American-raised children would inherit a proper place in society as "valued citizens." The country had the capability of providing salvation for all who had been deprived of their rights: "Let us be proud of the title, 'refuge for the oppressed of all nations.' . . . We do not entertain these views as Jews," he asserted, "but as American citizens."[22] He was not (he claimed), pleading for special interests—yet, in identifying what in his eyes were the common American values, he was selecting a set of values quite distinct from those of the "hundred-percent Americans" who no longer wished their country to be a haven for the oppressed. If the Jews were called upon to select America-compatible behaviors, America was called upon to be true to the regeneration formula.

Kaufmann Kohler (1843–1926), one of the leading exponents of Reform Judaism in America, echoed the Americanizing consensus of "uptown" in an address to the Council of American Hebrew Congregations in January 1911:

> Least of all could Judaism retain its medieval garb, its alien form, its seclusiveness, in a country that rolled off the shame and the taunt of the centuries from the shoulders of the wandering Jew, to place him, the former Pariah of the nations, alongside of the highest and the best, according to his worth and merit as a *man*, and among a people that adopted the very principles of justice and human dignity proclaimed by Israel's lawgivers and prophets, and made them the foundation stones of their commonwealth. . . . Behold America, the land of the future! . . . The land of promise for all the persecuted! [O]ut of the mingling of races and sects, nay, out of the boldest, the most courageous and most independent elements of society, a new, a stronger, a healthier and happier type of men and women should emerge. . . .[23]

Kohler, too, upheld the regenerative formula ("the best" and "the boldest"), holding the door open wide for his East European brethren to enter and partake. But in this sermon he also added another element: He claimed Judaic lineage for the American republic, so that the compatibility of the Jew and America was a mutual one, in which *America* is also compatible *with the Jew*.

It is clear from these three texts that Americanization, although a "mitzvah" incumbent upon the individual, was understood as impinging directly on the collective as well: the smaller, Jewish collective, as well as the larger, American nation.

The interplay of all these themes is graphically displayed on the masthead and cover illustration for an issue of the Yiddish-language journal, *Der idisher imigrant*, published by the Hebrew Immigrant Aid Society (HIAS). The artwork depicts an image of American Liberty opening the "gates of justice" for an impoverished Jew, superimposed over an endless trail of wandering, homeless Jews, bearing the burden of exile. The message is clearly one of redemption from exile, and while the Jew who enters the "gates of justice" is a solitary figure, he certainly is meant to represent the many of the historical collective (see illustration).

Moreover, the masthead logo includes two national banners, the Stars and Stripes and the Blue-White Jewish Star (no political Zionist connotation is implied—this flag was a general Jewish symbol). Over the flags the American eagle spreads its wings, and the Hebrew liturgical motto held in its beak reads: "Shelter us in the shadow of Thy wing." Once again, a Judaic symbol is wedded to an American one: the fulfillment of Jewish prophetic hope appears in American form.[24]

Probably one of the most intelligent and sensitive treatments of the subject of Americanization was penned by Israel Friedlaender (1876–1920). Friedlaender, himself an immigrant from Poland, and a professor of Bible at the Jewish Theological Seminary of America, published widely on contemporary Jewish issues and was an advocate of Diaspora Jewish nationalism (à la Dubnov). When asked to offer his educated advice on the problem of Americanization, he produced a manifesto in defense of Jewish tradition as the key to restoring to the dislocated immigrant a necessary source of psychosocial balance ("equilibrium"), a standard and rationale for moderation in all things, and a chance for successful acculturation in the long run. Bereft of tradition, of the ways and customs of the immigrant's former "natural environment" which had served as a social anchor, "a man is degraded into a beast . . . , he becomes

unnatural and unhappy, . . . in danger of becoming a moral wreck, a menace to himself and a menace to his neighbors." The social and religious moorings provided by one's own group are the foundations of self-esteem, and self-esteem is the basis for good citizenship.[25]

Thus, we return to the linked themes of human dignity, regeneration, and the individual; only here, with Friedlaender, the opportunity to "become a man" in America is predicated on the creative survival of the ethno-religious community. Friedlaender speaks of the need to modify the terms of Americanization so that it leaves room for the maintenance of "old country" cultures, for no immigrant is a "tabula rasa," lacking a personal history, positive values, and group attachments.

> It goes without saying that we must acquaint the immigrant with the conditions of the new land, not only to strengthen him in his struggle for existence, but also to enable him to realize the true foundations of American life and American culture. But it is just as important, if not more important, . . . that we make him again a social unit. . . .
>
> The Jewish immigrant, like all other human beings, cannot be made a new man. The human soul is *not* a *tabula rasa*. The impress of centuries is indelibly stamped upon it. . . .
>
> It is obvious, therefore, that our method of Americanization—an Americanization which is constructive and not destructive—must consist in restoring the impaired or destroyed equilibrium of the immigrant Jew. . . . We must then adapt the immigrant Jew to the new environment, but we must do so cautiously, gently, and sympathetically, ever alive to the dangers of a rapid and artificial Americanization which may destroy old values without building up new values in their stead.[26]

Dignity and self-esteem, both as components of the Jew's new stature as an American and as an aspect of the new "mode of living," were hardly the exclusive concern of do-gooders, spokespersons for the Jewish upper class, or Reform rabbis. Israel Zevin, a popular writer in the immigrant press in New York (under the *nom de plume* of Tashrak), and traditionally Orthodox, wrote a comprehensive etiquette manual for the Yiddish-speaking community, which will be discussed in more detail in the next chapter. Tashrak's guide sought to school his fellow newcomers in American standards of deportment, honor, and self-respect.[27]

The Orthodox Zevin was sufficiently impressed with the dignity and orderliness of services in American Reform temples that he held these up for emulation by his East European brethren.[28] In lecturing his audience, he advanced the argument for a Jewish American brand of civility: "In America we enjoy all civil rights and freedoms. What does freedom mean? It means self-control, [it means] following the rules of common decency. The Talmud teaches us: 'Who is truly respected? He who respects his fellow creatures,' that is, all people."[29] The path to self-respect and social respectability lay in regard for others' rights and comfort.

Although the stress here is on being a *mentsh* rather than on becoming a "man" (perhaps because in Zevin's view, only that extra bit of polish was needed, rather than a full-scale overhaul of the "ghetto" Jew), the importance of propriety, decorum, and dignified bearing is of a piece with other aspects of Americanization. Minding one's manners, whether in synagogue, in the street, or at home, was part of the "embrace of a new mode of life," a change to something new and better, in one's own interest and that of society at large. The honor of the group is linked to the self-improvement of the individual, and both are bound up in a sense of what was expected in bourgeois America. As an observer of the social history of New York Jewry has commented:

> Jews . . . displayed an intense concern for the rituals and routines of everyday life, investing cleanliness, table manners, diet, decor, appearance and privacy with profound cultural and social significance. . . . Jews were not unusual in cultivating social niceties which are, after all, commonly shared conventions. What distinguished their concern for such matters from that of society at large, however, was the extent to which New York Jewry's moral custodians elevated the observance of these social norms from the realm of private behavior to the level of a collective endeavor, promoting matters of manners and morals as vehicles of acculturation.[30]

That status-consciousness and bourgeois propriety became linked with what it meant to be American comes as no surprise if we consider America's image as a land of economic bounty. Even if Jewish immigrants arrived on the scene *en masse* after the "unappropriated wealth" of the agrarian Western frontier was enclosed, they nevertheless came with their own version of America as the land of limitless fortune. They called it the *goldene medineh* (the "golden land") and its "unappropriated wealth" was spoken of (metaphorically) as "gold in the streets."[31] Their "frontier" was urban, bounded by concrete and by neighborhood limits. If America did not quite live up to everyone's dreams, and if the new immigrant was not always welcomed enthusiastically into the "broad lap of our great *Alma Mater*," the immigrants nonetheless aspired to a higher status in America than that which they had held in Europe. If becoming American meant becoming "men," economic and social mobility was the essence of that process. Only through the "rewards of ample subsistence" did the new life confer regenerative qualities.

2. " . . . *The New Government He Obeys* . . . "

Just as Jews, by and large, did not go along with a static reification of Americanism and insisted instead that America remain open to all who wished to "become men" in the land of liberty, they likewise tended to favor a model of Americanization based on the salutary influence of a free system of government, rather than think in terms of classes of people who might be inherently fitter or less fit to become Americans. Social environment, rather than "race," was the determining factor. The essence and uniqueness of American nationhood, they believed, lay in its democratic ethos, and it was by living under American freedom that one came to appreciate and share in its blessings.

Addressing the Third Annual Meeting of HIAS, in January 1912, the organization's president, Judge Leon Sanders, enunciated the pro-immigration, liberal Jewish American credo as follows:

> I rejoice that the history of our people in this country is a living demonstration of the fact that the primal ambition of the Jew is to become assimilated in the mass of the population, to familiarize himself with the glorious traditions of liberty, which are the corner stone of the republic, and to become, in company with his fellow citizens of other faiths, a cog in the wheel of progress. I further rejoice that the history of our people is a living refutation of the malicious calumny that all immigrants remain alien to our customs, language, and institutions, but that, on the contrary, from the day he lands at Ellis Island, the Jewish immigrant is consumed with the desire to

hasten the approach of the day when he shall be qualified to enter upon the full enjoyment of the American franchise.[32]

In European debates over the Jewish question, apologists for the Jewish side "explained" or excused Jewish "defects" as the products of centuries of isolation and oppression. In America, a radically different legal-governmental and social environment was credited with an equally powerful potential, able to erase the negative effects of persecution and exclusion.

By extension, if Jews had been law-abiding subjects where they had been merely tolerated, in America they were not only honor-bound to love their country, but also eager to identify with its spirit.

Thus, Kaufmann Kohler's sermon on "American Judaism" noted:

> Look at any of the creeds and churches in our free land! They are all more tolerant, more liberal, more humane and sympathetic in their mutual relations than those in Europe. Our free institutions, our common school, our enlightening press and pulpit . . . enlarge the mental and social horizon and render progress the guiding maxim.[33]

Kohler created for his listeners an inspiring symmetry between the American people ("the youngest of the great nations of history") and the Jewish people ("the oldest"). In the American system, he declared, one found the ideal synthesis between "the world's two greatest principles and ideals . . . , the highest moral and spiritual and the highest political and social aim of humanity."[34] It was that synthesis that enabled a progressive Judaism to flourish, different in form (though not in essence!) from Judaism's "medieval garb," the "ark" in which it had been forced to take shelter in the lands of oppression. It was probably not coincidental that Kohler's words echoed those of the Puritan founders when he described America as "a new earth and a new heaven." The use of American vocabulary and allusion to American mythology was an important element in creating the rhetoric of Jewish Americanism: "Behold Judaism leaving the ark, because the flood of unrighteousness, of cruelty has ceased, and *looking out upon a new earth and a new heaven, wherein justice, liberty and peace reign in fulfillment of its seer's vision.*"[35] "Justice, liberty and peace," as the essence of righteousness and biblical faith, are thus equated with the essence of *both* America and Judaism. For Kohler, Americanism was clearly inherent in the quality of its institutions, not in the "blood" or religion of the nation's dominant social elements.

In a similar vein, David Philipson (1862–1949), president of the Reform movement's Central Conference of American Rabbis (CCAR), assured his colleagues in 1908 that progressive Judaism would eventually win the hearts and minds of even those East European immigrants—or else, certainly, of their children—who were still caught in "reactionism, romanticism, neo-nationalism, and neo-orthodoxy." "Let us have no fear," he said, "our Russian brethren, under the spell of *the spirit of our free institutions will be americanized.*"[36]

Ironically, one of those "brethren" who held the kind of views that Philipson called "perverse" and "distorted"—the socialist Yid-dishist writer, Chaim Zhitlowsky (1865–1943)—eagerly concurred in the Reform rabbi's assessment of the American system of government, precisely because it enabled him to champion his own program of Jewish national-cultural survival. Writing in 1915, he asserted:

> We live in one of the freest countries in the world, a country which cannot deny any group the right to live as it chooses, provided that it commit itself to the political and social progress of the land, and *on condition that this group love the free character of the country's institutions and laws,* to the extent that these indeed are free and just. We accept these conditions with the greatest joy, because no other nationality in the world is as eager as we are to see public life based upon freedom and justice.[37]

Zhitlowsky here enunciated the syllogistic formula of immigrant Americanism: America deserves Jewish love and loyalty because America is free; America is free to the extent that it allows its citizens a liberal measure of self-esteem and self-expression—that is, insofar as Jews may remain true to themselves; therefore, Jewish allegiance to America may be taken as a measure of America's faithfulness to itself. Should America fail to live up to those standards, Zhitlowsky intimated, Jews would be justified in leaving the country. But such a state of affairs was not realistically anticipated. America was to be regarded as a safe bet.[38]

Jewishness and Americanism were, thus, defined as mutually

reinforcing. But if the essence of Jewishness, according to Zhitlow-sky, was its *folk-ethnic* basis, the essence of America was its nature as a unique *polis*, as expressed in its "institutions and laws." The basis for American patriotism, then, did not lie in the *exchange* of one ethnic label ("Jew") for another ("American"), but in the maintenance of one's national-minority existence within the American system.[39] This was a far cry from Crèvecoeur's formula of "leaving behind . . . all ancient prejudices and manners" for the sake of receiving "new ones from the new mode of life [the American] has embraced."

Rather similar, though modulated by a greater sensitivity to America's national-cultural ambience, was Judah L. Magnes's defense of ethnic pluralism. Magnes (1877–1948), the San Francisco-born American Zionist, Reform rabbi, and leading figure in New York Jewry, devoted several sermons at New York's leading Reform temple, Emanu-El, in 1909 to the question of Jewish ethnic survival in the United States.

In one of these sermons, marking Lincoln's birthday, Magnes maintained that "Americanization" had turned from an open, rather simple idea that indicated the freedom enjoyed by the citizen, into a restrictive code word meaning ethno-cultural conformity. Citing the Great Emancipator as his authority, Magnes asserted that, "for him [Lincoln], an American was a freeman, at liberty to develop his spirit as he chose, so long as he obeyed the law." In words drawn from the Gettysburg Address (here, again, we see the appropriation of American vocabulary for Jewish polemical purposes), Magnes claimed that in his own day, however, the term "Americanization" was all too often "not conceived in liberty and dedicated to the proposition that all men are created free and equal."[40]

Americanization of the immigrant, when taken to mean a demand for abandonment of one's traditional religion or one's nationality (meaning one's native culture and group identity), was something bordering on the subversive. On the other hand, Magnes favored Americanization in terms of the cultivation of good citizenship:

It must be accepted as almost axiomatic that every one living in this land should be a citizen of the land. *If Americanization means this, that every inhabitant, native-born or foreign, assume the obligations of American citizenship,* then Americanization is a process that should be aided by us in every legitimate way. . . . The newcomers of the past generation and more have equalled their predecessors in the avidity with which they have entered into *political partnership with their fellow citizens.*[41]

To be a full-fledged American, then, was to enter fully into the social contract that was the founding principle of the nation. The emphasis, then, is clearly on "political partnership"—participation in the American system and the willing assumption of all corollary duties.

Yet, Magnes also recognized a dimension of American identity that went beyond political allegiance:

That process of Americanization that makes clear the privilege and the duty of American citizenship is something for which we may all be grateful. . . . Everyone . . . must seek to understand the spirit of [the country's] history, its laws, its institutions, its ideals. Everyone must, in greater or less degree, *saturate himself with the dominant culture of the land, which is English.*[42]

His solution, therefore, was one of *parallel* identities: "It is possible and it is desirable that parallel with a high appreciation of, and assimilation to English culture, a man cling with reverence to the national culture of his fathers." And here Magnes introduced the capping argument of his thesis: namely, that a multicultural America would be a better, richer America, in which democracy would not have an unfortunate leveling, homogenizing effect. America, he concluded, was "not yet a finished product." America was a dynamic process, an open-ended experiment in human coexistence. "American culture, American nationality can be made fruitful and beautiful by contact with the cultures of the various nationalities that are among us. America is not the melting pot."[43]

Thus, while acknowledging that American nationality entailed acculturation, not just citizenship, Magnes broadened the parameters of acculturation by suggesting the possibilities of "parallelism" and the dynamic encounter of multiple traditions. In effect, he wished to extend the sanctity of individual liberty to include group individuality as well.

Magnes elaborated on these ideas again in October 1909, in a sermon that rejected the model of assimilation depicted in Israel Zangwill's play, *The Melting Pot* (which had opened in New York the previous month). Mincing no words, Magnes referred to the melting-pot type of Americanization as "de-Judaization" and as "suicide" for an ethno-national-religious group such as the Jews. He called, once again, for a new understanding of Americanism, for a "republic of nationalities," and for an American "symphony . . . written by the various nationalities which keep their individual and characteristic note, and which sound this note in harmony with their sister nationalities."[44]

Magnes's agenda on these particular occasions was the legitimation of pluralism—that is, Jewish distinctiveness—within American society. On other occasions, however, he and his colleagues focused on another agenda: the legitimation of American principles of representative democracy within the Jewish community, particularly with regard to the custodial leadership of Jewish institutions. This, too, was an important facet of Americanization. The struggle for democratization of Jewish communal bodies led Magnes to head the New York Jewish Kehillah (from its founding until 1922), and it led Stephen S. Wise (1874–1949) and Louis D. Brandeis (1856–1941) to spearhead a campaign to establish a representative, elected American Jewish Congress.

It is undoubtedly true that the demand for a Jewish congress was a lever deliberately used by the Zionist movement against the American Jewish Committee, in the anticipation that it would reap political benefit from a defeat of the non-Zionist Jewish establishment.[45] Nevertheless, the pitched battle (that lasted throughout World War I and was resolved only when the Committee agreed to cooperate with a Zionist-led American Jewish Congress) was the first nationwide Jewish political "event" in the United States. It is therefore indicative and significant that both sides, both pro- and anti-congress, were moved to "Americanize" the arena of struggle.

The anti-congress forces, for their part, were loath to see the public affirmation of a national Jewish political interest, least of all under the Zionist-tinged title of a "congress," with its political-nationalistic flavor. Jews, as good American citizens, were supposed to be united by religious and philanthropic causes, but strictly American (i.e., concerned only with the greater good of the country, not with sectoral interests) in the political arena.[46]

The challengers, with Brandeis in the lead, seconded by Wise, also used the cudgel of American democratic values to support their case. The idea of a Jewish congress, they declared, was nothing but the people's vehicle for speaking its mind freely without having to accept the overlordship of self-appointed "bosses." This was the essence of democracy, the very spirit of American freedom. Thus, Stephen Wise declared at a meeting in Carnegie Hall in New York in October 1915:

> The question is whether American Israel is to be Jewish and American or un-Jewish and un-American. For un-Jewish it is to be distrustful and even fearful of the many; un-American it is to dread to summon the collective spirit of the people to an attitude of high self-reliance. The very resentment of the attempt of the masses to control their own affairs is proof of the anti-democratic spirit that has come over those good men who do not seem to understand the unimpairable passion of a people to direct its own affairs.[47]

In March 1916, addressing the Preliminary Conference for the organization of an American Jewish Congress, held in Philadelphia, Wise again stressed the American theme:

> We have chosen the name ["Congress"] because it is the American name, because its American associations have endeared it to us, native and adoptive children of the Republic alike. We have chosen the name Congress because it is an inclusive, all-American name, with no implication of partisanship or factionalism. . . .
>
> It were treasonable to be either un-Jewish or un-American, and we are Jewish in our determination to be self-succoring and American in the strength of our will to achieve the best for our people everywhere. . . .
>
> Are we forever to suffer men to think and act for us . . . because they have decreed that we are not fit to be trusted with the power of shaping our own destiny? Among the first of earth's peoples to advocate and to insist upon popular autonomy, shall we be the last to welcome the renewal of the spirit of democracy? Shall we in this democratic land renounce our democratic ideals . . .?[48]

The circle was thus completed: The American heritage of freedom was asserted as the birthright of American Jews—a birthright doubly theirs, by virtue of American *and* Jewish traditions. Allegiance to one justified allegiance to the other; to betray one meant betrayal of the other, as well. The rhetorical battle became a contest to prove which side was most true to the ideals of American freedom.

The rhetoric of Americanism indicates the extent to which the political allegiance of the Jewish citizen to the United States was the basis for a new American Jewish politics. Though chosen for effect, and thus, perhaps, revealing the *content* of the issues at stake only in part, the verbal ammunition was significant in its own right, reflecting the *context* of the debate. It was a context in which loyalty to America and its system of government was a key to legitimacy, even in an internal Jewish political setting.

3. "The New Rank He Holds . . ."

As alluded to in the preceding discussion, Jewish Americanizers took the view that the liberal social and political system in the United States provided the basis for the immigrant's progress toward a new stature and status. The dignity conferred by constitutional guarantees of equality and the political allegiance of grateful, free citizens to a system that offered them full civic participation would define the new Jew in the New World.

But there were those among the immigrants themselves who denied the assertions underlying this premise, for the reality of their lives as working men and women seemed to bar them from reaping any benefit from their new rank as citizens. Because of their class status, they had neither dignity nor an effective political voice. Their vital interests seemed to be neither represented in government nor protected in the courts.

Three years after writing his celebratory hymn to the Statue of Liberty, Avrohom Liessin wrote a scathing pre-Election Day editorial in 1900 in the socialist Yiddish New York daily, the *Forverts*, in which he underscored the disillusionment of the exploited immigrant worker. Regardless of who would enter the White House in the coming election, whether Bryan or McKinley, he argued,

> no change will come to the dark tenement districts. The poor, who have the right to determine the fate of America, will mortgage their

civic rights for four years with either of the two political "trusts,"
and—nothing! Back they'll go to bearing the yoke, . . . to making
more millions and billions for the greater glory of the nation, and to
contributing to their own misery, their premature old age, and their
premature death.[49]

These words clearly convey a thoroughgoing alienation from the
political process: indeed, a bitter hostility toward the system and
what it represented in the life of the Jewish immigrant worker. In
terms of the Crèvecoeur formulation, here was a flat denial of the
regeneration model, arguing instead the inverse proposition: that
the American way of life in fact *prevented* American workers from
achieving the status of "freemen," *reduced* their human stature,
and negated their basic human rights.

The phenomenon of Jewish socialism in America represents an
interesting counterpoint to the ideas of Americanization expressed
by other sectors of the Jewish community during that period. Moreover, in this instance we have not only a negative rejection of the
regnant model, but a positive projection of an alternative or rival
social utopia—one that was based on a transnational philosophy of
worldwide class consciousness. Thus, this example seems to be at
odds with other Jewish American ideologies, all of which uniformly
asserted an essential congruence between Americanism and their
respective principles.

And yet, the history of the immigrant Jewish Left in that period
as a whole is chiefly one of accommodation to American political,
social, and economic conditions. Students of the subject concur, for
the most part, in a model of moderation and adjustment over time,
in response to trade unionists' interests in immediate amelioration
in working conditions, wages, and social security—as opposed to a
militant struggle to denature or overthrow the capitalist system as
such. This was a course that brought Jewish socialist and labor
leaders into line with established American patterns.[50] Further, a
"functionalist" school of thought has interpreted the Jewish labor
movement's success in organizing and representing the Jewish
working class as having had an "Americanizing" effect (regardless
or in spite of intent) within the immigrant population, and, thus,
having served as an agency of Americanization. Two selected examples from an extensive literature will suffice to substantiate this

point, regarding the relative importance of latent effect over articulated intent:

> The truth of the matter is that for most East European Jews socialism was as much, or more, a bridge to Americanism as a road to revolution. Thus, future studies of socialism among Jewish immigrants must focus more sharply on [labor's role] as an agency of American acculturation.[51]

> The Jewish labor movement, the principal institution developed by East European Jewry in America, was forged on an anvil uniquely Jewish and American. Its development is evidence . . . that the Eastern Jewish–American amalgam was a stable one. . . . [Labor radicals were] instrumental in developing the first real power base for East European Jews in America. It was in that sense, in learning how to use power rather than building [utopian] castles in the air, that the Jewish labor movement was an important Americanizing agent.[52]

As against these "functionalist" historiographical interpretations, Irving Howe has argued for an "intentionalist" corrective. To capture not only the flavor of the socialist Left in the Jewish immigrant community, but also its immediate historical sense in its own context, attention ought to be paid to what socialist leaders actually said and intended to achieve. Howe would not have social historians diminish the unique qualities of Jewish socialism in America by treating it as a mere "vehicle of transition and acculturation" that enabled Jewish workers to "move into American society" and "integrated them into American political life."[53]

In a somewhat different sense, Arthur Liebman, too, is an "intentionalist" insofar as he stresses the radicalizing tendencies of the Jewish labor Left and its role in nurturing both a socialist Jewish "subculture" and "institutional bulwarks of socialism" in America.[54] Moreover, in accounting for the eventual shift toward accommodationism (what he terms "concession" and "socialism's decline"), Liebman eschews the theory of latent effect in favor of an intentionalist argument: namely, that "at the very time that . . . socialist union officials were espousing socialist ideals and supporting Socialist candidates, they harbored an even stronger commitment to pragmatism." Quite apart from structural "flaws" in the organization of the garment unions and apart, as well, from the socioeconomic mobility that drew Jews out of the working class within one generation, Liebman identifies a political-ideological accommodationism among the socialist leadership after 1900:

> [E]arly in their careers these leaders had already come to the conclusion that the capitalist system would be a lasting and durable one. Acting on this premise they chose to ensure their positions and the success . . . of their organizations by reaching an accommodation with the capitalist politicoeconomic system. . . . Once they had decided to participate in the American system, their commitment to the Left gradually but steadily weakened.[55]

Finally, yet another observer of the same problem, John H. Laslett, described what amounts to a synthesis between latent, spontaneous forces and political intent. East European Jews in the American labor movement, he argued, held sacred "the socialist ideal of the cooperative commonwealth." But, as the components of that ideal were elaborated (workers' education, women's suffrage, improved health care, etc.), these were "found in the end to be consistent with the native American tradition of reform." The "material benefits" of moderate unionism became "too valuable to discard" and gave union leaders an incentive for cooperation with employers.[56]

> As the [garment unions] matured and became more successful in the economic field, the revolutionary purposes for which many of these programs were designed were abandoned, and social reform became a sufficient end in itself. . . . America itself became an acceptable substitute for the [ideal-messianic] Promised Land.[57]

There would seem to be little substantive difference between "functionalists" and "intentionalists"—all conclude that the radical Left became more moderate and more "American" over time—other than the degree of sympathy they display for the Jewish socialists' original radical program. Nevertheless, Howe's point about taking Jewish labor radicalism at face value as a cultural-political phenomenon, Liebman's stress on the inherent duality or paradoxicality of Jewish radical unionism, and Laslett's position on the confluence of Jewish socialist praxis and American reformist liberalism do return our attention to the question of how Jewish socialists presented the case against (or for) America. Whereas the "functionalists" would have us understand Americanization in its broadest possible terms, including any process that directly or indirectly aided or abetted the adaptation of newcomers to their new environment, the "intentionalist" corrective requires us to take note of *conscious formulas* of adaptation.

Can we, then, identify an articulated Jewish-leftist Americanist formula, one that is explicit and argumentative in nature rather than just latent and structural, and that would be analogous to the formulas espoused by bourgeois Jewish elements? To answer that question, we will turn to material that appeared in New York's daily *Forverts*.

The *Forverts* was probably the most representative voice of the New York-based Jewish labor movement, both in terms of its mass circulation (over one hundred thousand) and its mainstream political position. After 1900, it backed the moderate revisionist line of the Socialist Party of America (opposing the radical wing, centered around the Socialist Labor Party). The editor of the *Forverts*, Abraham Cahan, has been properly associated with an Americanizing thrust within the Jewish immigrant community, not only because of his political point of view, but also because of his paper's role in educating the immigrants about American social mores, language, and culture. But what did Cahan's paper have to say on the subject of America itself, in an explicit rather than merely implicit way?

On this point we can discover much from *Forverts* editorials for significant dates on the American calendar: Thanksgiving, presidents' birthdays, Election Day, July 4, and so on. For the purpose of the present study, I will cite examples from the two most political of these national "days," Election Day and Independence Day, which serve as a sort of barometer regarding the issues at hand. On and around these days, the *Forverts* directly addressed its readers on the subject of American civil and political liberties, on the value of citizenship, and on the power of the ballot box.

The *Forverts* developed an editorial line that essentially argued the following: America's was an interrupted or incomplete revolution. It was inspired by the highest ideals, but it fell short of realizing them. Instead, the revolutionary spirit of freedom had been betrayed, subverted, and it was up to the American workers to complete the task begun in 1776. This they could and would do, but only if they could project a united voice onto the American political scene, through the instrument of the Socialist Party.

The following are a few samples of the rhetoric employed to flesh out this basic argument:

> Never are the wounds of the American nation as painful or as bloodied as when the nation celebrates its historical holidays and traditions. The birthday of American independence! Slaves may be entitled to celebrate their former freedom and independence, but only if they feel that they are struggling *in the present* to regain that freedom and that independence. But willing slaves, slaves in whom the spirit and the desire for freedom have become dormant, slaves like today's average American—dear heaven, have such as these the right to celebrate the birth of American independence?
>
> . . . Isn't it our only hope and expectation that the American people will finally throw off its slavish nature and the yoke of capitalist slavery? And this hope of ours shall be fulfilled. The American people will celebrate the true birth of freedom and independence in the future. (Emphasis in the original) [58]

Although, on the one hand, readers were told that "as workers, we have no share in the world's wealth: all we have is our bodies, our wives, and our children [all of which] we are forced to sell in order to feed ourselves";[59] on the other hand, they were urged to take political responsibility for their predicament: to exercise their right to vote "for your own good." "WORKERS, TOMORROW IS YOUR DAY. Remember all the suffering you've borne for the past 364 days and vote for your candidate [the socialist presidential ticket of Debs and Harriman]."[60] And they were warned: "When workers go out on strike after Election Day and they will be shot down by the capitalists' hired thugs, let them remember that on November 6th they helped load those guns with their own hands" by failing to vote for the Socialist Party.[61] "Today is the Day of Judgment [*yoym hadin*]. Today you have your sole opportunity to destroy the corruption that holds sway over the political life of this country . . . and to show your enemies and the whole world that you are no longer slaves, but free people."[62]

The paper had adequate cause to worry about its readership's readiness to "get out the vote." New York's Jewish and Italian immigrant districts showed the city's lowest proportion of registered voters per capita.[63] The immigrants were also often slow in filing applications for naturalization and the procedure itself was inefficient and complicated. Information on naturalization was disseminated by HIAS, and instruction in American civics was expanded in 1913 when evening classes were opened in the Bronx and Brooklyn, in addition to those in lower Manhattan.[64] By 1910, the Socialist Party had also decided to "help make citizens." Plans were drawn up to have the Party's local branch keep a close watch over procedures at the Naturalization Bureau, and the Bureau itself undertook to maintain a larger clerical staff and regular hours, to streamline operations.[65] In 1916 the Jewish unions sponsored their own Naturalization Aid League to encourage more Jewish workers to file their citizenship papers.[66]

The Jewish socialist vote on the Lower East Side of Manhattan remained numerically very small in this period, growing from 3,400 to 5,200 between 1908 and 1915. Moreover, this represented only 10–19 percent of the total Jewish vote in those election districts. Nevertheless, Jews contributed about a third or more of the entire Socialist Party winnings in Manhattan, until they succeeded in sending their own candidate, Meyer London, to Congress in 1914 (the second Socialist congressman, following Victor Berger's victory in Milwaukee in 1910).[67]

This "ballot box socialism" was one key to Cahan's "Americanization of Jewish socialist politics."

> Why are the Americans so happy about having declared their independence from King George 128 years ago when they are a thousand times more "dependent" today on the accursed King Dollar [than they ever were under King George]? True celebration will be in order only when the people rid themselves of this "king" . . . , when the people become independent in all aspects of their lives. How are we to achieve that? . . . Ballots, those little voting slips, when cast for the Socialist cause, are what can bring about the people's independence from King Dollar. . . . This year, the real "independence day" will be celebrated at the polls when Eugene Debs and Benjamin Hanford will run in the presidential elections.[68]

As the Socialist Party membership around the country grew (from 16,000 in 1903 to 118,045 in 1912),[69] exhortations to vote the Party ticket in New York grew more optimistic in tone: "While we wait impatiently for Election Day to arrive . . . , we can find great satisfaction in what we have already accomplished. . . . The unions have demonstrated their strength in this campaign," declared the *Forverts* in 1906.[70] With "three days to go" before the election, the Jewish voter was urged to consider carefully how to make the best use of "the great, sacred right of the citizen to have your say over how this country should be governed."[71]

The rhetoric no longer referred to "slaves," but to self-respecting and proud citizens, and the campaign was waged not only against the capitalist exploiters but against machine-politics bosses who delegitimized the voting process. In "A Word to You Non-Green-horns," the *Forverts* told its readers:

> You pride yourself, "Mister Citizen," on no longer being a greenhorn. No one is going to bluff you! Good. That is just what we are looking for: citizens who will not be made fools of by the bluffers. . . . Don't pride yourself on not being a greenhorn if you allow yourself to be led up the garden path by the [capitalist] parties. Don't throw your vote away!
>
> . . . By that I do not mean that you should sell your vote, either, but that you should get full value for it. The vote is the most precious right you possess. In that little piece of paper lies a power beyond your imagination. . . . The vote determines your future. It decides the fate of your children.[72]

The second key to the *Forverts*'s Americanist outlook was its identification with the *ideals* of American freedom, even as it deplored current realities. In doing so, it was able to claim for itself the flag, the Declaration of Independence, and the Constitution—while leaving to the "unfaithful" Americans their legacy of exploitation, boss-politics, and inequality. Standing thus on the high ground, the *Forverts* in effect claimed for the socialist immigrant the sole right to the name "American."

> Then [in 1776] everyone was inspired by the idea of equality . . . , but today America is divided between a "400" group whose lives are more opulent than those of any European count, and a mass of workers who don't know where tomorrow's breakfast is coming from. One hundred and twenty-six years ago all Americans fought together for the same ideal . . . ; but today millions are enslaved to a handful of overlords. . . . There are, however, some people in America in whose hearts the spirit of 126 years ago truly lives on—the spirit of 1776,

adapted to twentieth-century conditions. Only such people can celebrate the 4th of July wholeheartedly.[73]

Or, to quote another Fourth of July editorial:

The American Declaration of Independence is the world's first true
declaration of freedom for an entire nation: the first declaration of
complete equality for all. . . . At any time, so states this wonderful
declaration, the people can decide it no longer wishes to tolerate the
government. Then it has not only the right but the duty to throw it
out of power. Can you find any "Torah" as precious as this? True, this
is only a political teaching, but it is also the basis for the finest
morality in social relations: the source of all injustice is inequality;
among equals who possess equal power there is automatically
greater justice. . . .

And to commemorate this precious "Torah," all Americans devote
one holy day every year. How thoroughly suffused with the idea of
freedom, equality, and justice the Americans must be [so we used to
believe]! What a joy it must be to live amongst them! . . . But, oh,
what a disappointment! The world's worst tyrants celebrate on the
4th of July . . ., the most merciless oppressors. . . .

No, we would have nothing at all to celebrate today if it were only
the day on which a new rigid orthodoxy was "handed down." But on
this day, a new law was *demanded:* and that is our cause for celebration. It is the day on which an oppressed people *took* power for itself,
to better its own lot. That is mankind's cause for hope. (Emphasis in
the original) [74]

Thus, it was left up to those who truly grasped the meaning of
freedom and equality to complete the task of social revolution—or,
at least, to begin the process.[75] Rejoicing over the congressional
election victory in Milwaukee in 1910 and the doubling of the
socialist vote nationwide, the *Forverts* triumphantly declared that
"once it has won one victory, [socialism] is bound to take permanent root."[76] A "new chapter in American history" was proclaimed.[77]

It was in the name of a radical political program, one that
would challenge a new tyranny and would complete the unfinished
American revolution, that the major socialist Yiddish paper championed its own brand of Americanism. This was not just a pragmatism born after decades of collective bargaining, not merely the
accumulated sediment of practical experience and American labor
moderation. This was an ideology of liberation that preceded the

era of collective labor agreements by at least a decade, and that sought to confer the longed-for "new rank of freeman" on the Jewish worker in America, who would thus become fully human, fully American—a new person, a new Jew.

The fact that "the struggle" was presented as one of elections, strikes, and solidarity, rather than armed subversion, as in Russia, was due to the fact that, in the final analysis, American political institutions did offer even radical socialists greater scope than was available elsewhere. The paradox, if any, lay in the socialists' faith in American democracy, even when their strength was miniscule. Their own commitment (they believed) would extend the experience of regeneration to all those who still did not enjoy the fruits of "their new rank."

"What then is the American, this new man?" Crèvecoeur had asked. In concluding our *tour d'horizon*, we may well ask, "what then was the Jewish American?" In a simple sense, we can say, Jews in America tended to take the regenerative ideology seriously, no matter what their particular interpretation of that ideology may have been.

Probing a bit deeper, we find the ways in which Jews qualified their acceptance of any form of Americanism that would not leave sufficient room for Jewish particularism or Jewish sociopolitical interests. Their response to Americanist ideology was a creative, not a passive one. Jewish Americanism was a posture: standing with one's face toward America. It was also self-consciously expressed.

The fact that Americanism crossed all Jewish cultural and ideological lines is in itself of historical interest. While Jewish Americanizers were quick to discover that Judaism (or Jewish social ideals) and Americanism were mutually compatible, this kind of compatibility has also been claimed, at one time or another, for Judaism and German culture, Judaism and Zionism, Judaism and communism. Unless the Jewish variable in these equations is infinitely plastic, it is doubtful whether such propositions are "true" except in the subjective sense: in the eye of the beholder.

Perhaps, then, the across-the-board Jewish-American "symbiosis" did not indicate an inherent compatibility so much as it did the fact that (a) all Jews in America experienced an existential need to adapt to their new country, and (b) they felt obliged to defend their place in American society against hostile forces.

What strikes the observer about Jewish Americanism is that "America," as portrayed by Jews, was in large measure a projection of Jewish aspirations, self-image, and values. One finds in Jewish formulations *one version* of the American national ethos: that of a grand experiment in human and social relations. *Their* America bore little relation to the America envisioned by restrictionists, for example. Jews spoke in terms that were cosmopolitan, pluralistic, and egalitarian, rather than in terms of race purity. Jews stressed objective environmental factors over "immutable" traits. Jews held America accountable to "its own" principles as a haven for the oppressed or as the homeland of the democratic revolution. Jews used a Jewish filter to emphasize certain aspects of America over others. America, in that sense, was a mirror that the Jews held up in front of themselves. Little wonder, then, that what they saw in America was, indeed, *themselves.*

But there was more to it than the problem of subjective perception (which, after all, is a common human foible). There did exist a Jewish–American connection that was historically significant.

The American rhetoric of regeneration, enunciated by Crève-coeur and repeated again and again by American spokesmen,[78] offered considerable points of resonance with a variety of modern Jewish movements and ideologies. Modern Jews possessed their own rhetoric of emancipation, of emergence from the ghetto or from other forms of oppression; of emergence from oppressive forms of Judaism itself, when necessary. That was the rhetoric of the Haskalah and its offshoots.

That was why, when Jews looked at America, they tended to see themselves, or themselves as they wished to be. Modern Jews have sought auto-emancipation, liberation from their own past, and in America they found the same revolutionary impulse to self-reinvention. Modern Jewish ideologies are "revolts against destiny," a phrase that has been used by one recent historian to describe the American republic.[79] It was here, at a common juncture of modernity, that Judaism met Americanism—not just in the imagined ancient biblical commonwealth or an idealized image of the American revolution.

That is why Jews' visions of America seemed to corroborate their own inner vision. That is also why America could not be perceived as Exile, but—like the modern Jewish self-image—a repudiation of physical, spiritual, and existential servitude.

Ideal images and self-images may help us to understand the ideological aspects of Americanization in the Jewish community, but the encounter between the immigrant and the new society was not merely an abstract one. Real conflicts and real-life dilemmas had to be negotiated by the newcomers. As was alluded to in chapter one, much of this process had, of necessity, to be conducted and discussed in the immigrants' own languages. In the following two chapters, we will look at some of the media (books, pamphlets, and journals) that were generated within the immigrant Jewish community in the first half of the twentieth century, in both Yiddish and Hebrew, that reflected the Americanization process "on the ground." We will look at both popular and literary treatments of changing social mores, family and sex ethics, and the secularization of ethnicity, all of which were component aspects of Americanization. We will have occasion to observe, once again, how language choice and language use were intertwined with issues of political and cultural self-definition. Finally, in light of what has been said about self-reinvention as a common motif in modern Jewish history, we will discuss the attempts made by Hebrew writers, *maskilim* who found their way to American shores, to reinvent their literary tradition in the New World.

Guides for the Perplexed: Sex, Manners, and Mores for the Yiddish Reader in America

"What is culture?" asked Dr. Ben-Zion Liber, an early advocate of radical social reform, progressive health education, and preventive medicine, opening a short article on "Physical Culture."[1] Culture, he argued, is everything that enhances the quality of life. Taking a holistic view of human existence, Liber insisted—Jewish proclivities to the contrary notwithstanding—that culture is not confined to music, literature, art, and the sciences: aspects of culture that engage the mind. Rather, he argued, the concept of "culture" ought to include the "cultivation" and care of the body. Culture began with self-knowledge and involved, ideally, all of one's faculties.[2]

As we shall see, Liber understood "culture" as a society's (or an individual's) whole approach to living, and that necessarily included all areas that determined the conditions of people's lives, such as physical living and working conditions, and the economic and political systems that defined those conditions. As a leftist radical, he was determined to introduce change into the entire thinking of his fellow Jewish immigrants in urban America, asking them to care more about "their bodies, themselves," their social class, their gender, their existential predicament.

What historians generally speak of as "Jewish culture" is fairly narrowly and rigidly defined, and therefore there are some aspects of Jewish culture that are often overlooked. I am referring not only to the problem of "popular culture": I have in mind the fact that even popular or mass culture tends to be conceptualized as mass consumption analogues of "high culture" equivalents. Folklore and folk customs, popular music, the melodramas of the Yiddish stage, and serialized pulp novels are patently alternate, "poor man's" versions of the literature, religion, poetry, music, and art of the elite. Culture in the anthropological or social-historical sense— the sum total of a group's social behaviors and responses to its environment—is relatively underappreciated.

Such pedestrian matters as food, dress, sexual mores, family relations, and social etiquette go a long way toward defining a society. They might not appear quite as crucial as ideologies ?nd social movements, masterworks of scholarship, great literature, and other creations of the spirit; but they are matters of prime concern to the way most people live.

The following literary example, that exposes some of the major fault lines of cultural and social dynamics in modern East European Jewry, shows what I mean about the importance of these aspects of culture:

> Fradl . . . was a student in Zvihil. She liked to dress up and speak Russian. . . . This Fradl was considered the black sheep of the family. The khasidim, who were my grandfather's enemies, claimed that because of his contempt for their *rebeim* [rabbis] he had been cursed with a heretic granddaughter . . . who spoke gentile languages and wore patent leather shoes. . . . I gaped when she took a cigarette from Uncle Joseph's box and let the smoke drift from her mouth and nose at the same time, all the while bickering furiously with her father. . . . Uncle Joseph did not punish his daughter for her un-Jewish ways. But he did say that she was wasting her time going to school instead of staying home in Bilgoray and accepting a match with some eligible young man. Fradl shrieked in a way no decent Jewish woman would dare. . . . "Marry some Itche-Mayer and rot in this dump? Not me." . . . "Then what are you looking for?" her father asked, blowing smoke in her face. "To study and become a dentist," she shot back, blowing smoke in his face. . . . I could only keep staring at this fantastic creature . . . and wonder how she could be my blood relative.[3]

The combined abominations of a woman smoking, wearing alien clothes and shoes, blatantly and loudly challenging patriarchal authority, and rejecting social norms (not to mention speaking gentile languages!) marked this young woman as an outsider—practically "un-Jewish"—because these were behaviors that went against the grain of basic elements in Jewish society and culture.

The importance of these factors for an understanding of Jewish cultural and social history ought to be apparent to anyone approaching the topic of immigrant history in general, and the subject of Americanization in particular.[4] They do not readily fit into conventional definitions of religious life, but properly belong to the study of secular or ethnic culture.

The broader ramifications of this chapter, then, relate to our perceptions of a certain Jewish ambience: the secular culture of first-generation immigrants between roughly 1910 and 1930. I use the term "secular" in two senses: first, to denote cultural phenomena that do not necessarily derive from or directly relate to sacred institutions and traditions; second, in speaking about consciously antitraditional values and attitudes. To address these issues, I will look at them through the lens of "how-to" books and pamphlets that instructed small but substantial Jewish audiences in the ways of the world.

What this involves is not a study of culture in a static sense, but the dynamics of cultural change. We are dealing with a population that was undergoing culture shock. In its encounter with an alien environment, foreign values, and strange habits, that population came to internalize much of what it found in America and (to one degree or another) reshaped its life accordingly. But the conduits of cultural osmosis—apart from such obvious ones as public schools and the press—are not easily identified. The examples to be cited here may, therefore, shed light on an ill-defined area of social history.

Finally, a few words need to be added about secular Jewish culture as a concept and as a historical phenomenon. In the period under study, secular Jewish culture was still in its heyday, buoyed up by the cultural optimism that characterized the pre–"death of ideology," post–World War II era. The hallmarks of secularism were a critical stance vis-à-vis traditional norms (social as well as religious) and a pervasive individualism that sanctioned the ideal of personal growth. Secular Jewish culture, in that period, was expressed in Hebrew and Yiddish, in America as well as in Europe and Palestine. The parameters of that culture were much wider than many today might credit, and ranged from the agrarian-utopian experiments of young workers in Palestine (and their political supporters overseas) to secular schools and youth clubs in Eastern Europe, to such artifacts as I shall be examining here.

What made all of this "Jewish" was clearly not what is conventionally understood as "Jewish content." The Jewishness, very often, was in the medium and in the social context. Ben-Zion Liber noted, for example, that he wrote his book on sex and hygiene in Yiddish, precisely "to address the viewpoint of the Yiddish reader, whose needs I understand so well." *Dos geshlekhts lebn (Sex Life)*, therefore, was written "especially for the kind of Jew who would read such a book in Yiddish," and Liber dedicated the work as "A gift to the Jewish people." Interestingly, Liber reports (in the foreword to the third edition of his book) that it was only when he settled in America, in the congested immigrant district of New York, that the Jewish community became his chief arena of public activity, and it was only there, in the new Jewish metropolis, that he learned Yiddish. He did so in order to be able to speak directly to this mass audience.[5]

The materials to be examined here were sometimes translated from English. This made aspects of Anglo-American culture accessible to Jewish immigrant audiences. Though they may not rank with Yiddish classics in terms of cultural creativity or significance, they nevertheless helped to determine the patterns of Jewish cultural consumption and social behavior, and served to integrate Jewish with international cultural trends.

Forging such cosmopolitan links was, indeed, a prime function of secular Jewish culture. One reader's letter in Liber's monthly health journal, *Unzer gezund (Our Health)* criticized the local Jewish intelligentsia for organizing fine discussions on Ibsen and Nietzsche, but failing to organize "to clean the filth from the streets where they live."[6] Although neither Ibsen nor Nietzsche qualifies for the adjective "Jewish," the immigrants' encounters with them were undoubtedly Jewish encounters, filtered through the particular experience of uprootedness and of life in the slums—indeed, undertaken in an effort to transcend the squalor of tenement life. Secular culture, then, was an agent of cultural change because it mediated between the particular and the general.

Given how new, exciting, and different America was, it is no wonder that immigrant Jews needed a "user's guide" in the form of secular Jewish culture. But Ibsen and Nietzsche were hardly the most challenging or even the most novel paths to be negotiated. Such intellectual fare came right out of the familiar Russian tradition. Far more perplexing were the truly new, day-to-day challenges of private life. Guidebooks and manuals were written on parenting, sex education and sexual hygiene, love, marriage, and polite behavior. In such matters many immigrants were at a loss, in a double sense. Not only did they have to find their way in new surroundings and cope with children raised in an alien milieu, but in many cases they had to do all of that alone, without the cultural, social, and family support mechanisms that had been available back home. This much is suggested by the figures on Jewish immigration in this period, which show a preponderance of young adults and children.[7] Consider, especially, the predicament of single immigrant girls, young women, and new mothers, who had few people they could rely on for backup and guidance.[8]

It is true that neighborhood networks and the friendship-kinship ties of the *landsmanshaften*—fraternal hometown associations—could function as surrogate families. But guidebooks such as Margaret Sanger's "What Every Girl Should Know" (in Yiddish translation) still fulfilled a basic need and, therefore, found a ready market.[9] It was published twice (1916 and 1921) and sold for thirty cents. Ben-Zion Liber's *Unzer gezund* (later superceded by *Rational Living*) reached some four thousand subscribers in its first year and could not keep up with demand for reprints.[10] His book, *Dos geshlekhts lebn (Sex Life)*, went through four editions (1914, 1918, 1919, and 1927). On the topic of child-rearing, one could consult a Yiddish translation of Herbert Spencer's *Education (Di ertsiung: gaystig, moralish, un fizish)*, that also went through two editions.[11] The nouveau-bourgeois could turn to the popular writer Tashrak's *Etikette* (1912).[12] And those who needed to conduct their private and social lives by mail, or who wanted to impress someone with their mastery of formal and polite English, could use the model letters in Alexander Harkavy's *Amerikanisher briefen-shteller* (*American Letter Writer:* New York, 1902).

Lucy Dawidowicz once wrote about the wild sense of freedom that young immigrant Jews experienced in urban America: freedom from the limits and constraints of parental supervision, rabbinical chastisement, and social pressure.[13] This heady freedom was surely as disorienting as it was intoxicating. Redefining codes of behavior and absorbing new social models and ground rules became part of a larger cultural reorientation, a process that was aided by guides and handbooks like the ones I shall discuss.

Sex Education

The issue of sex education touched on a number of sensitive areas simultaneously. In the first instance, it was a particularly vexing aspect of intergenerational conflict and role-definition. In the second place, it was related to the desire to combat prostitution and reduce the spread of venereal diseases. The proliferation of the one and the transmission of the other to unsuspecting wives were held to be the products of an abysmal ignorance: "One reason why girls are driven to promiscuity is their utter lack of knowledge on sex and sexual relations."[14] Such ignorance was compounded by parents of adolescent boys and young men who encouraged their sons to seek "professional" sexual outlets before marriage, lest they fall victim to masturbation, nocturnal "pollutions," acne, and other alleged perils of unfulfilled manhood.[15]

But although these issues loomed large on the agenda of those who wrote sex education tracts, other matters were at stake as well. To Ben-Zion Liber, sex education was but one point (and a natural consequence) of his overall program, which he announced in the form of a credo:

Greater freedom for the individual to develop his personality. . . .

Greater freedom for the child, at home and in school; an open and free education for children. . . .

If one wants to accomplish something in life, one must first of all live rationally and do all one can to prevent disease. Enlightenment and science should be disseminated as widely as possible. . . .

Thinking people should regulate the number of children they have.

Never be enslaved by one's habits, theories or principles; they can change if one's convictions change.[16]

Margaret Sanger, too, adhered to a broad social vision which, she felt, was pertinent to her discussion of sexual development and to the education of girls generally:

Women must finally understand that they are not just mothers—they are people [in their own right], too. They are more than baby machines. Women have been taught to believe that their only mission in life is motherhood. . . . Today's woman is more fortunate. She is gradually liberating herself from such outmoded concepts. . . .

Another word about sexuality and the economic problems of our day: It is impossible to speak of prostitution, syphilis, etc. without mentioning that . . . the world is going through a great crisis. The entire edifice of our society is rotten. Capitalism is rotten. In today's society, young girls do not stand a chance of leading a pure life; youth is unable to develop its physical capabilities [properly]. . . .

Women will take their fate into their own hands. Women are the natural enemies of our rotten social order. All women must rise up as one against the prevailing system that enslaves women sexually. . . . We will declare war on the slavery that binds both men and women—a war of life and death.[17]

In short, these authors looked at the matter of sex education as one facet of a wide-ranging campaign to reeducate a new, liberated generation and to enlighten society at large. Sanger's pamphlet, therefore, was a treatise on how to raise a modern, progressive American girl—and herein lies its chief interest for us.

For instance, Sanger advocated a more open, equal, and friendly—that is, democratic, rather than authoritarian—parenting mode. An unembarrassed and educationally sound approach to children's questions on childbirth and sexuality was predicated on establishing trust and mutual understanding between the generations.[18] This counsel, though obviously meant originally for English readers, bore added significance (far beyond the specific point being made about sex education) for immigrant mothers facing a very real generation gap with their children.

A somewhat similar (if more Victorian) message comes across to the Yiddish reader of Spencer's *Education*, in the sections dealing with discipline, values, behavior, and parental authority.[19] The translator (a Dr. Morrison) noted that the entire subject of proper child-rearing was often discussed in what he called "intelligent circles," radical circles in particular, in terms of the need for "free" (i.e., liberal) education; but that precious little had been published in Yiddish on the subject. Hence, he believed, many would find the book of great use.[20]

Beyond building trust and friendship with their children, it was the parents' responsibility to be sensitive to the physical needs of growing youngsters. Liber was fanatic on the subject of the benefits of fresh air and proper ventilation. Alongside such aphorisms as, "The best cure for all diseases is social revolution," he warned readers of *Unzer gezund* to keep their windows open so as to ventilate their dank tenement apartments.[21]

Sanger, too, urged parents of working girls to see to it that, after factory or shop hours, their daughters had the opportunity to run, play, dance, and exercise in the open air in order to counter the deleterious effects of the work environment on bone structure, circulation, and posture.[22] On a related subject, she strictly warned against corsets, at least before age 21, because they could be harmful to the lungs, bone growth, and reproductive organs. "Every girl should consider the corset question very carefully, if she values her health."[23]

But above all, her pamphlet communicated to her readers an image of the robust, active, liberated American girl, raised to believe in and assert her independence and her own worth:

> Long ago, girls were supposed to be delicate, fragile, with underdeveloped breasts and small appetites. Those days are past. Nowadays we understand that a girl must be physically strong, healthy, and energetic. Today's girl does not wish . . . to sit home all day, sewing and playing with dolls. Mothers no longer require this of them. . . . We no longer worry if a girl learns to swim, ride, play ball and shoot [!]. . . . She *should* not be inferior to boys, and she *is* not inferior. Happy is the girl born in this day and age, who can calmly contemplate her physical development.[24]

At the same time, Sanger reacted very strongly against any impulse to stifle or inhibit young women's desires for self-adornment and self-expression of any kind (music, poetry, flights of fancy, dreams of fame and romance, etc.). This was something she warned parents against, stressing the great value of the feminine aesthetics of the young. She also held it against social reformers that they, out of patrician and disparaging attitudes toward the working class, denounced as "frivolous" and wasteful the money spent by working women on clothes. "It is high time that the social reformers stop trying to correct all the ills of our world and instead pay closer attention to the injustices they themselves perpetrate."[25] That must have rung a bell or two in the immigrant quarter!

Sanger dwelled on the question of love (and its distinctness from mere physical attraction) and on the sound bases for enduring relationships between husbands and wives.[26] But she also had encouraging things to say to single women regarding their potential role in social movements and about the new professional opportunities opening up for them. These, she maintained, were creating chances for fulfillment outside the conventional wife-and-mother framework.[27]

As a pamphlet addressed primarily to mothers of adolescent girls (and for the edification of single young women), "What Every Girl Should Know" did not take up subjects that would be encountered in literature addressed to married couples, and which were liable to violate obscenity laws that controlled the distribution of such materials through the mail. Sanger did not, for example, discuss sexual intercourse in detail, nor did she touch on birth control—a subject that concerned her deeply. In 1916, the year her pamphlet was translated into Yiddish, she opened her first birth control clinic on the Lower East Side of Manhattan.[28]

The topic of birth control was addressed, however, by Liber; indeed, planned parenthood and the promotion of smaller families was one of his chief interests.[29] Moreover, his book (in comparison with Sanger's pamphlet) was far more clinical and comprehensive, with three hundred pages of text and illustrations. It addressed the anatomy of male and female reproductive organs, pregnancy and childbirth, "normal" sexual relations, masturbation, eugenics, love, sex education for children, various sex-related problems ("anomalies") and diseases, and medical charlatanism in the field.

It is, of course, difficult to know how such publications (and public lectures)[30] actually impinged on immigrant culture and society. Perhaps their influence was restricted to a special class of reader, defined by their progressive and secular outlook. Still, in view of the fact that a market did exist for such materials (and we can assume that the number of readers exceeded the number of copies sold), it is safe to say that here we can pinpoint one conduit along which cultural information, American social values, and "radical chic" passed into the immigrant community.[31]

While gauging how well such ideas were received and implemented may be difficult, reader response is one indicator. Some people were sufficiently bothered by questions related to pregnancy, childbirth, and sexuality to direct queries to the relevant authors and health authorities. Liber's *Unzer gezund* published readers' letters and also an advice column, in which Liber answered medical questions. These ranged over various topics, but a significant proportion dealt with sex education, sexual development, and sexual performance. Naturally, as Liber explained, only a small portion of readers' queries could be answered in print; he was inundated by mail, and selected only those letters he felt were representative or likely to interest others.[32] It is worth noting that, at least geographically, *Unzer gezund* seems to have reached a diverse readership. Letters came from, among other places, Montreal, Boston, Paterson (New Jersey), Philadelphia, Providence, Milwaukee, Chicago, Detroit, Lynn (Massachusetts), and Liberty (New York), as well as from New York City, from the national Jewish sanitarium in Denver, and even from Paris and from Russia.[33]

Health officials in New York, too, were in a position to assess the relative impact of such literature on the consciousness of the immigrant quarter. The medical advisor to the venereal clinic run by the city's Health Department reported in 1914:

> For the past few months we have been somewhat mystified . . . by a certain class of cases which have come to us for advice. These cases all had a number of peculiarities: they were Hebrews, spoke English very indefinitely, and had very up-to-date views on eugenics [and] . . . asked many other questions which I could not hope to answer. Upon inquiring further, I found that they had been reading a journal called *Unzer gezund*.[34]

An interesting light is cast on our American evidence by comparing it with Yiddish tracts on sex, marriage, and related subjects that were published in Poland. For one thing, literature that was available to Jews in New York in the 1914–20 period seems to have become available to Jews in Warsaw only in the 1930s. For another, the European materials seem less concerned with prostitution, although promiscuity and venereal diseases are prominently discussed. On the other hand, there seems to have been a great concern in the European publications with problems of male impotence and sexual performance generally.[35] Also of note is the fact that, in Poland as in New York, there was a certain amount of reliance on translated materials. Finally, the publications from Poland do not seem to derive from politically radical sources, in contrast to the American cases we have looked at.

These distinctions and comparisons aside, there is internal evidence in some of the publications from Poland that suggests the appearance of such literature in Yiddish was linked to a process of sociocultural change, analogous to the situation facing East European Jews in America. Let us take one example, which seems to be representative, Dr. G. Weber's book, *Dos geshlekhts lebn fun mener un froyen (The Sex Life of Men and Women)*, published in Warsaw in 1936. The author contrasts the "clean living" generations of the past with the "dissipated youth of today," asserting that modern youth began sexual activity much too early in life, with the consequence of impaired virility in middle age, unlike their grandfathers' generation.[36] Similarly, he notes that modern couples seemed far too preoccupied with the material aspects of marriage, to the neglect of the "spiritual side"[37] (meaning, that family size was judged increasingly with a view toward maintaining a middle-class standard of living).

In addition, there are comments on the status of women in society, on women's employment outside the home, and on the respective roles of husbands and wives in household decision making, all of which clearly indicate a perceived change with regard to gender and social roles.[38]

As for birth control, Weber called this the "most burning issue on the agenda today," given the concern of middle-class families for planning, forethought, and material status. Modern couples, he asserted, were reversing the time-honored priorities, placing sexual gratification above procreation. Nonetheless, he refused to recommend, or even condone, most methods of contraception.[39]

Finally, it bears noting that what characterizes all the materials reviewed here—both from Poland and from America—is a deadly earnestness. Throughout, there is barely a suggestion that sex is to be enjoyed. Whether discussing "normal sex," masturbation, or venereal disease, they tend to preach at and intimidate the reader rather than simply inform. They are unrelievedly prescriptive, clinical, and, overall, make for dull reading.

"The Ordeal of Civility" or "Dos Past Nisht"

Guides to social etiquette remind us that culture is not only related to ethnicity but also to social class. Concern over propriety and conformity is conventionally associated with the middle-class ethic, although rather rigid codes of conduct are hardly the exclusive burden of those in the middle reaches of the social pecking order. The desire to know what is "the right way to act" in any given social encounter is a function of unfamiliarity with certain situations and the fear of not being regarded as acceptable in particular social sets. That is, a need to learn a code of etiquette reflects social mobility or aspirations to rise on the social ladder.

That such guides should have been published by and for Jewish immigrants in this period is consistent with what we know about their social and economic mobility. They were already heading toward middle-class status and they were unfamiliar with the ways "real" Americans behaved in society.[40] They were people in transition between the vaguely disreputable status of newcomers and the elusive goal of social acceptance.

Entrée into a new class and a new culture was not easily earned. Only mastery of the right gestures, passwords, choice of clothing, and proper eating habits could qualify one for membership. To "pass" as a native one had to know how to make the right signals. The goal of enhancement of status, understood in this way, is quite different from the type of goals held by radical writers (such as Liber and Sanger—although they, too, were talking about enhancement of status). The politics of middle-class conformity are another significant aspect of Americanization.

The author of one Yiddish handbook on the subject, *Etikette*, was a popular writer and well-known columnist in the Orthodox press, Israel Zevin, who went under the *nom de plume* of Tashrak (as already noted in the previous chapter).[41] He was well attuned to the nature of his audience:

> We often encounter people whose material standing . . . may not allow them to stick to all the niceties of fashion and worldly manners; but their clean and tidy appearance, their innate respect for others, their care and attention to others' comfort, [their consideration] for women and older people, make so fine an impression that we recognize them as true gentlemen and ladies, even if they are hampered by the lack of a certain polish. With the proper knowledge, they would surely be able to improve. That is the class of people who will find this book helpful.[42]

Tashrak pointed out that, ideally, ethics and etiquette ought to go hand in hand; in modern society, however, it was necessary to be educated in the outward forms of civility, even if one happened to naturally good-hearted and moral, so as to "avoid embarrassment."[43]

This field guide to good taste and good manners is incredibly detailed: from the proper form of the handshake to the art of conversation; from drinking and smoking etiquette to rules for train rides and ocean voyages; from the advisability of having clean fingernails to ballroom courtesies; from table manners to card playing; from the theater to the telephone. All contingencies are foreseen and accounted for. In addition, a full third of this three-hundred-page tome is devoted to matters of love, marriage, and family life.

What ties Tashrak's book to the problem of acculturation and to the question of culture itself (raised earlier) is the fact that it is as much about the acquisition of culture as it is about social refinement. Civility is the master key not only to being a fine human being, but to being a fine American and "a credit to one's race." The desire to Americanize, "civilize," and otherwise make the immigrant appear "less Polish and more polished" is something that historians have most often associated with the German-American uptown Jewish establishment, who looked askance at their plebeian kin. This is patently an oversimplification. *Etikette* is a good example of Americanization at work at the grass-roots level, within the immigrant community itself.

It is significant, for instance, that Tashrak begins with two introductory sections: one, a collection of proverbs and aphorisms on ethics and etiquette culled from the Talmud and ancient rabbinic lore; and the other, "George Washington's Rules of Polite Conduct—Wise and Useful Rules Written by the Father of His Country, that Still Apply Today."[44]

Or, again, we can take his treatment of decorum in the synagogue—the concern for which is often attributed to the more Americanized Jews of the German immigration stream, but to which East European Orthodox middle-class immigrants (and especially their children) were hardly indifferent.[45] Giving full credit where it was due, Tashrak commended the Reform temples for two things: first, for the dignity and decorousness of their services, which contrasted with the unfortunate picture he drew of the typical downtown prayer halls; and second, for the creditable way Reform Jews presented Judaism to their gentile neighbors and guests.[46] The good opinion of non-Jews, Tashrak argues, is not something to be dismissed lightly, and it was something that Judaism deserved because it was a dignifying, sacred, and uplifting faith.[47] The advice Tashrak gave was both Jewishly respectable and explicitly American:

> In America we enjoy all civil rights and freedoms. What does freedom mean? It means self-control, [it means] following the rules of common decency. The Talmud teaches us: "Who is truly respected? He who respects others," that is, all people. Whoever understands the concept of respect for others will understand how to behave correctly . . . in any social setting, but especially in . . . the house that is dedicated to the honor of God and the brotherhood of men.[48]

Self-control, tolerance, and following the rules—these were the key elements of American civility that Tashrak hoped to promote in his own community. Thus, in his section on behavior at public meetings we find counsel on "the obligation to listen to others," on the wisdom of keeping one's speeches short and to the point, on the duties of a president of an organization, and so on—matters of direct practical relevance to immigrant life, with its plethora of lodges, fraternal societies, and political groups.[49]

Indeed, alongside its emphasis on socialization into American ways, this book's strong points include a first-hand familiarity with the special circumstances and sometimes unique features of Jewish immigrant life. Returning to the section on the synagogue, for ex-

ample, the reader finds rules for nonbelievers who might have occasion to visit a house of prayer—a not unusual occurrence in the
complex world of the Jewish immigrant, in which ideological lines
could be blurry. The "freethinker" was urged to behave like "a
gentleman" and a guest, to refrain from open mockery or inappro-
priate clowning. "Even if he does not keep God's commandments,
he can still show that he is a decent human being."[50]

It has been suggested that Anglo-Saxon civility, which was basic
to the fabric of American culture, was especially foreign to the
Jew recently arrived from Eastern Europe, precisely because of its
differentiation between inner, unspoken feelings and outward appearances or expression—with the premium placed on the latter.[51]
Tashrak pointed out this distinction to his readers, but in mediating
between rabbinic ethics and American etiquette, he attempted
something of a synthesis. Etiquette, he claimed, was the natural
"daughter" of ethics, being based on the morality of "Do not do
unto others what you would not have done unto you." His point
throughout is that the external forms of refinement should reflect
sincere inner sensitivity—not mask a coarse interior. As far as he
was concerned, people who certainly appeared *salonfähig* (socially
presentable) could be "utter boors" in private, and thus miss the
essential point. The title of "lady" or "gentleman" had to be earned
through nobility of character.[52]

Of course, the standards of behavior that applied were taken
directly from the values of the American milieu. The "real American" was a master or mistress of moderation and restraint, under-
stated rather than ostentatious, never flashy, intense, or loud. Elegant evening wear might convey a superficial impression of
sophistication; but a woman with a shrieking laugh, no matter
how well attired, immediately gave away the fact that she was
"common" ("*a proste yente*").[53]

Although appearances could, thus, deceive, correct dress and
grooming were still an important component of good taste. The
stress here is on three elements of self-presentation: neatness, color
coordination, and sensible—rather than faddish—style. Everyone,
even those who could not afford new clothes, could take the time
to use a clothes brush before going out, our author admonished.
There was no excuse for slovenliness.[54] As for color and style, Tash-

rak tried to impress his female audience, especially, with the distinction between plebeian tastes and crass parrotting of the latest fashion craze, on the one hand, and "real American" sophistication, on the other. "Good taste is an art, and it takes talent to dress well."

It is actually among the poorer classes that women blindly follow the dictates of fashion. . . . It is well known that affluent American women prefer very simple clothing—of the finest fabrics, to be sure— and they are never the first to jump at a new style. . . . It is awful what poor taste most Jewish girls have. Consider the garish colors you can see on a Saturday or a holiday on Jewish streets. Any man with an ounce of taste can only shudder at the way girls and young women—who may otherwise be quite attractive—ape the latest fashions. . . . If fashion decrees that women should wear red [this season], does it follow that a woman with red hair and freckles must dress in a color that makes her look like a scarecrow?[55]

It should be noted that what we are dealing with here is obviously a stage at which European traditional garb had already been exchanged (in the younger set) for American clothing; Tashrak was hoping to take this transformation one step further.

Given the heavy involvement of immigrant Jews (both men and women) in the needle trades, it is hardly surprising that they, of all people, were keenly aware of the latest trendy styles. The point Tashrak was making is that a little knowledge could be a dangerous thing. To aid those without a trained eye, he included a guide to "harmonious color combinations," and also advised on the proper attire for young girls, elderly matrons, the businesswoman, and for maternity wear. Similarly, he addressed the questions of jewelry, perfume, and makeup, and the issue of how to spend money on clothes.[56] Finally, on the ubiquitous corset question, he gave his qualified approval:

A corset, if it is the right kind, made of good material and well constructed, is healthy to wear, quite apart from the fact that it smoothes the figure, makes a woman look slimmer . . . and improves her looks. Nowadays, there are scientifically designed corsets, known as "common sense corsets." There are even special corsets that may be worn quite safely by pregnant women.[57]

As already noted, a significant part of Tashrak's book is devoted to love, marriage, and family relations. It is worth pointing out that romantic love, as a social norm or ideal, was relatively new for East European Jews, and any advice on the subject was bound to reflect the adoption of standards and points of view from non-Jewish cultures.

The uninitiated were thought to be easily entrapped by the attendant dangers and pitfalls of romance, and therefore needed to be cautioned.[58] As for gender roles and ideal-types, Tashrak tended toward the Victorian: the gentle but manly and assertive male, and the educated, refined, practical and reliable, but modest, female.[59] He also gave pointers on the etiquette of betrothals, receptions, and weddings, and on relations with in-laws. In this connection, he also returned to the question of "freethinkers" and dealt with the issue of marriages that joined religious and nonreligious people[60]—something that was not a rarity in immigrant Jewish society. Secularization was a major component of the immigrant experience and deeply affected patterns of acculturation.

Turning to parenting, our author-advisor took his point of departure from the child-centeredness of the Jewish family, on the one hand, and the crucial early childhood experiences that would determine socialization, on the other. He emphasized the importance of play and of imagination, the child's need for playthings and art supplies, and the short attention span of young children.[61] At the same time, he advocated orderliness, firm guidance to discourage negative behaviors, strict attention to cleanliness, and punishment for lying.[62]

In light of the problems facing immigrant families in the area of parental authority, it is worth noting how Tashrak tried to deal with this issue, which he thought was a matter of projecting confidence, stability, and character:

> Parents' chief responsibility is to demonstrate their worthiness to exercise authority. They should never reveal to the child the unhappy side of life. They must not let on to their children if there is anything amiss between them. They must never utter words that children should not hear. They should set an example.[63]

Although it is hard to believe that children growing up in the immigrant quarter were quite that sheltered from strong emotions and negative experiences, what remains of significance here is the fact that parental authority could no longer be taken for granted, as it was in the traditional patriarchal order.

As in the case of the sex manuals, it should be pointed out here, too, that there were also European Jewish etiquette guides and even something of a tradition behind them. A very early example was a Hebrew work by Fayvl Shiffer, called *Mehalkhim 'im anashim* (*Behavior in Society*: Warsaw, 1866). It covered, in brief, some of the same aspects of social relations that we find in Tashrak's book, including relations between men and women, husbands and wives, parents and children—though Shiffer's perspective and cultural ambience were, of course, quite different. There was even a satirical work that parodied the posturing Jewish social climbers of the day: *Der mode ustav* (*A Course in Fashionableness*: Warsaw, 1894), by an author calling himself B.Z.

These works, in turn, were modern, secularized incarnations of even older forms of ethical conduct literature and social criticism, called *musar*, in which a heavy emphasis had been placed on the religious benefits of self-restraint, humility, and goodness.

Finally, a contemporary work fully parallel to Tashrak's guide was *Gutte zitn un sheyne manieren* (*Good Habits and Fine Manners*: Warsaw, 1930), by G. Whiteman. Like its American counterpart, this book was clearly intended for the novice. In the present context, it is impossible to go into a textual comparison between the two books, although a close examination would doubtless reveal interesting contrasts as well as similarities in bourgeois etiquette in the Old World and the New.

It is a fallacy to regard East European Jewish society as socially naive and homogenized: as one big shtetl, without a code of its own to define proprieties and outward formalities, class-based rituals and transactions, and subtle distinctions of status conveyed by details of attire and grooming.[64] (The passage about "Fradl," quoted at the beginning of the chapter, should be reread in this light.) The immigrants to America did not suddenly discover the importance of civility or style; rather, as they thought about moving into a different social class and began to make themselves over in a more "American" image, they needed to decipher and learn an intricate new choreography.

Conclusion

The importance of "culture" with a small c for social history is no longer a novel concept. In offering this small contribution to American Jewish social history, the main point I wish to make is that we ought not to overlook potentially rich sources of information.[65]

The problem, of course, is that we risk overlooking them only because we would never think of searching for them, if our own view of Jewish culture is blinkered or truncated. Yiddish sex manuals and guides to etiquette hardly fit the categories conventionally used to define Jewish culture; but once encountered, their existence makes eminent sense. To think of Jewishness as something limited by institutional, ethno-political, or religious definitions is to rule out automatically a rich vein of cultural media and experience whose Jewishness derives more from context than from content.

Along with the reservoir of knowledge we already have, such media can aid us in coming to grips with the issues we face when we ask ourselves about processes of social transformation. They also reveal, in fine detail, the substance of Americanization at the individual level of meaning and personal development.

Finally, in adding to our understanding of the links between culture, class distinctions, and social program, these materials illuminate the nexus between culture and politics that we have been observing in different forms. In the next chapter, we turn to a greater focus on language as an issue in ethnic existence and as a factor in the success or failure of Americanization.

CHAPTER 7

Against the Tide: The *American Hebrew Yearbook*, 1930–1949

Language preference, as was noted in the first essay in this volume, has manifold cultural and political implications. Loyalty to a minority language is a conscious ideological position entailing self-marginalization to one degree or another. In this chapter, we will explore a one-generation phenomenon of self-marginalization and ask why it did not endure. In the process, we will also have a chance to reexamine the Jewish "image" of America, this time from the less familiar perspective of a Hebrew "voice."

Despite the survival of Hebrew as a language of prayer and the pockets of Hebrew and Yiddish readers that exist in America today, American Jewry's cultural orientation is overwhelmingly toward English, which is the accepted medium for virtually all forms of communication. That is one of the measures of American Jewry's successful integration in American society, and may thus be regarded as one of its achievements.

On the debit side, of course, one may bewail the inevitable loss of direct access to the considerable cultural assets brought to the United States by the immigrant generation (or left behind in Europe). David Roskies has called American Jewry "the people of the lost book"[1] for that very reason.

For the most part, access to the Hebraic and Yiddish culture of the past is now mediated for the Jewish public by translators—both in the literal sense and in the metaphorical sense—whose function it is to restore the "lost books" to their rightful heirs. This is no vain attempt at artificial resuscitation or facile nostalgia, but a cultural project of potentially lasting significance; nor does "translation" begin to account for the bulk of Jewish cultural creativity in America. The Americanization of Jewish culture holds serious ramifications for American as well as Jewish culture, as Cynthia Ozick, Robert Alter, and Gershon Shaked have, in their different ways, suggested.[2] Art, literature, and scholarship in the American idiom, as well as more popular cultural forms, continue to find a large, home-grown market of cultural consumers in American Jewry. That, too, is a phenomenon worthy of analysis from the point of view of cultural politics.

Nevertheless, it is the theme of "lost books" that I wish to address here, with my focus on one such "book" in particular: the *American Hebrew Yearbook* or *Sefer hashanah liyehudei amerikah*. Edited for the most part by Menahem Ribalow (who also edited the Hebrew weekly *Hadoar*, that still publishes), the *Yearbook* appeared (somewhat irregularly) between 1930 and 1949. Altogether, nine volumes appeared—double volumes 8/9 and 10/11 covering the years 1946 to 1949. This was by no means the only important American Jewish publication in Hebrew in that period, but it did attract some of the best talent available in the Hebraist community in the United States, and may therefore be regarded as representative of much that was published by them and by others in various other journals. It was also a sustained effort, something of a success in the context of American Hebrew letters; and it covers a particularly fascinating period in American and world history.

Those who have examined the case of the American Hebraists have, in the main, drawn a rather depressing picture. Critical of their literary achievements, observers have in addition sought to explain why Hebrew literature was so ephemeral a phenomenon in American Jewish culture. Essentially, the argument centers on a double alienation: On the one hand, Hebrew writers and poets were immigrants who never succeeded in capturing the spirit of American literary consciousness, and therefore they were doomed to be transients in an alien land. On the other hand, they were also cut off from the main branch of Hebrew literary creativity in Eastern Europe and the Yishuv (Jewish community of Palestine).[3] Theirs was a cultural ghetto, if ever there was one.

In addressing myself to the work that was published in the *Year-

book, one of my tasks will be to ask whether this double alienation argument sufficiently explains what happened to Hebrew writers. Jewish immigrant writers were hardly the only ones to use the theme of alienation for their art; it is clear, in fact, that Jewish writers elsewhere and American authors and poets, writing in English, have made frequent and successful literary use of the outsider's experience, taken as symptomatic of the modern condition.[4] If we reason that our Hebraists wrote in Hebrew *because* they were alien and that they remained alien because they *continued* to write in Hebrew, we still have not penetrated to the social basis of their alienation.

I shall argue that—the double-alienation thesis aside—one may understand the plight of the American Hebrew writers (as reflected in the history of *Sefer hashanah*) better if we look, first of all, at their cultural-ideological program and secondly, at the question of their sociocultural function in American Jewry. It was their peculiar *lack of function* in the American context—mirrored in their lack of a market—that made them an endangered species, rather than their critical, alienated stance.

The Background: Out of the Haskalah, into the Melting Pot

Hebrew literature in nineteenth-century Eastern Europe was the metier and passion of a small elite. Functional literacy in Hebrew was fairly attenuated among the general Jewish public—normally confined to the male population, and even then generally reduced to the basics, which included the ability to recite psalms, daily prayers, and so on. This was the Hebrew of the sacred realm, popularly known as *loshn koydesh* (the holy tongue). The new modern Hebrew, on the other hand, that was just being invented, was something else again. The modern *maskilic* press and literature, that smacked of secular and heretical modern opinions, were spurned by large sections of the Jewish public, out of religious-ideological considerations.

Yet, in the East European context, Hebrew continued to function alongside Yiddish as a Jewish language, and its use as a literary medium—as circumscribed as it was—made sense. Even for the

barely literate, Hebrew provided a cornucopia of quotations, allusions, maxims, and puns, as well as a language of record for rabbinic and other classical or "official" media. As one observer has
put it, recourse to Hebrew was necessary in a society that communicated in a Jewish language, derived from a traditional, text-cen-
tered culture; thus, Yiddish preserved Hebrew.[5]

The early *maskilim* pioneered the use of Hebrew for a new,
secular purpose: art; and they championed a cultural vision that
embraced a humanist, universalist optimism. In the universal culture of the modern world, they firmly believed, the role of Hebrew
could hardly be negligible. In terms of the politics of culture, because the *maskilim* responded positively to modernity, they needed
to invent an appropriate language and literary medium for their
revolutionary purposes. The Hebrew they created served that
function.

Later in the nineteenth century, however, they confronted the
dismaying fact that many young Jews who had acquired Russian or
European educations had not only jettisoned their parents' Yiddish
(as the *maskilim* had advised), but no longer had any real use for
Hebrew, either. Polish, German, or Russian served them far better
as bridges to contemporary civilization. Disappointed old-line
maskilim like Judah Leib Gordon faced the devastating prospect of
having labored in vain ("For whom do I toil?" Gordon lamented in
a famous poem).

It was the nationalist Hebraists like David Gordon, Peretz Smolenskin, Eliezer Ben-Yehuda, and others, who began in the 1870s to
restore to Hebrew its secular, cultural, and political functionality.
As Gershon Shaked has remarked, their forward orientation toward
a political future for Jews in Palestine neatly complemented Hebrew's connecting links backward to a classical past, and these
combined elements lent Hebrew its functional significance for the
present.[6] As we saw in our examination of nationalist rhetoric in
chapter two, nationalist ideology required a usable past for the sake
of national-cultural renewal. Here, again, political ideology lent
new significance to language and culture.

Not only was Hebrew to be made over into a language of everyday communication, but in the realm of literature itself, there were
also major new developments. The new literary trends demanded a

more supple, streamlined language than the florid, stylized Hebrew of the Haskalah.

Thus, Hebrew literary creativity in Russia was just gathering new momentum when the emigration of Jews to the West began to take on the proportions of a mass movement. While Eliezer Ben-Yehuda found his way to Jerusalem to revamp the Hebrew lexicon, and while Odessa was becoming the capital of Hebrew letters in Russia, a different destiny cast a handful of adult Hebrew writers (and a more generous share of young, future writers) ashore in "the land of Columbus."

This is not the place to assess their paltry output. For the sake of a brief orientation, however, we might note that the literary historians agree on three points about the writers who were active in America from the 1870s until the eve of the First World War: The quality of their work was mediocre; none of their journals survived very long, though they valiantly kept on trying; and their poetry expressed, in the main, themes of estrangement and insularity.[7]

The social environment that had given Hebrew writers a certain scope in Eastern Europe, despite their relatively small numbers, was lacking in the United States. Primarily, they lacked not only colleagues, but readers. Coming just as the wave of immigrants from Eastern Europe was beginning, these writers found an English-speaking Jewish community of earlier migration vintage, Jews who hardly ever prayed in Hebrew anymore and who were spiritually far removed from the Russian Haskalah. In America, where the major strategy of acculturation revolved around a monolingual social policy, there was no equivalent to the bilingual symbiosis of Yiddish and Hebrew that had coexisted in Eastern Europe with a third, gentile language. Perhaps just as important, they had left the Russian heartland of Hebrew letters just prior to the great surge in creativity and modernism that was to take place there, and thus did not participate in a crucial phase in Hebrew literary development.

Judah Leib Gordon's disciple, Menahem Dolitsky, for instance, was to have been the torchbearer of the Haskalah to the New World, but he succumbed instead to "dull, grey pessimism and despair."[8] Economic privation and an inability to see the positive sides of America found literary expression in either bitter satire or mourning.[9] Although such themes, and that kind of exposed social and intellectual position, were certainly not out of keeping with the Haskalah tradition (and thus do not necessarily afford a ready explanation for literary decline), the new environment proved far less conducive.

A new phase began around 1914, when a new crop of writers came on the scene. These represented a generation who had arrived in America as children or adolescents in the 1890s or early 1900s, as well as more recent, youthful arrivals. Perhaps they were graced with greater talent and skill; perhaps they felt more at home in America, having grown up there or having a much larger immigrant Jewish hinterland around them; perhaps they were more directly influenced by the newer Hebrew literature of Europe. Their arrival, at any rate, was noticed.

Ephraim Deinard, a traditional Hebraist, who had himself arrived in the United States in 1888, found them insufferable. His bibliography of Hebrew books in America (published in 1926) opened with a diatribe against what he called "the modernists." He refused to dignify the scribblings of these semiliterate usurpers (as he saw them) with the name of "literature," and therefore decided against calling his bibliography *Sifrut yisrael beamerikah (The Literature of Israel in America)* as he had originally intended, using instead a vaguer, more neutral designation, *Kohelet amerikah* (roughly, *An American Collection*).[10]

In addition to their many other sins, it seems, the major crime of which the new writers stood accused in Deinard's book was their attempt to turn Hebrew into "Yiddish": that is, to pass off profane, everyday, mimetic speech as "pure" Hebrew. The "modernists" had "covered the land like locusts" and destroyed the few precious shoots that had grown up amid the alien corn. They were unmitigated camp followers of the accursed Ben-Yehuda, "the new Sabbetai Zevi, . . . the 'satan who had chosen Jerusalem,' " and newfangled "Bnei Moshe" types (i.e., adherents of Ahad Ha'am's cultural renaissance philosophy).[11]

Clearly, the younger Hebrew writers in America had a lot to answer for: most of all, perhaps, for pushing aside the work of the pioneer generation. As we shall see, their path was not strewn with roses, either. Most of them remained immigrant writers, transplanted on foreign shores with little chance for real success. For some of them, their own sense of marginality was profound.

One of these new poets, Shimon Ginsburg (whose work would soon be published in *Sefer hashanah*), tried hard to cope with the predicament of the newcomer who felt dwarfed and daunted by the "monstrous" power and grandeur of New York—the teeming symbol of modernity itself: "New York, a poem in prose, at once divine and satanic . . . , inscribed in verses of brick. . . . " The Jews there were "constantly tossed and buffeted between three worlds: the hemmed-in Exile of Europe, the open spaces of America, and the Promised Land."

Mining his *maskilic*, part classical-Hebraic, part modernist, cultural consciousness, he found that the crashing "full-throated" song of New York was one that "Jonah's ear never heard in Nineveh, a symphony of the gods that Wagner could not have imagined."

The poet, both repelled and attracted, observed the urban landscape from the safety of his foreignness ("from afar"), unsure whether "this is the palace of the king *(melekh)* or the House of Molokh," where human lives can be swallowed up into the abyss.

Yet, the pathos of his yearning to find kindred spirits and to become as one with the teeming metropolis comes across clearly in this passage:

> The night train carries me
> across Williamsburg Bridge . . .
> And all around . . . ,
> I see strands upon strands
> of small flickering lights,
> each beckoning and calling to the others.
> In that instant, my soul, too,
> plunges into the night,
> seeking its sisters,
> the flames, kindled like itself
> to light the night world. . . .

Alone, but enchanted, the night rider concludes on a note of optimism and salvation. Note the reference to "hidden lights," that recall the kabbalistic mysticism of the divine "sparks" which, when gathered together, can restore and redeem the world. Redemption is alluded to again in phrases lifted from Judaism's redemption liturgy, the Passover Haggadah (indicated here in italics):

> By whose design have so many secret lights,
> once hidden away by God, been kindled?
> Who recovered them and wove of them
> this blazing tapestry? . . .
> It is the heart of Man,
> on whom God bestowed His wisdom.
> I sensed the unseen, faithful, *mighty*
> *outstretched arm* (*yado . . . netuyah*)
> over this metropolis . . .
> *And all that night long* (*kol oto layil*)
> I was filled with *a new song* (*shir ḥadash*).[12]

Other voices, more confident and self-assertive perhaps, found it possible to bask in America without Ginsburg's ambivalence. Menahem Ribalow, the indefatigable editor of *Hadoar* who would found *Sefer hashanah* and guide it throughout its career, was enthusiastic about the prospects of Hebrew literature in America. In 1927 he issued a call for a new literature: "The Procrustean Bed or Boundless Freedom?" ("Mitat sedom umerḥav-yah"), that may well have been conceived as a defiant reply to Deinard. This cultural manifesto, bursting with the exuberance of the twenties, is worth a close examination here because it touches on a number of themes that figure in *Sefer hashanah* over the next twenty years.

Ribalow's point of departure was the sense of malaise that beset his fellow Hebraists in America, a malaise that stemmed from a lack of direction and purpose. The poetry of mourning and impotence had led to a dead end (alluded to in the essay's title). How could any writer worth his salt, he asked, remain so woefully out of touch with the mood of "these marvellous times"?[13]

The First World War, Ribalow argued, was a caesura as much for Jewish as for Western culture generally. The war and the Bolshevik Revolution that followed had swept away the remains of the nineteenth-century shtetl civilization that had for so long been the anchor and mythic universe of modern Jewish literature. Bereft of the one sure home (literally and figuratively) that they had ever known, Hebrew writers in America needed to discover a new artistic hearth.[14]

Moreover, as Ribalow correctly pointed out, the fructifying connection with Russian literature had also been severed. "Russia was our homeland in every sense," and Russian literature had been the chief influence on the younger Hebrew writers.[15] Without the Russian compass, Hebrew writers needed to hook into a different, but equally powerful, literary tradition. Why not the Anglo-American one? "America," he asserted, "with its vast potential for the future, is becoming the greatest, most vital center of Jewish life."[16]

Ribalow's admiration for America was boundless. With a Sandburgian hymn to industry and progress, he produced a Hebrew American equivalent of that ideology of rootedness-in-place that in Poland was called *doh-ikayt* (lit.: "hereness").

A kind of America-fever has gripped the world and is pushing it toward work and creativity. We [Jews in America] are at the center of the whirlpool. . . . The unleashed energy we are witnessing embodies the mystique of a new mythology, contains the seed of new life. . . . [America] has released great forces in humanity and has commanded them: Arise! . . . We have tied our fate to the fate of the world, and with its ascent, we will ascend. The land of Israel will be part of it, too, and our [Hebrew] literature—one blossoming branch on this tree of life. We will break out of the Procrustean Bed in which we are trapped and emerge into the freedom that calls to us.[17]

Ribalow was given to such grandiose outbursts, but behind the pontificating rhetoric, we may perceive several significant and serious ideas.

The motifs of "hereness," cultural optimism, and the role of Hebrew as a component of world culture are reminiscent of the Russian Haskalah of the mid-nineteenth century, and the exact opposite of cultural insularity or ghettoism. Haskalah ideology sought to transcend the alternatives of particularism and universalism by invoking a Judaism that would represent one stream within a single, universal, humanistic civilization. This was a position adopted by the best exponents of secular Zionist humanism to whom Ribalow was most closely connected.

In addition, Ribalow's faith in human progress and the positive cultural value of scientific and industrial endeavor bore more than a passing resemblance to the aesthetic outlook championed in the name of "futurism" in Soviet art and literature of the early 1920s.

Thus, Ribalow's celebration of postwar America (he himself arrived there only in 1921), and his call for a Hebrew literature attuned to the best in Anglo-American and world culture, were of a piece with the Russian Jewish traditions that had produced him. But his position also derived from the peculiar dilemma of Hebraists in America, where even the newest immigrants (and the second generation, much more so) were making the transition from a bilingual or trilingual to a monolingual, anglocentric culture. Choosing to work in Hebrew threatened to place the Hebraist writers in a cultural ghetto. They could operate within that ghetto—and remain with a literature of alienation and nostalgia—or they could try to connect with the world outside. Ribalow's message was a statement against marginality.

The only other option was a literature of vicarious experience: either dwelling in the receding European past or attempting to echo the Hebrew rebirth in Palestine. This was possible, of course, and was resorted to by some writers, but the approach risked artistic inauthenticity.

It remains to be seen whether the self-conscious Americanism expressed by Hebrew writers from the 1920s to the 1940s was equally vicarious and hence equally inauthentic. This, indeed, is the charge leveled at them by the literary historians, who conclude that this was one of the fundamental reasons why Hebrew writers in America were so transitory a phenomenon.[18]

Hebrew Humanism, the Depression Years, and American Judaism

By 1930, when the first volume of Sefer hashanah was published, the heady, "marvellous times" of which Ribalow had written had changed for the worse. The previous year had brought with it the onset of the Great Depression as well as serious Arab rioting in Palestine. By 1933, Hitler would come to power in Germany and Jewish confidence in universal progress had to be tempered. The first four volumes of the Yearbook (1930, 1935, 1938, and 1939) reflect both Ribalow's original program—Hebrew humanism and cultural optimism—and more sober realities.

We find, in terms of content, a veritable smorgasbord of intellectual fare in the premier volume, which ran to over three hundred pages. Contributors were drawn from Europe and Palestine, in addition to the American-based writers and scholars. This may have been partly caused by the scarcity of local talent, but a rationale was also articulated in the second volume of the *Yearbook:*

> We have sought to avoid being overly parochial in our Americanism . . . for we know that Hebrew literature is a world literature. It is not language alone that unites us, but also our common yearnings and the inner meaning of our writing, which derive from the self-same sources.[19]

Yet, together with this Hebraist-nationalist point of view, with its stress on Jewish national solidarity, a cosmopolitan-humanistic outlook is also strongly represented. The range of topics indicates a programmatic commitment to the universal, with an emphasis on Jewish involvement in the world of art and the sciences.

Zvi Rudy, for example, voiced what was a paradigmatic argument in an essay on Jews in contemporary philosophy. He submitted that there were no national philosophies in the substantive sense: philosophy transcended the lines of race and nationality. Nevertheless, because philosophy is a creative activity that takes place in particular linguistic and cultural milieux, one may speak (in terms of external forms) of German, Latin, or Anglo-American thought. "Our own wandering Jewish spirit" also might take its rightful place alongside such "national" philosophies.[20] The particular was a creative and individual aspect of the universal, and language was one of the chief bases of the particular.

Avraham Goldenberg's essay on Nahum Sokolow (the Zionist leader and probably the most prolific Hebrew writer of his day) hailed him, characteristically, as "the Jewish European." Noting the tendency of some nationalist writers to shun the influence of international culture and to reject its impact on Judaism, Goldenberg highlighted Sokolow's contrasting approach:

> He is a European through and through; he has no need to isolate himself in his Jewish ghetto, because his Europeanness does not negate his Jewishness. He is, however, not an unalloyed European— there has never been such a creature—but a *Jewish* European, just as there are German and Italian Europeans. . . . Sokolow is at once both "man and Jew" . . . "within his tent" as well as "without"

[paraphrasing Judah Leib Gordon's dictum: "Be a man abroad and a Jew within your own tent"].[21]

If the choice lay between universalism and particularism, then it was best not to choose at all.

The impact of shattering human experiences and world-shaking events comes across in the first volume of the *Yearbook* in two forceful statements: one, a war poem by Mordecai Goldenberg, reflecting much of the stereotypical literary images of the Great War (the mud and misery of trench warfare),[22] and the other, a new essay by Ribalow.

Ribalow's statement, though different in spirit, also sought to place the role of art—and of Hebrew literature in particular—within the context of a world that had somehow gone awry. At best, it had become less familiar and comfortable. No longer quite as optimistic as in his pre-Depression days, Ribalow noted that the social underpinnings of the old order—morals, justice, marriage, relations between parents and children—were being radically recast. He touched on Freud, atomic physics, anthropology, and their implications for "a new metaphysics" and a new understanding of human nature. Modernity, he concluded, was "a nettle" that must be grasped.[23]

In reverting to this minor key, Ribalow seemingly returned to the themes of alienation and dislocation which, as already noted, were part of the crisis of Hebrew literature that he had hoped to overcome. To counter that tendency, Ribalow continued to stress that the Jewish writer would have to meet head-on the rapid and extreme changes taking place in the world. Writers should "find the connecting link between humanity and our Jewishness that dwells within us and demands a resolution."[24]

The "Jewish person" (*haadam hayehudi*—again, a play on Gordon, and also a reference to the universal side of Jewish consciousness) faced a doubly difficult adjustment; for, in attempting to meet the new challenges of modernity, Jews, as a minority, had first of all to adjust to dominant majority cultures and to social situations that had lately assumed an ominous and even hostile character. "No wonder, then, that we tremble for our lives and for our creative spirit."[25]

The destructive potential of that very modernism whose praises he had sung in 1927 is more clearly recognized here, though Ribalow still favored an art that would struggle with new issues, rather than remain lost, angry, and impotent.

But literary reviewer A. Z. Ben-Yishai felt that the outlook for Hebrew in America was not bright. He did not impugn the talents of individual writers, but his pessimism was a judgment on the sum total of what had been produced, in relation to the resources and potential of American Jewry. American Hebrew writers—Ben-Yishai estimated their number then at 130—were altogether too complacent, too ready to pat themselves on the back, too eager to avoid real self-criticism.[26]

Here, then, was an acknowledgment of failure to reach beyond the confines of the Hebrew literary fraternity (curiously, though perhaps understandably, no female Hebrew writers were in evidence). With a Jewish community numbering in the millions, the impact of Hebrew writers remained woefully limited. Several years later, Nissan Touroff would also question the viability of a literature that remained within a circumscribed group of writers, virtually a cult that lacked a broader social connectedness.[27]

The first volume of the *Yearbook* was rounded off by several articles relating explicitly to Jews and Judaism in the United States. Azriel Chipkin reported on "Jewish Education in New York," with data comparing the situation in 1929 favorably with that in 1916.[28] Meir Waxman presented a sober report on "Rabbis and the Rabbinate in America."[29] Finally, Mikhl Ivensky contributed a survey of "The Jewish Labor Movement" in America. With the onset of the Depression, joblessness and work conditions had once again become major concerns. Ivensky's article focused on what had been accomplished for the Jewish worker by organized labor, and presented a *tour d'horizon* of the Jewish unions, the Jewish labor press, and the labor-oriented fraternal organizations. America, Ivensky enthused, was a "wonderful country" for getting things organized.[30]

In short, this first volume reaffirmed many of the values that animated the American Hebraist community: a commitment to Jewish culture and Jewish identity, a degree of social alienation, and a determination to overcome that alienation through an identification with broad humanistic values, Western culture, and the American social scene.[31]

An awareness of their beleaguered status is clearly evident in the preface to the 1935 volume. Here, the editors (Ribalow and S. Bernstein) expressed their desire to "continue what we attempted to do when we first began several years ago . . . to pluck from the stormy seas of America the scattered pearls of Judaism and, above all, to rescue the lonely Hebrew word from the din of foreign culture around us."[32]

The dichotomies (America versus Judaism, Hebrew versus foreign culture) are instructive. The Depression years brought with them a more somber assessment of America and of American Jewish life. By the end of the 1930s, this was compounded by a sense of doom surrounding European Jewry. But volumes 2, 3, and 4 of the *Yearbook* also continued to reflect the Hebraists' commitment to a humanistic worldview.

Thus, we find a continuing cosmopolitan motif in the wide diversity of subjects drawn from American and European intellectual life.[33]

The force of the Hebrew-humanist argument was most explicit, however, in an essay of Nahum Sokolow's that appeared in the volume for 1935: "Hebrew Nationalism through Humanism." Sokolow argued against political chauvinism, on the one hand (an attack against the Revisionist Zionists led by Vladimir Ze'ev Jabotinsky), and against the endless philosophizing about *kultura*, on the other hand—that is, the interminable debate in Zionist circles over Jewishness and national identity (a jab at the Ahad Ha'amist school). Both the one and the other were reflections of a *luftmentsh* mentality, unrooted in the real world, Sokolow maintained. Real work was needed to build a satisfactory social and economic infrastructure in Palestine. This work of construction—what Sokolow called "civilization"—was the way to respond to the present *human condition* of the Jews. Concentrating on technology, planning, and productivity, not on intellectual shortcuts or cheap imitations of European nationalisms, was the way to assure for the Jews both a soundly based national identity and equality among the nations.[34] He couched this advice in a general argument about the nature of humanity, the individual, and the nation, in which he stressed the great value of both group attachments and individual self-realization. This dualism was the essence of the human condition as Sokolow saw it, and this was the sense in which he understood the humanism of the Zionist enterprise: a balancing of individual and collective needs.[35]

Sokolow was primarily addressing the situation in Palestine, but the thrust of the argument was also bound to appeal to American Hebraists like Ribalow, who wanted to see Jewish pride rest on Jewish achievements in the free marketplace of ideas and the universal world of productivity.

The 1930s saw a new stress on Americanism among some of the Hebrew writers and poets. Israel Efros and Ephraim Lissitsky, for example, wrote their "Indian" poetry during this period.[36] Whether this turn to native American motifs was romantic escapism that signaled their marginality, a search for a pastoral setting more in keeping with the Hebrew literary tradition than the bustling urban context, or the expression of an affinity for other oppressed peoples,[37] may be of less consequence than the fact that such poets felt the need for "American" content and symbolism.

Other writers used local material that was closer to their own experience. Ginsburg's "New York" has already been quoted. Another poet of this period, Avraham Avi Halevy, also wrote a cycle called "New York," part of which was published in the 1939 volume of the *Yearbook*, under the title "Pigeons on the El." Halevy mingled disparate sound and visual sensations to evoke a raucous, dissonant, but lyrical New York morning:

> Morning's freshness slid down the skyscrapers . . .
> the tracks of the "el" glistened in the sun,
> flowing like streams. . . .
> The screech of a wild beast
> from the chain of wheels—
> is it a newborn day being murdered? . . .
>
> But the city cannot block out the sun
> or frighten off the new day,
> so long as there are pigeons
> singing their joy.
> Towers leap from their foundations
> and soar in mid-air.
> The city's uproar is stilled . . .
> and the world smiles its magic upon man.[38]

This highly individual, expressive, and sensual type of writing was characteristic of a whole group of poets (Gabriel Preil, Hillel Bavli, and others). Summing up trends in Hebrew poetry in the 1930s, Ribalow identified this "quiet" and "classical" approach as an *American* school of Hebrew verse, quite different from the sound and fury of national Hebrew poetry abroad (chiefly in Palestine), and comparable to the quiet romanticism of Edwin Arlington Robinson, Robert Frost, and Edna St. Vincent Millay.[39]

> Those looking for *Americana* in [Hebrew] poetry here will complain of the insufficient use of native material; but those looking first of all for *poetry* will find here those perennial themes that have always moved the hearts of poets. . . . After a long arid period, after years of fumbling versifiers, . . . a vibrant stream of *just plain poetry*, humanist and Jewish, had to emerge. . . . In this humanist Jewish poetry, we perceive the personalities of the poets as individuals, and when seen together it is evident that they are *American* poets.[40]

It bears noting that the kind of artistic sensibility described here matches quite closely the concerns of the younger Yiddish writers and especially poets in America in the interwar years, known collectively as *Di Yunge*.[41] The parallels can be striking, as we can judge from this observation about *Di Yunge* by Ruth Wisse: "Because of its deafening noise, unceasing motion, and thorough impersonality, the metropolis is the very place in which the individual may explore the moods of his solitude. . . . [T]hese immigrant Yiddish writers became conscious of their individuality against the looming skyscrapers and bridges and the rushing subways."[42]

It would seem reasonable, therefore, to propose a synoptic view of common cultural responses that transcended the bounds of the respective literary traditions of Yiddish and Hebrew.

The emergence of a Jewish American literature, whether self-consciously "American" or not, reflected more than the gropings of a few intellectuals. In the 1930s, domestic concerns became increasingly important to American Jews. This was partly the result of the Depression, which not only affected jobs and income in light industry, the building trades, and small business (fields in which Jews were heavily concentrated), but also created a new "relief class" of unemployed Jewish white-collar workers.[43] At the same time, alarming developments in Europe tended to underscore the contrast between American democracy and conditions overseas.

One writer in the *Yearbook* pointedly remarked on the vast difference between the New Deal, as the American response to economic crisis, and the corresponding German and Italian reactions. He took pride in the involvement of Jews in shaping and directing federal programs aimed at achieving economic recovery.[44] Another writer noted that sermons in American Orthodox synagogues no longer routinely cast aspersions on America as a setting for a viable Judaism (as they had done, prior to World War I). America's blessings were now being recognized.[45] To honor the 150th anniversary of the American federal constitution, the *Yearbook* published it in full in a Hebrew translation.[46]

That is not to say that the Hebraists, as a group, were sanguine about American Jewish culture. Shimon Ginsburg's narrative poem, "Memorial—An American Idyll," reflected mainly negative themes: the coarse materialism and philistine self-absorption of his fellow Jews, and the deleterious impact of the Depression on the Jewish social fabric. In addition, the poem dealt with the lonely struggle of the Jewish educator against the inroads of Americanization. (Many of the Hebrew writers earned their living in the field of Jewish education.) Ginsburg considered America to be "a land that devours its races" in a process of leveling (*erets okhelet geza'e-hah*—punning on the evil reports about the land of Canaan brought to Moses in the desert).[47]

Yet, despite the banality, vulgarism, and ignorance that he found in American Judaism, Ginsburg concluded on a note of sentimentality. Marveling that acts of goodness, devotion, and loyalty could exist in America as well, he called them a saving grace that might restore the soul of American Jewry and, in the process, provide the vindication and inspiration for Hebrew poetry in an alien land.[48]

Some of the fiction published in the late 1930s also reflected ambivalence about American values. Reuven Wallenrod's short story, "The Family Circle," was set in the Depression years and dealt with the conflict between an immigrant drugstore owner and his Americanized adult children. Though the story is heavy-handed, the ambience of the urban American Jewish neighborhood is carefully conveyed: the music on the radio in the living room; the immigrant mother's driving ambition for her American-educated children; the teenagers hanging out on the corner, where they skirmish with the grumpy storekeeper even as they buy his ice-cream.[49]

In Wallenrod's flexible Hebrew, we find words that Ben-Yehuda never dreamed of: *popsicles*, *fudgicles*, *payntim* (pints), and *ḥatsipayntim* (half-pints). Such adoption of street speech as a strategy for writers was pioneered, of course, by the popular Yiddish press.

The *Yearbook* now featured a regular section on American Jewish affairs, covering such topics as Jewish organizational life (*landsmanshaften*, fraternal orders, Jewish community centers, federations, and Jewish community councils),[50] Jewish education,[51] and an annual literary review. Articles devoted to the demographic impact of occupational change, the Depression, and the increasing proportion of American-born Jewish parents among the older generation voiced concern over shrinking Jewish birthrates and concomitant trends toward an aging Jewish population.[52]

Despite this considerable involvement with the American scene, the eyes of Hebraists in early 1939 (the fourth volume was published in March of that year) inevitably also turned toward Europe and Palestine. Eisig (Itshak) Silberschlag's play about Ferdinand and Isabella recalled past ages of expulsion and persecution,[53] while Yohanan Twersky's dramatized version of Theodor Herzl's encounter with the Kaiser in Jerusalem in 1898 illustrated the Zionist alternative to the Jewish fate in Europe.[54]

But the most compelling statement conveying a sense of hard times and impending doom was a poem by Gabriel Preil that took an unmistakably American symbol as its leitmotif: "Washington Remembers."[55]

Preil sets the scene in lower Manhattan near the East River, where an equestrian statue of George Washington dominates a bridge plaza. Young strollers have come out to enjoy some evening air on a sweltering night. There the poet also encounters the statue. Washington's once-youthful vigor, courage, and pride, it seems to him, are gone now: old age and feebleness prevent him from galloping through the night. Now, only the coming of daylight can drive away his fear, whereas once the evening had "framed his marvellous visage."[56]

Once he gazed upon the budding springtimes
of Jewish young men, and marked their course,
planting liberty throughout the land. . . .
Now the patience and wisdom
of the commander of Valley Forge
no longer suffice unto the dream. . . .
Young mothers put children to bed,
destined to be killers and casualties
in the approaching future of blood. . . . [57]

The Life of the Mind in Dark Times

The 1930s, even more than the First World War, severed the American Hebrew writers from Europe and all that it represented. Conscious of this separation throughout the interwar years, some writers were left culturally stranded, while others were driven to seek their new literary moorings in the New World—in the throbbing urban landscape, in the natural beauty of the countryside,[58] or even in the old West of Indians, the frontier, and the Gold Rush.[59]

But regardless of whether they chose to write of the New World or the Old, the land of the Bible or the land of opportunity, many of the writers had been imbued with a sense of mission vis-à-vis the maintenance of a Hebrew literary tradition. There was thus positive value that grew out of a sense of historic responsibility.

The Second World War, and with it, the Holocaust of European Jewry, intensified these reactions.[60] This time, the destruction was far greater than it had been in 1914–21, although this only became evident after the first two or three years of the war. On the one hand, these events demanded a more direct identification with the Jewish people in its hour of tragedy. By 1943, certainly by 1944, this identification with the fate of Europe's Jews tended to diminish the value of such themes as humanism and Americanism. On the other hand, it also imposed on those writers who were far from the "city of slaughter" an onerous responsibility: to preserve intact the thread of continuity of cultural creation.

In recent years, we have come to appreciate the various forms of what has been called "spiritual resistance" offered by the Jews of occupied Europe against the Nazis, including art in all its forms.

Literary and scholarly activity in wartime America, though hardly belonging to the same order of things, nevertheless fits into a general framework that might be called the Jews' refusal to submit to fate and succumb to despair.

As the war began, it was again Menahem Ribalow who signaled (albeit obliquely) the type of response that the times seemed to call forth. Taking the author of *Kohelet* (Ecclesiastes) as his point of reference, Ribalow observed: "There is in him a fine and sophisticated balance between individual and collective sorrow, faith and doubt, darkness and light, . . . life and death. Life ultimately triumphs and even conquers the deep despair of Kohelet, because this poet-sage, after all, *was a Jew*."[61]

At the beginning of the war, this faith in survival and the commitment to art and culture "in spite of everything" seemed to dominate much of what was published in the *Yearbook*. There is almost an air of business-as-usual in some of the work that appeared. Poems by Hillel Bavli, for example, dealt exclusively with the theme of art itself and the search for beauty and creativity.[62] We find essays on purely historical topics, such as those on Rashi, for instance, written by Meir Waxman and Shmuel Mirsky;[63] and a speculative article about "Theories of Physiognomy" by Nissan Touroff, that dealt sympathetically with a subject perilously close to racial theories.[64]

Even material that dealt specifically with the war and the gathering tragedy of European Jewry tended to emphasize the Jews' mystical ability to survive throughout their history, despite painful losses. Aharon Zeitlin's poem "Revenge and Recompense" recalled the pogroms of the First World War, reminding readers that the Cossacks who had shed Jewish blood had been cursed with defeat on the battlefield.[65]

The paradigm of the First World War and its consequences still dominated the thinking of those who wrote about the more recent fate of Polish Jewry, for example. In an article entitled, "The Destruction of Polish Jewry," S. Rosenfeld was not speaking about mass physical extermination per se (though the massacre of thousands was included in what he meant by "destruction"). Rather, he was referring mainly to the idea that Polish Jewry, as a social and historical entity, would never again be reconstituted in any recognizable form or return to "normal." His assumption was that the Allies would win the war and that, once again, as in 1918, a significant Jewish population would then face the prospect of life in an independent Poland. But this time, he forecast, most Polish Jews would choose to emigrate, given their failure to become integrated and accepted as equals in interwar Poland.[66]

Finally, the *Yearbook* also dealt with America's role in accepting Jewish refugees, beginning with the influx from Germany in the 1930s. A discussion of the plight of the wartime refugees expressed hope and confidence (in retrospect, woefully misplaced) in President Roosevelt's ability to win Congressional acquiescence in a humanitarian refugee policy.[67]

None of this sets the mentality of this group of Hebrew writers apart from ideas generally propounded in American Jewry at the time. Most of these writers had been living in the United States for some thirty years or more, and there is no evidence to suggest that their perspective or consciousness was any different from that of their American Jewish peers. I stress this point because I think it illuminates, from yet another angle, the issue of the American Hebraists' alleged isolation or alienation from America and American Jewry.

Echoes of the theme of *iberlebn*—of the Jews' ability to surmount virtually all threats to their survival—continued to reverberate in the *Yearbook* for several years. Examples of this appear in the poem, "Here," by A. S. Shvarts ("You cannot burn the spirit of a people the way you burn a stick of wood");[68] in the quite conventional and traditional treatment by A. Hefterman of the theme of messianic faith in the face of adversity;[69] and even in a report on wartime atrocities and postwar prospects for European Jewry, that estimated Jewish losses at the end of 1943 at between 2.5 and 3 million, but focused on the postwar tasks of rehabilitation of survivors and emigration.[70]

A similar theme, though not central to the work in question, was incorporated in the epic "Hidden [or "Lost"] Tablets," by Zalman Shneour. (Shneour, probably the most important Hebrew poet at that time, had escaped from Paris in 1940 and lived in the United States from 1941 to 1951.) The basis of the poem was an iconoclastic counterscripture—a modern, subversive pseudepigraphon of sorts.

The historical frame provided for the newly "rediscovered" texts was the first destruction of Jerusalem and the determination of the king of Judea and his priests to salvage for posterity the records of Israelite culture. These "tablets" or "scrolls," destined not to be found again for centuries, were lost to the biblical canon but represented a hidden, perhaps truer tradition than the expurgated canonical version.[71]

Though the main point of this work is unrelated to the Holocaust, a number of key passages refer to the immortality of the cultural treasures set down in Jewish writings. This message held particular resonance for writers during the years of the new ḥurban habayit (Destruction) of the twentieth century: the life of Jewish creativity, recorded in books, would outlive the awful conflagration.

Not all writers, to be sure, could find comfort or literary inspiration in the theme of survival. To Gabriel Preil, for example, poetry had to come from life, not death: there was no poetic answer to mass slaughter. In "There Are No Words," he replied to those who "look to me [in vain] for words of flint, words like burning embers, that might soak up the blood of my people, heal it with balm. . . . Alas, in lawless times, words become birds with broken backs."[72]

No dam would ever stop the rivers of blood, no channel could restore the flow of life to the severed veins of slaughtered infants, and there was not even any comfort in somehow being spared, only to bear witness to such a death. Therefore, "words, too, have failed, no new suns will shine in them, no old wines will ever again bubble forth from them."[73]

The war revealed what is commonly called the "bestiality" of human beings. Nissan Touroff attempted to provide the Hebrew reader with some understanding of this phenomenon from the point of view of social psychology. To what extent, he asked, were aggression, violence, and war an indelible part of the human psyche? Delving into various aspects of the problem, from classical history to the erotic side of sadism and masochism, to the psychology of the soldier facing death, he acknowledged that war was, in fact, deeply rooted in the human experience and perhaps even "normal."[74]

Providing a passionate counterpoint to this depiction of perpetual conflict and of the human capacity to inflict death without compunction, Abraham Joshua Heschel's essay, "Piety" (or "Fear of God") attempted to reaffirm humanist values and to restore the ideal of the sanctity of human life.[75]

It took moral courage to sustain that belief in the transcendental meaning of life—and the possibility of overcoming the brutality of death—in the very darkest hour of Jewish history. Others were far less willing than Heschel to believe that the moral universe he described could ever again be affirmed.

Two poems by Israel Efros, published in the *Yearbook* in 1944, expressed Jewish contempt for Europe and all its murderous history of Jew-hatred, and at the same time vented Jewish rage at conventional Judaic theodicies. In the first poem, "In Old Germany," Efros chose a medieval setting to underscore the idea that nothing had changed in hundreds of years of persecution. He also alluded with savage irony to Jewish ritual and flaunted phrases from the laudatory "'Aleinu" prayer (which thanks God for having singled out the Jews from all other peoples), which he used both to castigate the Germans and to give Jewish "chosenness" a devastating twist—the Jews are uniquely victimized.[76]

In the second poem, "A People," Efros conveyed his sense of helplessness in the face of the bloodbath that was relentlessly destroying his people and human civilization. And, alluding to God's role in history (again, partly through a phrase from "'Aleinu"—indicated in italics), once more he posed the question of meaning in human history:

> Up now, slash us, let the hot blood spurt—
> we are captive,
> led away from the inner circle . . .
> There stands a Great One,
> keeper of terrible mysteries.
> Like Joseph's sheaves we bow in a circle
> to him, we
> prostrate ourselves before his majesty,
> and with passion and with burning breath
> we whisper:
> Thine is the flesh and the spirit—spare neither.
> With blades we expose our hearts and entrails to him
> until he is drenched with our blood. . . .
> Is he a creature of God
> or the work of the Devil?

And so we empty the wine of our veins
into his shadow, as we sing,
"We who are about to die salute you!"
and we *bow down to (nikhr'a modim bifnei)*
that syllable or sound,
as the universe takes a bridegroom
in a marriage of blood.[77]

Thus did the Holocaust make a mockery of all human, religious, and literary values in a pagan blood orgy, leaving the Hebrew poet with only one voice: that of the madman.

Looking for Something to Live For

Two more volumes of the *Yearbook* appeared, in 1946 and 1949, in which the American Hebraist community had the opportunity to mourn, to reassess their position in the world, and, finally, to celebrate the birth of the Jewish state.

(The faltering continuity of *Sefer hashanah* may be partly explained by the fact that Menahem Ribalow, who had been sole editor of all the volumes since the third, was involved in several other major publishing projects between 1944 and his death in 1953, in addition to his work at *Hadoar*.)[78]

Israel Efros contributed several more poems to the 1946 volume that expressed the feelings of those, like himself, who had not personally experienced the Holocaust, but who, nevertheless, were emotionally scarred by it.

His "More Silent Than a Dream" told of the numbing shock and silence that burdened the remnant of his people: "Dumbstruck, as if in a trance, we go on living. . . . "[79] In "Tomorrow God Will Appear" (the title is ironic), he contrasted the victorious, postwar world, washed spanking-clean, with the Jew's inability to share in the general rejoicing: "As for me, all my wounds will cry out in this sparkling, better world, and wherever I tread I will drip blood that finds no solace, and for which there can be no atonement."[80]

Finally, in "After Mourning" came reassessment: a new understanding of how "brittle and hollow" was the life of culture that Jews had built up over the centuries. With fewer illusions now, perhaps, they were fated nonetheless to continue to plough the same furrow over again, in the same old rhythm of "Jewish time," which knew a tempo all its own.[81]

Another series of post-Holocaust poems was contributed by Aharon Zeitlin. In his turn, he wrote of the difficulty of facing the world and life again; of the renewal of the spirit that writing might bring; of his yearning for his destroyed Warsaw home, almost palpably real but locked forever in incorporeal memory; and finally, of the ultimate futility of grief, prayer, and poetry:

> Even if God himself tried
> to wrest a cry from His lips—He could not.
> As the slaughtered millions are silent,
> so would the son of Hilkiah [Jeremiah]
> be left wordless before the ineffable.
> Now even crying aloud is useless:
> tears turn to mere literature,
> all prayers are for nought.[82]

Gabriel Preil, whose expressionist style did not easily lend itself to "national" poetry, found himself overtaken by an unaccountable, wintry melancholy in the midst of a spring day: "Then come, desolate tear, find yourself a nest in the corner of my eye, come, whisper; even the future is trapped and swallowed up in the maw of the night."[83]

As for fiction, a short story by Benjamin Ressler ("A Soldier Returns from the War") narrated a tale of an amputee who returned from the war with a new sense of his Jewishness. Gentile America, symbolized by the soldier's non-Jewish girlfriend, is left standing at the doorstep, as the Jewish family becomes more central.[84]

Altogether, the effect of the Holocaust on the intellectual world of these writers was traumatic. The literary section of the 1946 volume returned to themes of alienation and despair that had characterized American Hebrew literature in its infancy.

Outside the realm of belles lettres, however, the trauma was less in evidence. In the sections devoted to research and criticism, the stress was on continuity, not breakdown. Intellectual concerns ranged from the religious philosophy of Franz Rosenzweig, to Judaic liturgical development, to kabbalah and Jewish mysticism. Literary critics reviewed the work of Ephraim Lissitsky, Yosef Haim Brenner, Zalman Shneour, and Uri Zvi Greenberg.

The American scene, too, remained an abiding concern. Jacob Lestchinsky's essay on the "Economic Development of American Jewry" was a summary of trends and occupational stratification that brought up to date the evaluations published in the 1930s.[85] Rabbi A. Hefterman presented a gloomy picture of Jewish affiliation and identification in suburbs and small communities, sounding a note of near-panic with regard to the galloping intermarriage rate.[86] (This perception conflicts with the findings of social scientists gathered in the late 1940s and early 1950s.) [87]

Ribalow devoted a separate section in the volume issued in 1949 to the new State of Israel, beginning with a "Hymn to the State" by Aharon Zeitlin.[88] The chief interest for us, however, lies in Ribalow's own essay, that bore the triumphalist title, "Entering the Third Commonwealth." [89]

In his grandiloquent way, Ribalow sang a hymn of his own to the new state and celebrated its potential as a source of renewed life for the Jewish people and for Hebrew culture in particular. It was, he said, time for a literary awakening, for a new scholarship, and for new horizons in all fields of Jewish life.

It would not do, he argued further, merely to return to ancient or traditional forms. Harking back to modernist and "futurist" themes he had expressed in 1927, he reaffirmed the cultural and even religious value of the new life to be created in Israel, and with it, the "new breed" of Jew who would emerge there.[90]

Ironically, then, it was Israel's national and military triumph that allowed Ribalow to return to the positive humanist-universalist ideas of twenty years earlier. The world had gone through an astonishing revolution in technology and in social values, he declared. The new civilization was vastly different from that of the nineteenth century:

> And we are part of this great humanity, caught up in the travails of servitude and liberation. . . . We are the children of this great world, . . . with all its tragic conflicts and its awesome achievements. . . . "When God brought us back to Zion, it was as if we were dreaming." We dream about the glorious past that has been resurrected, and we dream about the future, our future and that of all the world. We want to pour all of our 2,000-year-long experience into our present lives. And we want the universalist understanding that we acquired

in our years of being a "world people" ['am 'olam] to become the
criterion of our new life, in Israel and in the lands of the Diaspora.[91]

As for the Hebrew language, new challenges awaited it. What
would be the link between the Hebrew literature of the past and
the new literature to be created by a free generation? How would
Hebrew, as the language of an elite, be transformed as it became
the common language of the masses? What would be the impact of
trends in Israel on creativity in the Diaspora and—who knew?—
what influence could the Diaspora writers bring to bear on Hebrew
culture in Israel? Ribalow foresaw a fructifying symbiosis between
the two, enriched by the youthful vigor of Israeli writing.[92]

The triumphalist tone of Ribalow's message was qualified by a
continued brooding on the great tragedy that the Jewish people had
just endured. Ephraim Lissitsky, for example, wrote on "Hitler before the Seat of Judgement."[93] A. S. Shvarts composed a narrative
poem that alluded to the traditional liturgy in order to form an
analogy between modern and ancient martyrs.[94] And A. R. Malachi's essay on the chroniclers of the mass slaughter of Jews in
Poland three hundred years earlier, during the Chmielnicki revolt
of 1648–49, bore obvious relevance to the generation of the Holocaust.[95] Perhaps most impressive of all, in this area, was a detailed
essay on what has become known as Holocaust literature, that
analyzed and quoted from Jewish poetry written in the ghettos,
camps, and forests.[96]

The sum total for the last *Yearbook* was thus a mix of vindication and dejection. The open wounds of the Second World War
could not be healed, but the establishment of the State of Israel
was—against that background—so much more extraordinary and
encouraging.

In the years that followed, a number of Hebrew writers left America
to make their home in Israel (notably Shimon Halkin, Israel Efros,
Yohanan Twersky, Avraham Regelson, and Zalman Shneour). A
number of others died during the 1950s (Menahem Ribalow, Nissan
Touroff, Shmuel Simcha Cohen, Herman Frank). Under the circumstances, the community that they had created around the *Yearbook*—many of them had contributed to more than one volume—

fell apart.[97] While less ambitious journals, including *Hadoar* and *Bitzaron*, and specialized professional journals such as *Shvilei haḥinukh* carried on, none was able to match the breadth of vision and achievement that had infused *Sefer hashanah liyehudei amerikah*.

Conclusion

Those who have commented on Hebrew literature in America until now have tended to agree that it was an émigré literature, that its practitioners were raised (or at least born) in Europe, and that, therefore, it never succeeded in developing indigenous roots in American culture. It remained a literature of alienation and marginality, lacking an understanding of American realities and unable to connect with American literature as a whole. Hence, it did not survive.

I wish to take issue with the notion that it was a lack of alertness to the American scene that doomed Hebrew literature in America. I believe I have shown that this argument does not do justice to the degree of American influence on the agenda of American Hebrew writers.

Nor is it clear that the stance of alienation and the fact of cultural marginality would have prevented these writers from voicing something authentically American. For one thing, they were not the only "outsiders" in the literary world. Marginality as such is no bar to literary creativity or success, and there are some contemporary writers (even native-born American ones) who clearly find their inspiration in such situations. Cynthia Ozick has pointed out that, in her own mind, marginality coexists with at-homeness: she feels "perfectly at home [in America] and perfectly insecure, perfectly acculturated and perfectly marginal."[98] Moreover, marginality was not something that *Sefer hashanah* cultivated: quite the opposite.

More persuasive than the general "alienation" argument is the suggestion made by Robert Alter, that Hebrew literature in America was always a sideshow, while the "main event" took place in Palestine-Israel.[99] The fact that some of the leading Hebrew writers in America left for Israel during the 1940s and early 1950s tends to bear out this thesis.

Much more basic, however, is the fact that American Hebrew literature failed *not because it could not communicate American ideas*, but because *American Hebrew writers lacked a readers' market*. Their problem was not that they were poets of disenchantment and alienation, but that they were isolated by a semantic wall from their only potential public. That is why virtually none of them earned their living as writers.

Hebraists in America wrote for themselves and to one another, not to a general public. Without a readership of any numerical significance, without critics, standards, without writing for the theater or the cinema—the entire social framework that supports modern literary activity—Hebrew literature in America could never become self-sustaining. This was pointed out back in 1901 by Mordecai Raizin and indicated by Nissan Touroff in the late 1930s.[100]

Without a social context to work in, American Hebrew writers could not serve a social function. Thus, they became craftsmen dedicated to perpetuating a lost art—which strongly implies a built-in obsolescence. Although they sensed that they had a mission to fulfill—to carry the torch of Hebrew letters that Russian Jewry was prevented from carrying—it was not in America but in the Yishuv that the mission would one day come to fruition. When Israeli statehood was established, American Hebraists were relieved of a burden, in a sense, and could hand the torch on to others.

If American Jewry is indeed the "people of the lost book," *Sefer hashanah* merits being placed on the bookshelf of those lost books that need to be recovered. Although short-lived, the phenomenon of American Hebrew literature has cultural and historical significance. Retrieving the message of the American Hebrew writers is one more way to find the interface that existed between American Jewry and European Jewry when American Jewry was still largely an immigrant community, and thus to illuminate for American Jews an important part of their own heritage.

The experiment of a cosmopolitan and American-oriented culture, expressed not in English but in a minority language, raises wider issues about the politics of culture in American history, the interplay of cultural conformism and national identity, and the parameters of "otherness" in American society. Far from fading away in the interwar and immediate postwar era, these questions have reemerged in recent years in the debate over the legitimacy of minority culture and multiculturalism within American society. Although the Hebraists' experience does not seem to offer a positive paradigm in this regard, it is at least relevant to raise the issues again. In the final chapter, these threads and others will be drawn together in a consideration of Jewish studies in the American academy today.

CHAPTER 8

Afterword: The Politics
of Cultural Transmission,
the Legacy of Simon Dubnov,
and Jewish Studies

Simon Dubnov, the preeminent historian of East European Jewry in the first half of the twentieth century, was killed along with thousands of other Jews under the Nazi occupation of Riga, Latvia, in 1941. As an ideologue of Jewish autonomism, he personally elaborated one strategy for Jewish collective existence in Diaspora lands. As a historian, he did much to create a place within the Western academic tradition for Jewish history. The following remarks are intended to explore the relevance of Dubnov to current discussions about multiculturalism and Jewish studies.

To Simon Dubnov, the study and the writing of Jewish history was a mission, not a career. The questions I would like to address here relate to this particular aspect of Dubnov's legacy:

To what extent, if at all, can Dubnov, the engagé Jewish intellectual, serve as a model for Jewish academics today?

To what extent, if at all, did Dubnov's personal and political agenda limit the long-term value of his work as a historian?

And, in the contemporary American context, what political and personal attitudes underlie our own enterprise as Jewish historians?

I raise these questions as much for my own sake as for anyone else's, since Dubnov has always been one of my culture-heroes. His discovery of Jewish historical scholarship as a medium for expressing his authenticity as a Jew—his blending of the existential and the academic—struck a chord of sympathy in me when I was still an undergraduate. I imagine that Jewish historians who seek, through the study, teaching, and writing of Jewish history, to give form and content to their Jewish attachments, will always find in their hearts a special affinity for Dubnov.

Part of what prompts me to consider the problems of commitment, mission, and politics in the context of Jewish historiography are two unrelated encounters that I had during a year I spent recently in the United States. The first of these encounters occurred at an academic conference, in which a heated political debate was sparked. The speaker pointedly challenged one particular school of thought concerning American Jewish intellectual history (the "world of our fathers" approach, referring to a penchant by certain liberal intellectuals for looking back with nostalgia to the cradle of Jewish leftism in America), calling such an approach a form of filial piety that was devoid of a sense of real ("parental") responsibility toward the community and its interests today. The problem (beyond the particular challenge to a liberal writer by a conservative one) raises the wider issue—that goes back to the case of Dubnov—of "disinterested" scholarship. Does it legitimately exist in the Jewish academic community, and if it does, what are its limits?

The second encounter involved a private discussion with an undergraduate who was taking my class in modern Jewish history. The young man in question came to me for help in working through his personal conflicts over his Jewish identity, perhaps through the writing of a paper for the course. In the course of our conversation, the student (who bears the surname of an old, illustrious Italian Jewish scholarly and literary family) explained at length what was troubling him: that his own home had provided little guidance, except for negative input about the family's suffering during the years of Italian fascism. Was Jewishness worth all the trouble (he asked), if it was only about the Holocaust, only about victimization, only about surviving against the odds? It was clear that what this student wanted from me went beyond the academic: He wanted me to provide a satisfactory "answer" to his personal crisis.

That encounter, like the first, prompted me to consider the role of Jewish academics in America, and to look back again at Dubnov as a model of the engagé intellectual. Dubnov's historiographical labors, after all, were an expression of his deep national commitments and values. His political work on behalf of democracy in Russia, his championing of the causes of Jewish emancipation and national-cultural autonomy, his work to promote the enterprise of Jewish scholarship among his fellow Russian Jews, his role in the founding of the YIVO Institute for Jewish Research in Vilna (today located in New York)—all of these are central to understanding Dubnov, the man and the historian.

I would therefore pose the following questions:

- How does our scholarly agenda compare with Dubnov's?
- Do we, like Dubnov, see the work of Jewish history as a collective mission to document, preserve, and reinterpret a national culture?
- Is our intellectual quest also a quest for personal authenticity, and if so, how does that affect what we write and how we teach? Do we integrate the roles of scholar and community member, or compartmentalize them? Are our basic commitments to our discipline, to Jewish culture, or to both?
- And what is the primary role of the academy in society: to transmit and sustain culture, or to objectify, relativize, and question human experience through distancing oneself from the object of study? To translate the past into modern idiom, or to let the past be the past and speak for itself?

To make the matter perfectly clear, these are dilemmas that Dubnov faced and attempted to resolve in his own life and work. His solution was on the side of an integration between scholarship and personal authenticity; on the side of programmatic commitment and active, didactic intervention in cultural and political processes. His politics were a fulfillment in practice of his intellectual ideals, and his historiography was part and parcel of the "new Judaism" that he saw emerging from the cultural and social turmoil of his age. He chose topics of research that suited and promoted his

Diaspora-nationalist-autonomist program, and his legacy is therefore a selective interpretation of Jewish history (though it purports to be a comprehensive one).

In short, Dubnov was a secular-humanistic Jew, a nationalist *maskil*, and a liberal democrat, as is immediately apparent to anyone who reads his historical oeuvre. He permitted himself to write judgmentally and critically of those who opposed human freedom and human enlightenment, in a way that was much in vogue at the time, but became rare in Western scholarly discourse in the postwar generation. Nevertheless, such value-laden and controversial issues as racism, poverty, sexism, ecological destruction, and other social abuses in modern society have reentered and reshaped the scholarly agenda in recent years, in a way that would have suited Dubnov.

Let me begin to address some of the issues I have raised with a few observations about Dubnov's historiography, because that will inevitably color our assessment of Dubnov's legacy in other areas.

Dubnov was an innovator, the first major Jewish historian to challenge the regnant Germanocentric and idealist historiography of the Jewish *Wissenschaft* school. Though he could be lachrymose with the best of them, Dubnov's was truly a counterhistory (to borrow a phrase from David Biale). Dubnov parted company with his predecessors in the way that he championed the history of the "folk," the *narod*, against that of the elite.

He readjusted our historical vision in two ways: first, by establishing an East European focus in modern Jewish historiography to balance the prevailing West European, Iberian, and Semitics orientation; and second, by bringing into play a social-historical methodology that represented the birth of modern Jewish social history and sociology. Even a cursory glance at the way Jewish history has been "done" since Dubnov will demonstrate the continuing influence of his point of view. His appreciation for the importance of communal frameworks in Jewish society, for example, and his understanding of the central significance of economics and demography, pointed the way toward new methodologies, new interests, new ways of looking at Jewish historical research, that have remained in the forefront ever since.

His thesis that preeminent Jewish "centers" of population and culture define successive epochs in Jewish history has lost little of its plausibility in the post-Holocaust period, when Israel and American Jewry can both be fitted into such a theory.

Indeed, it is remarkable how close the scholarly agenda among Jewish East Europeanists remains to what we discern in Dubnov. The fact is, that the losses due to Sovietization of Jewish scholarship in Russia in the 1920s and 1930s, compounded by the tragic losses sustained during the Holocaust (including Dubnov himself), created a semivacuum in this field that has only begun to be filled in recent years. The irony is, that the fate of East European Jews under the Nazis has so overshadowed the social-historical work that Dubnov began one hundred years ago, that what might have become a major focus in modern Jewish studies has remained something of a minor field. Perhaps the lament of students who suffer from an overexposure to negative messages is related to this phenomenon, and perhaps Jewish academics ought to take note.

Dubnov, of course, was not only a historian of Eastern Europe. Indeed, he was one of that rare breed who was able to gaze upon all of Jewish history at once and articulate an all-embracing vision of it. He belongs in a class with his illustrious predecessor, Heinrich Graetz, and with contemporaries and successors like Salo Baron, Gershom Scholem, Yehezkel Kaufman, and Ben-Zion Dinur. We mourn the passing of that age of giants: It is as if the tyranny of specialization has robbed us lesser mortals of the aspiration to do what they did (even if we were able to). Perhaps that ability was reserved for the European-trained.

Yet, having said that, I do not wish to imply that we do not aspire to do what Dubnov did *solely* because of lack of sufficient intellectual resources. In large measure, I believe, that kind of history on a grand scale is a model we no longer *choose*. To write a comprehensive history requires the selection of a red thread of continuity, an organizing principle or theme. It means going back to the notion of an "essence" of the Jewish experience that can be distilled from the whole. It means imposing a superstructure based on that essence, choosing a defining characteristic of each successive "stage" of development. It is, in fact, a teleological model that departs only slightly from traditional, Judaic theological models, and goes back to the old Hegelian triad. Dubnov used that schema because he believed in the teleology of a new Judaic synthesis in the modern world: the Jews would survive as a "spiritual nation," living in compact, self-sustaining (but at the same time integrated) minorities within modern society.

But there is a quality of "unbearable lightness" to such interpretations. Most of us today have far less trust in absolutes, in overarching schemes, in eternal essences. When we try to do justice to the multiplicity and uneven nature of the Jewish experience, we unavoidably take a different path from that of the great masters. That is why Baron, who may be said to have tried to perfect Dubnov's concept (in his *Social and Religious History of the Jews*), actually achieved something different. Despite the range and scope of Baron's concept, the trim lines of a unified history are undermined by the "heaviness" and sheer volume of discrete data. So, if Dubnov may be compared to Tchaikovsky, and Baron to Mahler's Ninth, it seems that we are bound to go back to the quartet.

But our problems with Dubnov really begin where his programmatic outlook is concerned. In retrospect, it is clear (as it could not have been clear to Dubnov himself) how limited was the application of the autonomist scheme of national minority rights that he espoused. As a political program, autonomism has not fit the post-Holocaust Jewish world, dominated as it is by the Western-type, voluntary Jewish community on the one hand, a sovereign Jewish state on the other, and communities under pressure, on the third, for whom emigration has been the chief or only safe option.

The meshing of Dubnov's historiography with his politics, however, means that in reassessing the latter, we unavoidably find cause to critique the former, as well. His *folkist* reading of Hasidism is a prime example of how ideology determined historiography. There is still much value in reading his *Toldot haḥasidut*, but it is even more fascinating to read it as a document of ideological populism than as a study of religious experience and phenomenology. The same may be said of Dubnov's overall outlook on the development of the Jewish people through successive stages, from territorial to spiritual nationhood—an outlook that owed much to his *Wissenschaft* forebears and bore the unmistakable imprint of nineteenth-century notions of "national spirit" and "national character."

Despite such caveats, Dubnov's achievement is to have produced a coherent picture of the past whose lasting value transcends issues of ideological content.

How, then, does the Dubnovian model illuminate options and dilemmas that face the Jewish historian today, particularly in the area I indicated earlier: the social purposes of the Jewish scholarly agenda? What is the nexus between academic Jewish studies and the entire problem of contemporary Jewish identity?

First, it is important to note that the myth of academic neutrality and objectivity is something that has been more honored in the breach, and has been rather openly debated in the United States at least since the late 1960s. The politics of learning and of research agendas, the choice of what to teach and what not to teach, the critique of Eurocentric political and cultural bias in textbooks, the pros and cons of affirmative action in both student and faculty recruitment, the political and economic affiliations of universities—all these have been the bread and butter of the open discourse of academic life for years.

The dramatic growth of Jewish studies on the American campus is one facet of this overall change in the nature of higher education in the United States, as it is a reflection of the different expectations of university students today, as compared with those of generations past. American society itself is in the midst of a fundamental debate over national identity that shows no immediate signs of petering out; quite the contrary. Within that context, Jewish studies make a statement about cultural diversity in American society that cannot be entirely separated from the wider political-cultural debate.

Jewish historiographical trends in the past have been politically linked: The genesis of modern Jewish historical scholarship is rooted in the project of Jewish emancipation in Central and Western Europe. Dubnov and his East European colleagues, of whatever ideological stripe, were similarly motivated by a politics of culture, rooted in Jewish nationalism.

Scholars today also follow an implicit agenda, one that stems from our own historical moment, which lies beyond both emancipation and nineteenth-century nationalism. We stand after the catastrophe, and we are engaged—when viewed collectively—in a salvage project: to preserve and interpret the record of our parents' and grandparents' world for those who can never enter that territory themselves.

Dubnov urged students to go out and collect records from the Jewish communities around them, because modernization threatened to rob posterity of direct access to the world of the past. But it was still possible, then, to collect and to observe directly. We, in contrast, do our work at one remove. Our access to the past is chiefly through paper and ink. Moreover, access to these texts is available only to those with the requisite language skills, who must transcribe, translate, and reinterpret for everyone else. We cannot bring the past back to life—that goes against the grain of the historical enterprise—but we can try to forge links between past and present.

By doing so, we commit ourselves to a more-or-less explicit survivalist program—and that applies, of course, to all fields of contemporary Jewish scholarship, not history alone. Thus, in the introduction to his book of essays, *Voices of Jacob, Hands of Esau*, Stephen Whitfield could remark, as if the assumption were self-evident, that, "Like virtually every other book about contemporary American Jewry, this one takes for granted the validity of Jewish life and the importance of its preservation."[1]

In a different field, the late sociologist Marshall Sklare used to characterize the postwar crop of American Jewish sociologists as basically "survivalist" in orientation, as compared with an earlier "assimilationist" perspective that doubted the long-term ability of any minority ethnic group to persist under conditions of technological, urban modernization.

One may go so far as to say that the survivalist posture is pervasive in American Jewish communal life: in politics, in religion, in philanthropy—what Jonathan Woocher calls the "civil religion" of *Sacred Survival*. It is not surprising, then, to note the presence of this posture among the academics produced by that community.

To go back to Whitfield (who is so often insightful on these matters): He offers several examples of what he calls the "outer limits of Jewish sensibility and belief"[2] that indicate the boundaries of objective or noncommitted discourse among Jewish intellectuals. Thus:

Whatever their reservations about the trial of Adolf Eichmann in Jerusalem in 1961, it did not occur to Jewish writers to reach for comparisons with the trial of Jesus, [as did Protestant] theologian William Stringfellow. . . . Nor would many Jews, no matter how antagonistic to communism, have agreed with W. Averell Harriman's view in 1945 that "Hitler's greatest crime was that his actions had resulted in opening the gates of Eastern Europe to Asia." These statements may help define the boundaries of even the pluralism of the intellectual enterprise among American Jews.[3]

This, if you will, is a partial indicator of what is deemed "politically incorrect" on our own little patch of academic turf. The need to set boundaries at all may seem offensive in principle; but it is merely the negative flip-side of a committed, engagé scholarship that cannot be neutral on questions of the affective purposes of learning.

The essential point is not the posting of red lights of thought control, which can indeed become oppressive—and ultimately ineffectual. The point, rather, is the positive intellectual quest—the survivalist quest to salvage an authentic and usable past for the sake of the present and the future. In the process, we will be making the value judgment that (as Whitfield put it), Jewish life is "valid and important"; that cultural diversity in American higher education is a good thing; that, just as teaching in the humanities is ultimately a project in shaping the cultural options of a society, so, too, is engaging students in Jewish scholarship. It is by nature different from training them for careers in business, law, or physics.

Dubnov's example is instructive in two ways: first, in the intellectual integrity he found in integrating scholarship and cultural-political concerns; and second, in his political commitment, as a Russian and Jewish intellectual, to press his society to meet certain basic standards in human development and cultural freedom.

Notes

Notes to Chapter One

1. Pertinent details and remarks about the nexus between language issues and Jewish national politics in Eastern Europe are to be found in Israel Bartal, "Midu-leshoniyut masortit leḥad-leshoniyut leumit," *Shvut: yahadut brit-hamo'atsot umizraḥ-eiropah* 15 (1992): 183–93.

   The frequent and explicit connections between language and politics also come across very clearly in the following observations by sociolinguistics expert Joshua A. Fishman:

   > The history of organized language consciousness, language loyalty and language maintenance on behalf of vernaculars in the Western world . . . reveals many instances of popular democratic triumphs in which submerged and deprecated tongues threw off the social and intellectual shackles of superimposed languages and became languages of governments, languages of culture, of commerce, and of diplomacy. . . . The history of organized language consciousness in the West is part of the history of the Renaissance, the Reformation, the growth of nationalism and the consolidation of nation-states, the rise of industrialization and of the city, the spread of colonialism and of post-colonial internationalisms, neo-colonialisms, and independence movements. The printing press and universal literacy, religious and political liberty, a world made "safe for democracy," and the self-determination of peoples—these are all intertwined with the rise of successive "lower" languages. . . . There are many instances in which language loyalty provided the momentum, the unity, and the devotion which carried libertarian movements of an avowedly sociopolitical nature to their successful conclusions. . . . [O]ne must also grant that religious and temporal wars, expansionism as well as Balkanization, irridentism and animosities, genocide and cultural subjugation have also been associated with language loyalty. (Joshua A. Fishman et al., *Language Loyalty in the United States: The Maintenance and Perpetuation of Non-English Mother Tongues by American Ethnic and Religious Groups* [The Hague, 1966], 25–26)

2. The phrase "language loyalty" comes from Fishman.
3. Henry Feingold, *A Midrash on American Jewish History* (Albany, 1982), 94.

4. See A. Z. Ben-Yishai, "Yevul sifruteinu bishnat tara"ts," *Sefer hashanah liyehudei amerikah* 1 (1930): 268–69.

5. See Mordecai Altshuler, *Hakibuts hayehudi bivrit hamo'atsot biyameinu* (Jerusalem, 1980), 206–34; Zvi Gitelman, *Jewish Nationality and Soviet Politics* (Princeton, 1972), 321–78; Alfred A. Greenbaum, *Jewish Scholarship and Scholarly Institutions in Soviet Russia, 1918–1953* (Jerusalem, 1978); Benjamin Pincus, *Yehudei rusiah uvrit hamo'atsot* (Beer-Sheva, 1986), 214–38; Elias Schulman, *A History of Jewish Education in the Soviet Union* (New York, 1971); Chone Shmeruk, "Hapirsumim biyidish bivrit hamo'atsot bashanim 1917–1960," in *Pirsumim yehudiim bivrit hamo'atsot, 1917–1960*, ed. Chone Shmeruk (Jerusalem, 1961), 55–131.

6. A recent official formulation of the role of Hebrew *reading* competency in the life of the "ideal Conservative Jew" relates to the quality of spiritual and intellectual experiences: "The . . . ideal Conservative Jew is . . . a learning Jew. One who cannot read Hebrew is denied the full exaltation of our Jewish worship and literary heritage." *Emet veemunah: Statement of Principles of Conservative Judaism* (New York, 1988), 57.

7. Chaim Zhitlowsky, "Unzer tsukunft doh in land," *Gezamelte shriften* vol. 10 (New York, 1919), 88–89, as quoted in translation in Paul Mendes-Flohr and Jehuda Reinharz, eds., *The Jew in the Modern World* (New York and Oxford, 1980), 389.

8. See Jonathan Frankel, *Prophecy and Politics: Socialism, Nationalism and the Russian Jews, 1862–1917* (Cambridge, 1981), 118–19, 172–74; J. S. Hertz, *Di yidishe sotsialistishe bavegung in amerike* (New York, 1954), 39–43; Moshe Mishkinsky, *Reshit tenu'at hapo'alim hayehudit berusiah* (Tel-Aviv, 1981), 151, 159, 172, 174, 176; Moses Rischin, *The Promised City: New York's Jews, 1870–1914* (New York, 1970), 115ff.; E. Tcherikower, ed., *Geshikhte fun der yidisher arbeter-bavegung in di fareynikte shtatn*, vol. 2 (New York, 1945), 285ff., 411ff.

9. Apart from the use of various European languages, international Zionist meetings even spawned their own argot based partly on Yiddish. See Raphael Patai, "The Languages of the Jews," in Patai's book, *Tents of Jacob: The Diaspora Yesterday and Today* (Englewood Cliffs, 1971), 128: "Yiddish, or rather a mixture of Yiddish and German, humorously referred to as *Kongressdeutsch*, still served as the *lingua franca* of the Zionist Congresses. . . . Even Hebrew had difficulty in making headway against *Kongressdeutsch* until . . . the Zionist Congresses were transferred to Israel."

10. On Yiddish and Zionism in America, see, e.g., *Geshikhte fun der tsionistisher arbeter bavegung in tsofn amerike* (New York, 1955), esp. vol. 1, 261–73; Shulamit Nardi, "Yiddish as Catalyst in American Zionism," in *Contemporary Jewry: Studies in Honor of Moshe Davis*, ed. Geoffrey Wigoder (Jerusalem, 1984), 79–83 (English section).

11. On the Evsektsiia and anti-Hebrew campaigns, see Mordecai Altshuler, *Hayevsektsiah bivrit hamo'atsot, 1918–1930* (Tel-Aviv, 1981), 290–93; Gitelman, *Jewish Nationality and Soviet Politics,* 276–86. On the status of Hebrew-language education and literature in the Soviet Union in those years, see Pincus, *Yehudei rusiah,* 221–22; Yehuda Slutsky, "Hapirsumim ha'ivriim bivrit hamo'atsot bashanim 1917–1960," in Shmeruk, *Pirsumim yehudiim,* 55–131.

12. Note, for example, the case of the sometime socialist, sometime anarchist, sometime Zionist, Ben-Zion Liber, a medical doctor who was active in political affairs in Romania prior to his emigration to the United States in 1904, but did not learn Yiddish until he came to New York and was eager to communicate directly with the multitudes of destitute immigrant Jews. See chapter 6 in this volume.

13. David G. Roskies, "The People of the Lost Book: A Cultural Manifesto," in *Orim, A Jewish Journal at Yale* 2, no. 1 (1986): 31.

14. Ibid.

15. See, e.g., the HIAS publications, *The Jewish Immigrant* and *The Jewish Immigration Bulletin.* On the issues of language, nationality, patriotism, and civic loyalty in the United States during the First World War, see Julius Drachsler, *Democracy and Assimilation* (New York, 1920).

16. One might also cite here the example of Louis Marshall, the Jewish establishment figure par excellence (leader of the American Jewish Committee and the American Jewish Joint Distribution Committee), who did not actually "cross over" in this manner, but who cooperated effectively with East European Zionists during the Versailles peace talks of 1919. Marshall was also prepared to address the immigrant public in its own language, learned Yiddish, and set up a newspaper, the *Yidishe velt* (1902) for that purpose.

17. See Patai, "Languages of the Jews," 107–30.

18. Hillel J. Kieval, "The Social Vision of Bohemian Jews: Intellectuals and Community in the 1840s," in Jonathan Frankel and Steven J. Zipperstein, eds., *Assimilation and Community: The Jews in Nineteenth Century Europe* (Cambridge, 1992), 246–75; idem, "Education and National Conflict in Bohemia: Germans, Czechs and Jews," *Studies in Contemporary Jewry* 3 (1987): 49–67; idem, *The Making of Czech Jewry: National Conflict and Jewish Society in Bohemia, 1870–1918* (New York, 1988).

19. Quoted in translation in Michael Meyer, *Response to Modernity: A History of the Reform Movement in Judaism* (New York, 1988), 248. The source is Kaufmann Kohler, ed., *Dr. David Einhorn's Ausgewaehlte Predigten und Reden* (New York, 1881), 65, 90. Cf. Naomi Cohen, *Encounter with Emancipation: The German Jews in the United States, 1830–1914* (Philadelphia, 1984), 58–63. Cohen quotes another prominent German rabbi in America, Bernhard Felsenthal, speaking in 1901: "Racially I am a Jew. . . . Politically I am an American. . . .

Spiritually I am a German" (*Encounter*, 63). Cited from Emma Felsenthal, *Bernhard Felsenthal* (New York, 1924), 19.

20. See Peter Y. Medding, "Segmented Ethnicity and the New Jewish Politics," *Studies in Contemporary Jewry* 3 (1987): 36, who quotes from the
1984–85 Joint Program Plan of the National Jewish Community Relations Advisory Council:

> Jewish community relations activities are directed toward the enhancement of
> conditions conducive to secure and creative Jewish living. Such conditions can
> be achieved only within a societal framework committed to the principles of
> democratic pluralism; to freedom of religion, thought and expression; equal
> rights, justice and opportunity; and within a climate in which differences
> among groups are accepted and respected, with each free to cultivate its own
> distinctive values while participating fully in the general life of the society.

Medding elsewhere also describes the political ramifications of Jewish distinctiveness in America:

> Christianity is the formative cultural system for the vast majority of Ameri-
> cans. . . . Jews see American society as Christian, despite the formal constitu-
> tional guarantees aimed at insuring the state's religious neutrality. Indeed, for
> American Jews, Christianity is not merely the religion of the majority of their
> fellow Americans—a relatively neutral aspect of social diversity—but is rather
> a fundamental feature of their own status definition. . . . To be Jewish in
> America means, among other things, not to be Christian. This translates politi-
> cally into a strong commitment to the separation of church and state. While
> many other Americans share this conviction, its meaning for American Jews is
> fundamentally different. No other identifiable group in America has a greater
> investment in separation than the Jews . . . because to breach separation is to
> Christianize America, relegating the Jews to second-class citizenship. A prime
> concern of Jewish politics in America is ensuring that this does not occur.
> (*The Transformation of American Jewish Politics*, Jewish Political Series, The
> American Jewish Committee/Institute of Human Relations [New York, 1989], 2)

In a 1985 survey, 86 percent of American Jews agreed with this
statement: "Whatever I may feel personally about nonconforming
groups—like black activists, feminists, homosexuals, and radicals—I
think Jews are much better off in an American society which can be
truly open to and tolerant of groups such as these" (Cited from Charles
S. Liebman and Steven M. Cohen, *Two Worlds of Judaism: The Israeli
and American Experiences* [New Haven, 1990], 106).

21. The integration argument is advanced in Medding, "Segmented Ethnicity," 40–44; cf. Charles Silberman, *A Certain People* (New York,
1985), 101–5; and Ze'ev Chafets, *Members of the Tribe: On the Road in
Jewish America* (New York, 1988), 38, and (quoting an actual AIPAC
[American Israel Public Affairs Committee] "pitch"), 46: "You have
representatives in the House and Senate, and they want to hear from
you. Your job is to let them know what you want. Remember, that's
your right as American citizens."

22. Commenting broadly on the experience of ethnic and religious groups in American society vis-à-vis questions of acculturation and linguistic-cultural distinctiveness, Fishman notes the coexistence of both strategies:

> The two processes—de-ethnization and Americanization, on the one hand, and cultural-linguistic self-maintenance, on the other—are . . . neither opposite sides of the same coin nor conflicting processes. Frequently the same individuals and groups have been simultaneously devoted to both in different domains of behavior. (Fishman, *Language Loyalty*, 15)

Notes to Chapter Two

1. Jacob Neusner explains the paradox of divine control and human responsibility as follows: salvation (according to the rabbis of the talmudic era) could only be achieved through becoming holy, and this meant absolute submission to the rule of God, including a humble acceptance of gentile rule in Exile: "Israel has the power to save itself by giving up its arrogant claim to be able to do anything to save itself. . . . Since the spiritual condition of Israel governs [the fulfillment of salvationist hopes], Israel itself holds the key to its own redemption. But this it can achieve only by throwing away the key." (*Messiah in Context: Israel's History and Destiny in Formative Judaism* [Philadelphia, 1984], 185, 210.) Cf. ibid., 114–15, 152, 211, 224, 231.

2. Jacob Neusner, "From Theology to Ideology: The Transformation of Judaism in Modern Times," in *Churches and States: The Religious Institution and Modernization*, ed. Kalman H. Silvert (New York, 1967), 14 (emphasis added).

3. See, e.g., Jacob Talmon:

> The salvationist hope was desperately needed by the Jews to explain to themselves and to others why the chosen people had been abandoned by God. The very idea of providential justice hinged upon it. The [Jews'] stubborn will to retain [their] uniqueness and the refusal to merge with the peoples around lacked all rationale without the sustaining vision of choice, sin, trial, atonement and salvation." (*The Myth of the Nation and the Vision of Revolution* [Berkeley, 1980], 175)

On theodicy, see Peter Berger, *The Social Reality of Religion* (London, 1969), 53–80.

4. Shlomo Zalman Landa and Yosef Rabinowicz, comps., *Sefer or layesharim* (Warsaw, 1900), 8, 23–25.

5. See, e.g., Ben-Zion Dinur, *Sefer haẓiyonut: mevasrei haẓiyonut* (Tel-Aviv, 1938), vol. 1, bk. 1, 4ff.; Yosef Klausner, *Hara'ayon hameshiḥi beyisrael mereishito ve'ad ḥatimat hamishnah* (Tel-Aviv, 1950), 229ff.; Yisrael Klausner, *Behitorer 'am, ha'aliyah harishonah merusiah* (Jerusalem, 1962); cf. David Myers, "History as Ideology: The Case of Ben-

Zion Dinur, Zionist Historian 'Par Excellence,' " *Modern Judaism* 8, no. 2 (May 1988): 167–93.

6. Jacob Katz, "Orthodoxy in Historical Perspective," *Studies in Contemporary Jewry* 2 (1986): 11, 16.

7. Jacob Katz, "The Jewish National Movement: A Sociological Analysis," in *Jewish Society through the Ages*, ed. Hayim Hillel Ben-Sasson and Shmuel Ettinger (New York, 1971), 269.

8. Gershom Scholem, "Toward an Understanding of the Messianic Idea in Judaism," in his *The Messianic Idea in Judaism and Other Essays in Jewish Spirituality* (New York, 1971), 35.

9. Stephen Sharot, *Messianism, Mysticism and Magic: A Sociological Analysis of Jewish Religious Movements* (Chapel Hill, 1982), 221.

10. See Eli Lederhendler, *The Road to Modern Jewish Politics: Political Tradition and Political Reconstruction in the Jewish Community of Tsarist Russia* (New York, 1989), chap. 5.

11. See Eli Lederhendler, "Politics and Messianism in Traditional Jewish Society: A Reconsideration," *YIVO Annual* 20 (1991): 1–22.

12. Lederhendler, *Road to Modern Jewish Politics*, chap. 5.

13. On a parallel use of rhetoric to create new political myths, see Lynn Hunt, *Politics, Culture and Class in the French Revolution* (Berkeley, 1984):

> Certain key words served as revolutionary incantations. *Nation* was perhaps the most universally sacred, but there were also *patrie*, constitution, law, . . . regeneration, virtue, and vigilance. . . . Revolutionaries placed such emphasis on the ritual use of words because they were seeking a replacement for the charisma of kingship. (21)

My thanks to Richard I. Cohen for bringing Hunt's book to my attention.

14. For discussion, see, e.g., Shmuel Almog, "Hameshihiyut keetgar laziyonut," in *Meshihiyut veeskhatologiah*, ed. Zvi Baras (Jerusalem, 1983), 433–38; Israel (Yisrael) Kolatt, "Ziyonut umeshihiyut," ibid., 419–32; Azriel Shochat, "Shemot, semalim vehavai behibbat ziyon," *Haziyonut* 9 (1984): 359–72.

15. David Gordon, "Beshuvah venahat tevashe'un," *Hamaggid* no. 14 (1863): 105–6.

16. Ibid., 106.

17. David Gordon, "Davar be'ito," *Hamaggid* no. 27 (1869): 214; cf. Yosef Salmon, "David Gordon ve'iton 'hamaggid': hilufei 'emdot laleumiyut hayehudit, 1860–1882," *Ziyon* 47 (1982): 153; and Isaac Barzilay, "'Hamaggid' vereishit hatenu'ah haleumit," *Bitzaron* 37 (1957–58): 179–82.

18. David Gordon, "Davar be'ito," *Hamaggid* no. 28 (1869): 222.

19. Mordecai Ben-Hillel Hacohen, "Dor holekh vedor ba," *Hashahar* 9 (1876–77): 124.

20. Yitzhak Kaminer, "Leumiyut yisrael," *Hamaggid* no. 38 (1879): 299.
21. Peretz Smolenskin, "'Et la'asot," *Hashaḥar* 4 (1872–73): 72 (repr., idem, *'Am 'olam* [Vienna, 1873], 130).
22. Smolenskin, " 'Am 'olam," *Hashaḥar* 3 (1871–72); repr., idem, *'Am 'olam.*
23. Smolenskin, " 'Am 'olam," 206–7 (repr., 44–45).
24. Ibid., 207 (repr., 45).
25. Ibid., 665 (repr., 97).
26. Ibid., 670–71 (repr., 102–3).
27. Ibid., 671–73 (repr., 103–5).
28. On Smolenskin's attitude toward Berlin Haskalah and German Jewish intellectuals, see Isaac Barzilay, "Smolenskin's Polemic against Mendelssohn in Historical Perspective," in *Proceedings of the American Academy for Jewish Research* 53 (1986): 11–48.
29. Alter Druyanov, ed., Shulamit Laskov, rev. and ed., *Ketavim letenu'at ḥibbat ẓiyon veyishuv ereẓ yisrael* (Tel-Aviv, 1982), vol. 1, 49–51, doc. 2.
30. David Gordon, "Yishuv ereẓ yisrael," *Hamaggid* no. 46 (1880): 386.
31. Ibid., (article in installments) no. 47 (1880): 396.
32. S. H., "Hadat vehaleumiyut," *Hashaḥar* 12 (1883): 40.
33. "Brit 'am," *Hashaḥar* 12 (1883): 205–6.
34. David Gordon, "Yom livnot gedarayikh," *Hamaggid* no. 18 (1881): 143.
35. Alexander Zederbaum, "Bin badavar vehaven bamareh," *Hameliẓ* no. 20 (1881): 405.
36. Peretz Smolenskin, "Mishpat 'ami," *Hashaḥar* 12 (1883): 11.
37. Mordecai Ben-Hillel Hacohen, "Kumu vena'aleh ẓiyon!" *Hamaggid* no. 24 (1881): 197 (emphasis added). And see the comment by "Ben Shem," in *Knesset yisrael* 1 (1886): 922: "The fundamental idea of those who preach for love of Zion is not to [promote the idea of] miracles and wondrous acts, not to bring the End closer, and not to revel in fantasies; nor do they seek for themselves the crown of Providence."
38. On the use of historical analogies, see Shavit, "Shivat ẓiyon," *Haẓiyonut* 9 (1984): 359–72.
39. Gershom Scholem, *Major Trends in Jewish Mysticism* (New York, 1941), 329–30; idem, "The Neutralization of the Messianic Element in Early Hasidism," in his *Messianic Idea in Judaism*, 176–202; cf. Rivka Shatz, "Hayesod hameshiḥi bemaḥshevet haḥasidut," *Molad*, n.s. 1, no. 1 (1967): 105–11; idem, *Haḥasidut kemistikah* (Jerusalem, 1968), 52, 168–76.
40. Scholem, *Messianic Idea*, 194–95.
41. Ibid., 195–96.
42. Ibid., 202; Hillel Zeitlin, *Haḥasidut* (Warsaw, 1910), 29; cf. Yaakov Hisdai, ed., *Sifrut haderush kemakor histori biyemei reshit haḥasidut* (Jerusalem, 1984), 106 (passage from *Meor 'einayim* by Rabbi Nahum of Czernowitz).

43. Scholem, *Messianic Idea*, 200–201; Shatz, "Hayesod hameshiḥi," 105–6.
44. Meir Orian, "Ḥazon hageulah vehagshamato bemishnat haḥasidut," in *Geulah umedinah: hakinus hashenati lemaḥshevet hayahadut* (Jerusalem, 1979), 35–36. (No editor named.)
45. Sharot, *Messianism, Mysticism and Magic*, 155–88.
46. Ben-Zion Dinur, "Reishitah shel haḥasidut," in his *Bemifneh hadorot* (Jerusalem, 1972), vol. 1, esp. 159, 170, 181–88, 207–27; or, in my translation, "The Origins of Hasidism and Its Social and Messianic Foundations," in *Essential Papers in Hasidism: Origins to Present*, ed. Gershon David Hundert (New York, 1991), 86–208.
47. Aryeh Morgenstern, *Meshiḥiyut veyishuv ereẓ yisrael bamaḥaẓit harishonah shel hameah hatesh'a 'esrei* (Jerusalem, 1985).
48. Ibid., 32–35, 66–113; cf. Dinur, "Hayesodot haideologiim shel ha'aliyot bishnot t"k-t"r [1740–1840]," in his *Bemifneh hadorot*, vol. 1, 69–79; Mordechai Breuer, "Hadiyun beshalosh hashevu'ot," in *Geulah umedinah*, 50.
49. Morgenstern, *Meshiḥiyut*, 71–72, 74–78.
50. Ibid., 38–65; Jacob Katz, " 'Al shnat t"r keshanah meshiḥit vehashpa'atah 'al pe'ilut haperushim lekiruv hageulah," *Kathedra* 24 (1982): 73–75; Abraham Duker, "The Tarniks (Believers in the Coming of the Messiah in 1840)," in *Joshua Starr Memorial Volume*, Jewish Social Studies Publications, no. 5 (New York, 1953), 191–201 (published by the Conference on Jewish Relations).
51. Morgenstern, *Meshiḥiyut*, 122–32, 156–59, 212–15, 220–40.
52. This entire thesis, as outlined by Morgenstern, is the focus of much scholarly dispute. On doubts raised about the impact of the "Lithuanian" group, their special character and their messianist motivation, see Menahem Friedman, "Lesheelat hatefisah shel talmidei haGra be'ikvot kriah bamekorot," *Kathedra* 24 (1982): 70–72; Israel Bartal, "Ẓipiyot meshiḥiyot umekoman bameẓiut hahistorit," *Kathedra* 31 (1984): 159–81.
53. Jacob Katz, "Demuto hahistorit shel harav Ẓvi-Hirsh Kalisher," in his *Leumiyut yehudit* (Jerusalem, 1982), 291–98 (first published in *Shivat ẓiyon* 2–3 [1952]); idem, "Meshiḥiyut uleumiyut bemishnato shel harav Yehuda Alkalai," *Leumiyut yehudit*, 310–28 (first published in *Shivat ẓiyon* 4 [1956]); idem, "The Jewish National Movement," 271–75; Sharot, *Messianism, Mysticism and Magic*, 218.
54. Yosef Salmon, " 'Aliyatah shel haleumiyut hayehudit bemerkaz eiropah uvema'aravah," *Haẓiyonut* 12 (1987): 8–9.
55. See David Vital, *The Origins of Zionism* (Oxford, 1980), 12–15; Katz, "Demuto hahistorit," 297; idem, "Orthodoxy in Historical Perspective," 10; Michael Graetz, *Haperiferiah haytah lamerkaz* (Jerusalem, 1982), 281–87.
56. The phenomenon has been noted by Azriel Shochat in "Hitrofefut haẓipiyot hameshiḥiyot eẓel rishonei hamaskilim berusiah vehahatḥa-

lot lesheifat hishtalvut baḥevrah harusit," *'Iyun uma'as* 2 (1981): 205–11.

57. Isaac Ber Levinsohn, *Te'udah beyisrael* (Vilna, 1828), dedication; idem, *Efes damim* (Vilna, 1837), 15; idem, *Beit yehudah* (Vilna, 1839), 333, 364.

58. Avraham Ber Gottlober, *'Anaf 'eẓ 'avot* (Vilna, 1858), 12, 61; idem, *Mizmor letodah* (Zhitomir, 1866), 10.

59. Adam Hacohen Lebenson, *Kelil yofi* (Vilna, 1856), 28.

60. " 'Ikva demeshiḥa," suppl., *Hamaggid* no. 37 (1859).

61. Yaakov Shmuel Halevi Trachtman, "Maamar me'ein yemot hamashiaḥ," suppl., *Hamaggid* no. 42 (1862).

62. *Hameliẓ* no. 20 (1869): 228–29.

63. "Davar be'ito: 'ikva demeshiḥa," *Hamaggid* no. 24 (1863): 189.

64. Michael Stanislawski, *For Whom Do I Toil? Judah Leib Gordon and the Crisis of Russian Jewry* (New York, 1988), 73; cf. 71–73, 100–102, 120–21.

65. Ibid., 121.

66. Ibid., 102.

67. This attitude typified many illustrious Russian *maskilim* and writers, including Isaac Ber Levinsohn, Avraham Mapu, Israel Aksenfeld, Ayzik Mayer Dik, Avraham Ber Gottlober, Joachim Tarnopol', and Alexander Zederbaum. See Mordecai Levin, *'Erkei ḥevrah vekhalkalah baideologiah shel tekufat hahaskalah* (Jerusalem, 1975), 228–31; Azriel Shochat, *Mossad harabanut mita'am berusiah* (Haifa, 1975), 69–70.

68. Shavit, "Shivat ẓiyon"; and see his essay, "Realism and Messianism in Zionism and the Yishuv," *Studies in Contemporary Jewry* 7 (1991), 100–127.

69. Shochat, "Shemot, semalim vehavai," 243–45.

Notes to Chapter Three

1. Harris Pearlstone (Yeshaya Heshl Perelstein, 1870–1947), "Zikhronot shel na'ar to'eh" (unpublished ms: privately owned copy in the possession of the family; photocopy in my possession—E. L.). The original handwritten copy was recently typed, and the typed copy runs 69 pages. I translated the memoir into English as "Memoirs of an Errant Young Man" (hereafter, *Memoirs*). The circumstances of the original composition of the memoir and of its later revision are mentioned by the author in his introduction (1–3 of the English version).

   I would like to express my gratitude to the family of Harris Pearlstone who have granted me permission to publish the relevant part of the manuscript, and in particular to Robert Raphael.

2. See Marcus Moseley, "Jewish Autobiography in Eastern Europe: The Prehistory of a Literary Genre" (Ph.D. dissertation, Trinity College,

Oxford University, 1990). Cf. David G. Roskies, "The People of the Lost Book," *Orim, A Jewish Journal at Yale* 2, no. 1 (1986): 27–28:

> For those of us raised from the start on and in Western culture, it is hard to imagine what a tremendous impact this discovery [of the self] had on Jewish self-perception in the last decades of the nineteenth century. For prior to that time there was no readily available language to describe the journey of the soul in search of perfection—save in the esoteric realm of Jewish mysticism which, unlike today, was then accessible to very few. Suddenly the confessional autobiography appeared, charting the painful break with traditional faith and practice. Suddenly the measure of a hero's success was the distance travelled from his place of birth; from the shtetl to Breslau and Berlin; from the yeshiva to the secular city; from Europe to America.

3. *Memoirs*, 16, 47–48.
4. Ibid., 9–10.
5. Ibid.
6. Ibid., 24.
7. Ibid., 71–73, 76–77.
8. Ibid., 15, 66–67, 75.
9. The memoir contains several instances in which the author takes obvious pride in his accomplishments, expressed in a kind of ingenuous one-upmanship (69–70, 72–77), a motif that appears in the fragments presented here, as well.

Notes to Chapter Four

1. See, e.g., Shlomo Zalman Landa and Yosef Rabinovich, *Sefer or layesharim* (Warsaw, 1900), 23ff.
2. See my book, *The Road to Modern Jewish Politics: Political Tradition and Political Reconstruction in the Jewish Community of Tsarist Russia* (New York, 1989), chap. 1, and cf. 68–83, 118–19.
3. On Orthodox politics in Russia in 1917 and in the immediately preceding years, see Mordecai Altshuler, "Hapolitikah shel hamahaneh hadati vehaharedi berusiah bishnat 1917," *Shvut: yahadut brit-hamo'atsot umizrah-eiropah* 15 (1992): 195–234. On the question of Orthodoxy and politics generally and the evolution of various Orthodox political models in twentieth-century Poland see Gershon C. Bacon, "Rabbis and Politics, Rabbis in Politics: Different Models within Interwar Polish Jewry," *YIVO Annual* 20 (1991): 39–59. On parallel contemporary issues in the East European immigrant community in Palestine, see Yehoshua Kaniel, *Hemshekh utemurah: hayishuv hayashan vehayishuv hehadash bitekufat ha'aliyah harishonah vehasheniyah* (Jerusalem, 1982).
4. Catalog number L2073.
5. The appeal itself is undated, but it bears a censor's approval dated 26 June 1903 (old style).

6. Israel Klausner, *Vilna, yerushalayim delita: dorot aharonim, 1881–1939* (Tel-Aviv, 1983), vol. 1, 21.

7. Ibid., vol. 2, 409–10; Henry Tobias, *The Jewish Bund in Russia from its Origins to 1905* (Stanford, 1972), 150–51.

8. Jonathan Frankel, *Prophecy and Politics: Socialism, Nationalism and the Russian Jews* (Cambridge, 1981), 140, 583 n. 22.

9. Chaim Weizmann to Theodor Herzl, in Weizmann's *Letters and Papers*, vol. 2, 307, cited by Frankel, *Prophecy and Politics*, 140.

10. Frankel, *Prophecy and Politics*, 140.

11. Klausner, *Vilna*, vol. 2, 409. Klausner also notes that the Vilna Bund was sufficiently strong in 1902–3 to fend off an attempt by the Zubatov-inspired "Independent" (legal) trade union party to establish itself among Vilna's Jewish workers.

12. Frankel, *Prophecy and Politics*, 140; Tobias, *Bund*, 150.

13. Klausner cites the case of Vilna Jewry's official preacher, Rabbi Zvi-Hirsh Rabinovich, who intervened in a cigarette-workers' strike in 1894 (*Vilna*, vol. 2, 400–401). And our own document notes that the local rabbis had issued an antisocialist statement in 1901.

14. Avraham Aeber Hirschowitz, *Beit avraham* (Jerusalem, 1923), Sermon no. 10, 51–52: "Eulogy at Congregation Ansche Knesseth Israel in Chicago, to Mourn the Martyrs who were Killed in the Cities of Russia." On Hirschowitz, see the obituary in *The Australian Jewish Chronicle*, 11 December 1924, 14. My thanks to David and Shari Satran for bringing Rabbi Hirschowitz's sermon to my attention.

15. Cited in Altshuler, "Hapolitikah," 199.

16. See Lederhendler, *Modern Jewish Politics*, chap. 1, esp. 33–35.

17. Klausner, *Vilna*, vol. 1, 23.

18. Ibid., 21.

19. Ibid., 29.

20. Tomashpol' was a small town, thirty-three miles east of Mogilev-Podolsk. In 1897, the census listed a total population of 4,972, of which 4,515 were Jews (*Evreiskaia entsiklopedia* [St. Petersburg, 1908–15, 16 vols.], vol. 14, col. 906).

21. Schocken Library (henceforth: SL) *Nun/59/5414*. Dated 28 December 1876, the document is a duplicate copy retained by Rabbi Yerusalimsky. (Telegrams to and from Yaakov, Yerusalimsky's brother, in December 1897, report on the younger Yerusalimsky's release from military service: SL *Yod het/325–28/2168*).

22. Biographical details on Moshe Nahum Yerusalimsky (hereafter: MNY) are taken from *Evreiskaia entsiklopedia*, vol. 8, col. 650.

23. See the capsule biography of MNY written by his son, David-Yona, in 1898: SL *Khaf-bet/169–72/2590*.

24. Ostrolenka, a district city in the Lomza province, had 12,949 inhabitants in 1897, of whom 4,823 were Jews (*Evreiskaia entsiklopedia* vol. 12, col. 152). According to the contract agreed to by the community

and MNY, the rabbi was to receive a salary of 20 rubles per week (1,040 rubles per annum) in addition to a residence and other fees (SL *Heh*/1–2/413, dated 20 Tammuz 5658 [=summer 1898]).

The contract was signed by thirty-two community officers (*parnasim* and *gabbaim*), including twenty-nine men representing the voluntary associations (*ḥevrot*) and the Hasidic congregations of the town. The list of associations gives a good sense of the subdivisions and manifold activities maintained even in so small a community at the end of the nineteenth century, as well as an indication of the communal authority wielded by the rabbi:

Mishna Association	Midrash Association
Ḥovat halevavot [Ethical studies] Association	Poor-Relief Fund
	Travelers' Welfare Association
The Great *Beit Midrash*	Burial Association
The Small *Beit Midrash*	Free Loan Association
Poor Brides' Welfare Fund	Gur [Ger] Hasidim
Aleksander Hasidim	*Shas* [Talmud] Association
Convalescent Visiting Association	
Talmud-Torah Association	
Torah Association	

25. SL *Heh*/31–34/422, dated 7 Tishrei 5659 (=1898), is an agreement between the Jewish community of Kamenka and MNY, obligating the community to repay everything that was owing to the rabbi (1,000 rubles), and prohibiting the hiring of any other rabbi until such time as the debt was cleared. Until that time, MNY remained the official rabbi of Kamenka. He deputized a local young man, one Kalman ben Dovid Tabachnik, to act as his stand-in. The document bears 218 signatures. Subsequently, the young man took over the post of rabbi in his own right, thus incurring the wrath of his mentor (SL *Lamed-alef*/127/3282, 131–33/3284, 161/3291).

26. Kielce had a Jewish population of 6,399 in 1897. Yerusalimsky's contract with the community stipulated that he would receive an annual salary of 1,500 rubles, in addition to the customary fees (the contract is SL *Heh*/13–14/417).

27. SL *Dalet*/419–20/389. David-Yona himself lived in Khorol', Poltava province, another small Ukrainian shtetl (population in 1897: 8,000; Jewish population: 2,056—*Evreiskaia entsiklopedia* vol. 15, col. 661).

28. *Evreiskaia entsiklopedia* vol. 8, col. 650. MNY authored the following: *Leshed hashemen* (Warsaw, 1881); *Minḥat moshe* (Warsaw, 1882); *Birkat moshe* (L'vov, 1886); and *Be'er moshe* (Warsaw, 1901).

29. Azriel Shochat, *Mossad "harabanut mita'am" berusiah* (Haifa, 1976), 93–97, 132–38.

30. See, e.g., the letter from MNY to several colleagues in the summer of

1906, in which he relays a call for a public fast *(ta'anit zibur)* issued by "the great rabbis of Kovno, Vilna and Telz"—SL *Mem gimel*/419/4726.

31. The advice was passed along by R. Salanter to R. Lifschitz, from Lifschitz to R. Isaac Elhanan Spector, and then relayed to hundreds of rabbis in Russia and Poland. See Shochat, *Mossad "harabanut mita'am,"* 96.

32. On the relationship between the Orthodox and the non-Orthodox or secularized Jewish leadership, see my essay, "Modernity without Emancipation or Assimilation? The Case of Russian Jewry," in Jonathan Frankel and Steven J. Zipperstein, eds., *Assimilation and Community: The Jews in Nineteenth Century Europe* (Cambridge, 1992), 327–37.

33. The Rabbinical Commission met in 1910, from March 2 to April 4 (old style). On the Commission, see Lederhendler, *Modern Jewish Politics,* 73–74, 76, 97, 135, 150–52; Shimshon Dov Yerushalmi, "Va'adot uve'idot harabanim berusiah," *He'avar* 3 (1955): 86–94. (Shimshon Dov Yerushalmi was originally Yerusalimsky, either a younger son of MNY or his grandson.)

34. SL *Mem-alef*/102–4/4387: *Sheilta* to MNY from Rabbi Nahum-Meir Fish, rabbi of Chęciny (Khentshin), and responsum by MNY, dated 13 Iyar 5664 (early summer 1904).

35. SL *Yod-alef*/431–32/1159.

36. SL *Mem*/355/4322. Henryk Sliozberg (1863–1937): lawyer and Jewish affairs advisor to Baron Horace Günzburg; a founder of the "Society for Equal Rights for the Jews in Russia" (1905) and the liberal (Kadet-affiliated) "Jewish People's Group" (1907). He was active in Jewish political life and closely involved in the business of the Duma.

37. SL *Dalet*/335/365. In the nineteenth century the Russian government designated official (or "crown") rabbis for each Jewish community who were subordinate to the local administration and were responsible for keeping communal records in Russian. The Jewish communities, however, continued to maintain their own rabbis, who were known as "spiritual" rabbis (to distinguish them from the official rabbis). On the dual rabbinate and problems associated with it, see Shochat, *Mossad harabanut mita'am;* cf. Lederhendler, *Modern Jewish Politics,* 51, 87, 91–92, 95, 99. On Rabbi Katzenellenbogen, see *Evreiskaia entsiklopedia* vol. 9, col. 392.

38. SL *Mem*/345/4318.

39. SL *Mem-zayin*/86/5190.

40. SL *Mem-zayin*/84/5188. The rabbis to whom the letter was addressed were, in all likelihood, R. Haim Soloveitchik of Brest-Litovsk and R. Haim-Oyzer Grodzensky of Vilna, both of whom were leading figures in the events in question.

41. SL *Lamed-vav*/227/3806.

42. SL *Mem-bet*/263/4530.
43. SL *Mem-zayin*/61/5165.
44. The date is according to the old Russian—Julian—calendar used in Russia until the end of 1917.
45. SL *Khaf-dalet*/420/2811.
46. SL *Dalet*/462/408: "*Kol koyre.*" On the scope of the desertion problem in the United States during this period, see Ari L. Fridkis, "Desertion in the American Jewish Immigrant Family," *American Jewish History* 71, no. 2 (Dec. 1981): 285–99; Reena S. Friedman, "Send Me My Husband Who Is in New York City," *Jewish Social Studies* 44, no. 1 (Winter 1982): 1–18.
47. SL *Nun-gimel*/67/5677. Rabbi Segal was selected as "chief rabbi" by twenty congregations of Galician Jews in New York City in 1892, in part out of opposition to the "Litvak" congregations that had selected Rabbi Jacob Joseph of Vilna as their "chief rabbi." Segal had lived in New York City since 1875. See Avraham Karp, *Ḥayei haruaḥ shel yahadut amerikah* (Jerusalem, 1984), 97–98.
48. SL *Khaf-gimel*/547, 553/2727.
49. SL *Mem*/315, 321/4311. The honorific terms employed suggest that the addressee is a hasidic leader. Along one side of the first page of the draft appears the Russian inscription "to Sheinfeld." On the political circumstances surrounding the Duma deliberations on municipal self-government for Congress Poland and the restriction of the Jewish franchise, see Stephen D. Corrsin, *Warsaw before the First World War: Poles and Jews in the Third City of the Russian Empire* (New York, 1989), 89.
50. Samuel Dickstein (1851–1939): mathematician and pedagogue, representative of Jewish "assimilationist" circles in the Warsaw city council, 1884–1918 (*Encyclopedia Judaica*, vol. 6, cols. 22–23). The Natansons were a prominent Warsaw family of bankers, industrialists, and scientists. Dr. Ludwik Natanson had been the head of the Warsaw Jewish community board from 1871 to his death in 1896. His brother, Henryk, was vice president of the Warsaw stock exchange. Ludwik's sons, Władysław and Edvard, were both prominent in public life, and were Dickstein's colleagues in the publication of the journal, *Prace matematyczno-fizyczne*. The reference in our document to "Natanson" may be to Władysław, or possibly to another family member, Henryk's son, Kazimierz, a lawyer and banker. See Jacob Shatzky, *Geshikhte fun yidn in varshe* (New York, 1953), vol. 3, 85, 410; Corrsin, *Warsaw*, 63, 91.

Notes to Chapter Five

1. Frederick Jackson Turner, in his famous lecture of 1893 to the American Historical Association ("The Significance of the Frontier in American

History"). The essay appeared in Turner's *The Frontier in American History* (New York, 1920), and has been reprinted numerous times.

2. J. Hector St. John de Crèvecoeur, *Letters from an American Farmer* (London, [1912] 1945), 41–43.

3. Ibid., 44.

4. John Higham, "Social Discrimination against Jews in America, 1830–1930," *Publication of the American Jewish Historical Society* 47, no. 1 (September 1957): 8–10; Moses Rischin, *The Promised City: New York's Jews, 1870–1914* (New York, [1962] 1970), 261ff.; David A. Gerber, "Cutting Out Shylock: Elite Anti-Semitism and the Quest for Moral Order in the Mid-Nineteenth-Century American Marketplace," in Gerber, ed., *Anti-Semitism in American History* (Urbana, 1986), 201–32; Naomi W. Cohen, *Encounter with Emancipation: The German Jews in the United States, 1830–1914* (Philadelphia, 1984), 249–78.

5. Hannah Arendt, *The Origins of Totalitarianism* (New York, new edn., 1973), 54.

6. Ibid., 55.

7. See Cohen, *Encounter*, chap. 6; John Higham, *Strangers in the Land: Patterns of American Nativism, 1860–1925* (New Brunswick, 1963).

8. *Temporary Suspension of Immigration*, Sixty-Sixth Congress, 3rd Session, House of Representatives, Report no. 1109, Dec. 6, 1920. Reprinted in Paul R. Mendes-Flohr and Jehuda Reinharz, eds., *The Jew in the Modern World* (New York, 1980). On annual immigration figures and percentages, see table 3 in Gerald Sorin, *The Jewish People in America: A Time for Building: The Third Migration, 1880–1920* (Baltimore, 1992), 58; cf. *The Jew in the Modern World*, Appendix, Table 6, 530.

9. *Temporary Suspension* (see note 8).

10. Ibid., Appendix A. Cf. "Hearings: Emergency Immigration Legislation" (Senate Committee on Immigration), Sixty-Sixth Congress, 3rd Session, 10.

11. Quoted in Martin E. Marty, *Modern American Religion*. Volume 2: *The Noises of Conflict, 1919–1941* (Chicago, 1991), 60, from *U.S. Congressional Record* (1924) 68:1: 5865, 5868–69.

12. Marty, *Modern American Religion*, 63–64, quoting André Siegfried, trans. H. H. Hemming and Doris Hemming, *America Comes of Age: A French Analysis* (New York, 1927), 3.

13. Oscar Handlin, *The Uprooted* (New York, 1951), 294.

14. On discrimination against Jews and on its gradual waning in the postwar period, see Henry L. Feingold, *Zion in America* (New York, 1974), 261–75; Charles H. Stember et al., *Jews in the Mind of America* (New York, 1966), esp. "Introduction," and 259–72 (Morton Keller, "Jews and the Character of American Life since 1930"); Marcia Graham Synnott, "Anti-Semitism and American Universities: Did the Quotas Follow the Jews?" in Gerber, *Anti-Semitism*, 233–71; Benjamin B. Ringer, *The Edge of Friendliness: A Study of Jewish-Gentile Relations* (New

York, 1967); Ronald Bayor, *Neighbors in Conflict: The Irish, Germans, Jews and Italians of New York City, 1929–1941* (Baltimore, 1978), 29; Eli Ginzburg, *My Brother's Keeper* (New Brunswick, 1989), 33–47, 110–16; Charles E. Silberman, *A Certain People: American Jews and Their Lives Today* (New York, 1985), chaps. 2–3; and Higham, "Social Discrimination."

15. Avrohom Liessin (Valt), *Lider un poemen* (New York, 1938), 287–88.
16. *Jews in the South*, ed. Leonard Dinnerstein and Mary D. Palsson (Baton Rouge, 1973), 7.
17. Quoted in Moses Rischin, *The Promised City: New York's Jews 1870–1914* (New York, [1962] 1970), 100 (emphasis added). Minnie Louis was a founding member of the National Council of Jewish Women.
18. Ibid. (emphasis added).
19. *Menorah Monthly*, August 1889, 92–93.
20. Ibid., August 1890, 65–67.
21. Ibid., September 1890, 158.
22. Ibid., August 1891, 61–66.
23. Kaufmann Kohler, "American Judaism." Reprinted in Mendes-Flohr and Reinharz, *The Jew in the Modern World*, 372–73.
24. *Der idisher imigrant* (New York), vol. 2, no. 1, January 1909.
25. Israel Friedlaender, "The Americanization of the Jewish Immigrant," in Friedlaender, *Past and Present: Selected Essays* (New York, 1961), 229–45. The article was first published in *Survey*, May 5, 1917, and was based on a memorandum submitted to the board of the Educational Alliance, a leading Jewish institution engaged in Americanization work.
26. Ibid., 241–44.
27. Tashrak, *Etikette* (New York, 1912). Zevin immigrated to the United States from Russia in 1889, at age seventeen. On him, his book, and the issues involved in this genre of immigrant literature, see infra, chap. 6, "Guides for the Perplexed: Sex, Manners and Mores for the Yiddish Reader in America."
28. Tashrak, *Etikette*, 114–18.
29. Ibid., 117.
30. Jenna Weissman Joselit, " 'A Set Table': Jewish Domestic Culture in the New World, 1880–1950," in Susan L. Braunstein and Jenna Weissman Joselit, eds., *Getting Comfortable in New York: The American Jewish Home, 1880–1950* (New York, 1990), 21.
31. The phrase "unappropriated wealth" occurs in David Potter's discussion of Turner's frontier thesis: David M. Potter, *People of Plenty: Economic Abundance and the American Character* (Chicago, 1954), chap. 7, esp. 160. Potter credits Walter P. Webb with the "explicit recognition that the very essence of the frontier was its supply of unappropriated wealth."
32. Cited in Hebrew Sheltering and Immigrant Aid Society, *Addresses De-*

livered at Third Annual Meeting at the Auditorium of the Educational Alliance, New York, Sunday, January 21, 1912 (4).

33. Kohler, "American Judaism," 372–73.

34. Ibid., 373.

35. Ibid. (emphasis added). Reference to the Puritans is implied in the allusion to the following passage from Edward Johnson's *Wonder-Working Providence of Sions Saviour in New England:* "Know that this is the place where the Lord will create a new Heaven, and a new Earth in, new Churches and a new Common-wealth together. . . . " See Perry Miller and Thomas H. Johnson, eds., *The Puritans,* rev. edn. (New York, 1963), vol. 1, 145.

36. David Philipson, "Message of the President," Proceedings of the Nineteenth Annual Convention of the CCAR, *Yearbook of the CCAR* 18 (1908): 145–46 (emphasis added) (reprinted in Mendes-Flohr and Reinharz, *The Jew in the Modern World,* 387).

37. Chaim Zhitlowsky, "Unzer tsukunft doh in land," *Gezamelte shriften,* vol. 10 (New York, 1919), 89 (emphasis added).

38. Ibid.

39. Ibid., 88–89.

40. Judah L. Magnes, "A Republic of Nationalities," *The Emanu-El Pulpit,* Feb. 13, 1909, 5 (reprinted in Mendes-Flohr and Reinharz, *The Jew in the Modern World,* 390–93).

41. Ibid. (emphasis added).

42. Ibid. (emphasis added).

43. Ibid.

44. Magnes, "The Melting Pot," Oct. 9, 1909, *The Emanu-El Pulpit,* vol. 3, 1909, reprinted in Arthur A. Goren, ed., *Dissenter in Zion: From the Writings of Judah L. Magnes* (Cambridge, 1982), 101–6.

45. See Ben Halpern, "The Americanization of Zionism," *American Jewish History* 69, no. 1 (September 1979): 27: "Accordingly, while Brandeis and his aides employed the rhetoric of a clash between 'democracy' and 'plutocracy' with vigor and conviction, they fought for the American Jewish Congress less for ideological reasons than because of the advantage they hoped to gain for the specific objectives of the Zionist organizations."

46. See Naomi W. Cohen, *Not Free to Desist: A History of the American Jewish Committee, 1906–1966* (Philadelphia, 1972), 90–96; idem, *Encounter with Emancipation,* 129ff.

47. Stephen S. Wise, "Jewish Conference or Congress: Which and Why?" Address given before the Free Synagogue at Carnegie Hall, October 3, 1915. *The Case of the Jewish People,* Addresses Delivered before the American Jewish Congress, by Dr. Stephen S. Wise. The American Jewish Congress, New York, 1922, 19.

48. "American Israel and Democracy" by Rev. Dr. Stephen S. Wise. Issued by the Executive Organization Committee for the American Jewish

Congress, New York City. Address delivered at the Preliminary Conference for the organization of an American Jewish Congress, held at the Hotel Walton, Philadelphia, March 26, 27, 1916, 4, 7, 11.

49. *Forverts*, Nov. 4, 1900, 4.
50. See Feingold, *Zion in America*, 169–72; Rischin, *Promised City*, part 4; Arthur Liebman, *Jews and the Left* (New York, 1979); Will Herberg, "The Jewish Labor Movement in the United States," *American Jewish Year Book* 53 (1952), 58, 65–66; John Bodnar, *The Transplanted: A History of Immigrants in Urban America* (Bloomington, 1985), chap. 3.
51. Melvin Dubofsky, " 'The Political Wilderness,' " *American Jewish History* 73, no. 2 (1983): 160.
52. Feingold, *Zion in America*, 158, 178. Cf. Rischin, *Promised City*, 236; Arthur A. Goren, "The Promises of *The Promised City*: Moses Rischin, American History and the Jews," *American Jewish History* 73, no. 2 (1983): 177–78.
53. Irving Howe, *World of Our Fathers* (New York, 1976), 321–22.
54. Liebman, *Jews and the Left*, 207–12, 219–25.
55. Ibid., 225 and 212; cf. 226–36.
56. John H. Laslett, *Labor and the Left: A Study of Socialist and Radical Influences in the American Labor Movement, 1881–1924* (New York, 1970), 135.
57. Ibid.
58. *Forverts*, July 4, 1900, 4.
59. Ibid., Nov. 3, 1900, 4.
60. Ibid., Nov. 5, 1900, 1.
61. Ibid., Nov. 6, 1900, 4.
62. Ibid., Nov. 8, 1904, 4.
63. Abram Lipsky, "The Number of Jewish Voters in New York," *American Hebrew* 92 (Nov. 1, 1912): 5.
64. *Jewish Immigration Bulletin*, January 1913, 12.
65. *Forverts*, Nov. 16, 1910.
66. Thomas McLean Henderson, "Tammany Hall and the New Immigrants, 1910–1921," Ph.D. dissertation, University of Virginia, 1973, 113.
67. Ibid., 148; cf. *Forverts*, Nov. 9 and 10, 1910; Nov. 4, 1914.
68. *Forverts*, July 4, 1904, 4.
69. Gerald Sorin, *The Prophetic Minority: American Jewish Immigrant Radicals, 1880–1920* (Bloomington, 1985), 86.
70. *Forverts*, Nov. 1, 1906, 4.
71. Ibid., Nov. 3, 1906, 4.
72. Ibid., Nov. 5, 1910, 4; Nov. 6, 1910, 4.
73. Ibid., July 4, 1902, 4.
74. Ibid., July 4, 1910, 4.
75. Ibid., Nov. 7, 1910, 4.
76. Ibid., Nov. 10, 1910, 1, 4.
77. Ibid., Nov. 9, 1910, 4.

78. See, e.g., address by Senator Penrose to the Third Annual HIAS Meeting, January 1912 (see above, note 32), 14–15; and President Woodrow Wilson's address at naturalization ceremonies in Philadelphia, May 10, 1915, in Julius W. Muller, ed., *Presidential Messages and State Papers*, vol. 10: Wilson (New York, 1917), 114–16.
79. Paul A. Carter, *Revolt against Destiny: An Intellectual History of the United States* (New York, 1989).

Notes to Chapter Six

1. Ben-Zion Liber, "Fizishe kultur," *Yidishe kultur*, March 1955, 37–39. Liber, who immigrated to the United States from Romania in 1904, was a medical doctor with political ties to socialist, Zionist-socialist (Poale Zion), and anarchist groups. He wrote prolifically and lectured widely on public health and hygiene, vegetarianism, art, and education. He died in 1958 in New York City, where he was professionally associated with the New York Psychiatric Institute and was professor emeritus of psychiatry at the New York Polyclinic medical school. At his death he was eulogized by *Yidishe kultur*, in the inimitable style once perfected by the socialist press, as "[a man] who was well-known and much beloved among the broad working masses." (*Yidishe kultur*, June–July 1958, 58). See Ephraim Auerbach, et al., eds., *Leksikon fun der nayer yidisher literatur* (New York, 1963), vol. 5, cols. 53–54; Zalman Raizin, *Leksikon fun der yidisher literatur* (Vilna, 1927), vol. 2, cols. 117–19.
2. Liber, "Fizishe kultur," 37.
3. I. J. Singer, *Of a World That Is No More* ([New York, 1971] London, 1987), 124–25.
4. I understand that a major project on the cultural impact of Americanization on immigrant women is being undertaken by Hannah Kliger and Barbara Schreier, both of the University of Massachusetts. Dr. Kliger presented a paper on Yiddish etiquette manuals at the Tenth World Congress of Jewish Studies, Jerusalem, August 1989.
5. Liber, *Dos geshlekhts lebn* (New York, 1918), 13, and "Foreword" to the 1919 edition.
6. *Unzer gezund* 3 (1910): 213–14.
7. Simon Kuznets, "Immigration of Russian Jews to the United States: Background and Structure," *Perspectives in American History* 9 (1975): 94–100. Among Jews immigrating between 1899 and 1914, 24.4 percent were under age 14, 69.8 percent were between age 14 and 44, and only 5.8 percent were over age 45. In 1913, 28.8 percent of all Jewish arrivals were single adults (HIAS, *Annual Report* 1913, 56, Table 3).
8. Figures on the arrival of unaccompanied women were compiled by representatives of the Hebrew Sheltering and Immigrant Aid Society (HIAS). Figures for the year 1913 show that a total of 16,093 "unaccompanied Jewish girls" had arrived in the United States (at five major

ports—the majority having arrived at New York: 13,588)—constituting a quarter of all female Jewish immigrants. Of these, 9,000 (56 percent) were met by family members; 6,533 (40.6 percent) were met by other relatives; and 555 were met by friends or intended husbands (3.4 percent). HIAS, *Annual Report 1913*, 56, 60 (Tables 3 and 16).

For the first five months of 1914, a total of 4,813 (28.7 percent of all arriving Jewish females) were in the "unaccompanied" category. Of these, 55.9 percent were met by family members, 41.2 percent by other relatives, and 2.9 percent by friends or intended husbands. *Jewish Immigration Bulletin* 4, no. 7 (July 1914), 9 (Table 11).

The isolation of the immigrant woman from home and family, and the attendant need for other sources of advice and guidance in such matters as love, marriage, and parenting, contributed to the usefulness of advice columns in the Yiddish press. This point is stressed by Maxine S. Seller in "Defining Socialist Womanhood: The Women's Page of the *Jewish Daily Forward* in 1919," *American Jewish History* 76, no. 4 (1987): 429–31.

9. *Vos yedde meydl darf visn*, 71, translated from the English by K. Tepper, published by the Max N. Maisel Press for Literature and Knowledge, at 424 Grand Street on Manhattan's Lower East Side.

10. *Unzer gezund* 4 (1911). *Unzer gezund* was sold to subscribers at the price of ten cents per monthly issue, or one dollar a year. The printing cost per copy came to twenty-five cents each for a press run of one thousand copies; twenty cents each for a press run of two thousand. Liber sold out his entire stock of the first issue, which (if the ten-cent charge is a proportional reflection of printing costs) can be estimated at four thousand copies. He received many requests for reprints (see ibid., 286). Liber's first edition of *Dos geshlekhts lebn* (1914) was also sold out within the first few months. See "Foreword to the Second Edition," 12.

11. Also the work of the Maisel Press, the book appeared in 1910 and 1911.

12. Hebrew Publishing Company, also a Lower East Side enterprise.

13. Lucy Dawidowicz, "From Past to Past," *Conservative Judaism* 22, no. 2 (1968): 24, 26.

14. Sanger, *Vos yedde meydl darf visn*, 5. Cf. Liber, *Geshlekhts lebn*, 33. On the salience of the prostitution problem in urban America and in the Jewish community in particular see Edward Jay Bristow, *Prostitution and Prejudice: The Jewish Fight against White Slavery, 1880–1939* (Oxford, 1982), 146–80, 220–25, 233–35; Jenna Weissman Joselit, *Our Gang: Jewish Crime and the New York Jewish Community, 1900–1940* (Bloomington, 1983), 45–53; Arthur A. Goren, *New York Jews and the Quest for Community* (New York, 1970), 139ff.; Judith L. V. Joseph, "The Nafkeh and the Lady: Jews, Prostitutes and Progressives in New York City, 1900–1930," Ph.D. dissertation, State University of New York at Stony Brook, 1986.

15. Liber, *Geshlekhts lebn* (1918 edn.), 29–33. The physiological "necessity" for young men to have sexual relations was "one of the first things a young man learns" (ibid., 32). This passage was censored by the U.S. Post Office in the 1927 edition.

16. Ibid., 19–20. See also the "foreword" to the 1919 edition. Other points in Liber's credo included: "The Jewish people will be free only when it lives in Eretz Israel on such a basis that no capitalist institutions will exist there. . . . More art for everyone, and greater artistic freedom. . . . All religions are dangerous and are an obstacle to progress and freedom. . . . People with any sense of justice should not eat meat. . . . With enough determination, it is always possible to avoid bloodshed."

17. Sanger, *Vos yedde meydl darf visn*, 70–71.

18. Ibid., 6, 9. Cf. Liber, *Geshlekhts lebn*, 32, 135ff., 146–47.

19. Spencer, *Di ertsiung*, 182–88.

20. Ibid., translator's introduction. Yiddish works on the subject appeared somewhat later: e.g., H. G. Salutsky's *Gaystige ertsiung fun kind* (New York, 1920).

21. "One of the first principles of a modern education ought to be: the child must be taught the benefits of following the rules of proper health habits, so that the need for fresh air becomes ingrained in him. . . . Radical parents—remember this!" *Unzer gezund* 3 (1910): 167; cf. ibid., 170, 177–79, 187ff.

22. Sanger, *Vos yedde meydl darf visn*, 12. Exercise and lots of outdoor physical activity were also recommended as a way to tire girls out before bedtime, which would minimize the risk of masturbation (ibid., 31–34).

23. Ibid., 10–11. See also the cartoon about corsets in *Unzer gezund* 3 (1910): 171.

24. Sanger, *Vos yedde meydl darf visn*, 10.

25. Ibid., 15–17.

26. Ibid., 36.

27. Ibid., 36–37.

28. Seller, "Defining Socialist Womanhood," 433–34. Cf. Mari Jo Buhl, *Women and American Socialism, 1870–1920* (Urbana, 1981), 276.

29. Liber, *Geshlekhts lebn*, 14, 159ff., 180ff. Sections on birth control were banned by the Post Office and deleted from the 1927 edition.

30. E.g., Liber's lectures on childbirth and on "Parents, Children, and Physical Hygiene" in New York in January 1911, and on "Normal Sex Life" and "Sexual Diseases" in Boston later that same month. See *Unzer gezund* 4 (1911): 287.

31. There is some anecdotal evidence on the popularity of Margaret Sanger among young Jewish women in New York. See Neil M. Cowan and Ruth Schwartz Cowan, *Our Parents' Lives: The Americanization of Eastern European Jews* (New York, 1989), 170, 172, 183.

32. *Unzer gezund* 4 (1911): 278.
33. One of Liber's correspondents was Emma Goldman, who supported his efforts (see *Unzer gezund* 4 [1911]: 282).
34. Printed in the front matter of the second, third, and fourth editions of *Dos geshlekhts lebn*.
35. E.g., Ivan Bloch, *Dos geshlekhts lebn fun unzer tsayt* (Warsaw, 1934–36); G. Weber, *Dos geshlekhts lebn fun mener un froyen* (Warsaw, 1936); idem, "Kreftungs-mitlen in geshlekhts lebn" (pamphlet: Warsaw, n.d.); Reinhold Gerling, "Der mansparshoyn mit velkher [*sic*] men tor nisht khassene hobn" (Warsaw, 1928); H. Grinboym, *Di bavustzinike shvangershaft* (Warsaw, 1937); G. Vandeli, *Vi azoy dergreykht men erfolg in der libe?* (Warsaw, 193?); T. Veld, *Libe un hayrat* (Warsaw, 1930); Emil Jason, *Dos seksuele lebn bay mener un froyen* (Warsaw, 1934); B. Mannheim, "Vi azoy farhit men zikh fun onanizm" (Warsaw, 1934); Alexander Parczewski, *Moreh nevukhim: menlikhe geshlekhts-shvekhe iz a kultur-krankhayt fun unzer tsayt* (Warsaw, 1937); Lev S. Friedland, *Vegn vos me redt nisht: notitsn fun a doktor vegn geshlekhts laydn* (trans. from Russian, Warsaw, 1931).
36. Weber, *Geshlekhts lebn*, 9–10; "Sadly, these days only a small proportion of young men are chaste until their wedding night" (52).
37. Ibid., 29–30. One consequence of the preoccupation with material success was the postponement of marriage, especially among males. Weber recommended that women marry between age 21 and 26, and that men marry between ages 27 and 31. He noted, however, that the average age at marriage among middle-class couples was 26 for women and 30 for men. Among working-class couples the respective ages were lower.
38. Ibid., 30–32, 44–45, 92–96.
39. Ibid., 71–76. A more helpful attitude may be found in a TOZ (Jewish Health Organization) pamphlet, "Yidishe froy, dervakh! Vi azoy zikh tsu farhitn fun ungevunshener shvangershaft" ("Jewish Woman, Awake! How to Prevent Unwanted Pregnancies" [Lemberg, 1934]).
40. Thomas Kessner, "The Selective Filter of Ethnicity: A Half Century of Immigrant Mobility," in David Berger, ed., *The Legacy of Jewish Migration: 1881 and Its Impact* (New York, 1983), 172, 178. Between 1880 and 1905, the share among Russian Jewish heads of household employed in upper white-collar jobs rose from 5.2 to 15.1 percent, and those in lower white-collar jobs rose from 15.8 to 25.1 percent. Among their offspring, 58.1 percent filled white-collar jobs by 1925.
41. Israel Joseph Zevin (Tashrak) immigrated to the United States from Russia in 1889, at age 17. He edited and wrote for two Orthodox Yiddish newspapers in New York, the *Tageblatt* and the *Morgen zhurnal*. Many of his popular articles appeared in the latter paper's "Home and Family" column. In addition, he wrote numerous short stories and feuilletons, mostly humorous vignettes of immigrant life in America, and also wrote compilations of *midrash*. He continued his association with the

Orthodox community, serving as a warden (*gabbai*) in an Orthodox synagogue. See Raizin, *Leksikon*, vol. 4, cols. 902–12.

42. Tashrak, *Etikette*, 36; cf. 14–15.

43. Ibid., 36.

44. Ibid., 26–30.

45. Jeffrey Gurock points out the importance of this issue to the young, American-raised Orthodox Jews of Harlem when they set out to found their own synagogues in the early years of the twentieth century. See his book, *When Harlem Was Jewish* (New York, 1979), 117.

46. Tashrak, *Etikette*, 114–18.

47. Ibid., 114. Among his criticisms of the Orthodox immigrant *shul* or *beys medresh* were the following: too much gossip, business discussions and joking during services, disorder, a lack of English-speaking ushers, and the frequently dirty appearance of prayer shawls. "Cleanliness is godliness ("getlikhkayt") and courtesy is human decency ("menshlikhkayt")," he summed up (118).

48. Ibid., 117.

49. Ibid., 107–13.

50. Ibid., 117.

51. John Murray Cuddihy, *The Ordeal of Civility* (New York, 1974), 12–14:

> The differentiations most foreign to the *shtetl* subculture . . . were those of public from private behavior and manners from morals. . . . Civility requires . . . the bifurcation of private affect from public demeanor. . . . "Niceness" is as good a name as any for the informally yet pervasively institutionalized civility expected—indeed required—of members (and of aspirant members) of that societal community called the civic culture. Intensity, fanaticism, inwardness—too much of *anything*, in fact—is unseemly and bids fair to destroy the fragile solidarity of the surface we call civility. . . . [Civility] is not merely regulative of social behavior; it is an order of "appearance" constitutive of that behavior.

52. Tashrak, *Etikette*, 15, 31.

53. I.e., coarse; ibid., 33. Interestingly, the internalization of this middle-class American view of loudness has been noted in the Yiddish socialist press as well by Seller, "Defining Socialist Womanhood," 436.

54. Tashrak, *Etikette*, 35.

55. Ibid., 42–43. American women, he asserted, were known the world over as the best dressed. Here, again, it is noteworthy that Tashrak's objections to loud dress and to overattention to fashion were also echoed in the socialist *Forverts:* see Seller, "Defining Socialist Womanhood," 434.

56. Tashrak, *Etikette*, 44–63, 248–49, 303–7.

57. Ibid., 305.

58. Ibid., 145–55, 170–71, 176–81, 238–45, 307–10. On divorce, see 263–71. On the perils of love, see also Seller, "Defining Socialist Womanhood," 429–30.

59. Tashrak, *Etikette*, 155–68, 228–38.
60. Ibid., 196–228.
61. Ibid., 249.
62. Ibid., 252–56.
63. Ibid., 254.
64. Cuddihy (*Ordeal of Civility*, 14) makes this error, and approvingly quotes Irving Howe's poetic assessment of shtetl life: "Having love, they had no need of politeness." Howe, "Sholem Aleichem: A Voice of Our Past," in his *A World More Attractive: A View of Modern Literature and Politics* (New York, 1963), 215.
65. I myself stumbled on this material by chance, spotting Liber's book at a used book sale.

Notes to Chapter Seven

1. David G. Roskies, "The People of the Lost Book, A Cultural Manifesto," *Orim, A Jewish Journal at Yale* 2, no. 1 (1986): 7–34.
2. Robert Alter, in "The Jew Who Didn't Get Away: On the Possibility of an American Jewish Culture," *Judaism* 31 (1982): 274–86; Cynthia Ozick, "Toward a New Yiddish," in her book, *Art and Ardor: Essays* (New York, 1983), 153–71—even in the caveat added (151–52) in 1983 to the views she had originally expressed in 1970 (see Ozick, "America: Toward Yavneh," *Judaism* 19, no. 3 [1970], 264–82); Gershon Shaked, *Ein makom aḥer* (Tel-Aviv, 1988), "Alexandria," 138–84.
3. See, e.g., Robert Alter, "The Inner Migration of Hebrew Prose," in David Berger, ed., *The Legacy of Jewish Migration: 1881 and Its Impact* (New York, 1983), 100–101; J. K. Mikliszanski, *Toledot hasifrut ha'ivrit beamerikah* (Jerusalem, 1967), 8–29; Jacob Kabakoff, *Ḥaluẓei hasifrut ha'ivrit beamerikah* (Tel-Aviv, 1966), 11–15; Menahem Ribalow, ed., *Antologiah shel hashirah ha'ivrit beamerikah* (New York, 1938), Introduction: "Hashirah ha'ivrit beamerikah," 2–7; Ephraim Epstein, *Soferim 'ivrim beamerikah*, 2 vols. (Tel-Aviv, 1952), vol. 1, 5–8.
4. The ubiquitous nature of this theme, from Wasserman to Kafka, from Delmore Schwartz to Philip Roth (and see the comment by Cynthia Ozick quoted at the end of this essay), can be extended to include many American writers, including black writers and others.
5. Mikliszanski, *Toledot hasifrut*, 7–8.
6. Gershon Shaked, at a symposium on American Judaism, "Babylonia or Alexandria?" held at Hebrew Union College, Jerusalem, 23 April 1990.
7. Ribalow, *Antologiah*, 3; Alter, "Inner Migration," 100. Even their contemporaries were not terribly impressed with their work. Mordecai Ze'ev Raizin wrote, in 1901, that "American Hebrew literature will not be able to raise itself from its current low level," although he allowed for the chance that the new immigration from Russia would bring

fresh talent to American shores. M. Z. Raizin, "Sefat 'ever vesifrutah beamerikah," *Hashiloah* 8 (1901): 549.

8. Ribalow, *Antologiah*, 4–5.
9. Ibid.; Kabakoff, *Haluzei hasifrut*, 14.
10. Ephraim Deinard, *Kohelet amerikah* [English title: *Koheleth America: Catalogue of Hebrew Books Printed in America, 1735–1925*] (St. Louis, 1926), 1.
11. Ibid., 1, 10, 13, 17–18, 30, 50, 56–57.
12. Shimon Ginsburg, "New York," in Ribalow, *Antologiah*, 163–66.
13. Ribalow, "Mitat sedom umerhav-yah," *Sefer hayovel shel "Hadoar"* (New York, 1927), 10.
14. Ibid., 10–11, 14.
15. Ibid., 10, 14.
16. Ibid., 14–15.
17. Ibid., 11, 15.
18. Alter, "Inner Migration," 97: "[W]ith very rare exceptions, their efforts to acclimate Hebrew literature to the American scene were strained, self-conscious and artistically unconvincing." See also Epstein, *Soferim*, vol. 1, 5, 8–9; Mikliszanski, *Toledot hasifrut*, 122 (and see note 37 below).
19. *Sefer hashanah* (hereafter SH) 2 (1935), "Lasefer" ["Preface"], unpaginated.
20. Zvi Rudy, "Hayehudim bapilosofiah shel yameinu," SH 1 (1930): 117–18.
21. Avraham Goldenberg, "Hayehudi haeiropi," SH 1 (1930): 16. The allusion is to a line in Gordon's poem, "Hakizah 'ami": "Be a man abroad and a Jew in your home. . . . " (to which Ahad Ha'am replied in his essay, "Haadam baohel" ["Be a Man in Your Home"]).
22. Mordecai Goldenberg, "Shirei milhamah," SH 1 (1930): 213–15.
23. Ribalow, "Havai hehayim vehavayat hasifrut," SH 1 (1930): 7.
24. Ibid., 8.
25. Ibid., 9.
26. A. Z. Ben-Yishai, "Yevul sifruteinu bishnat tara"z," SH 1 (1930): 268–69.
27. Nissan Touroff, "Hayahid veharabim baomanut uvasifrut," SH 4 (1939): 193–214.
28. Azriel S. Chipkin, "Hahinukh ha'ivri benyu-york," SH 1 (1930): 291–308.
29. Meir Waxman, "Harabanut veharabanim beamerikah," SH 1 (1930): 309–16.
30. Mikhl Ivensky, "Tenu'at hapo'alim hayehudim beamerikah," SH 1 (1930): 324–25.
31. It is not clear why it took five years to produce the second volume, and why a further three years elapsed between the second and third volumes. It is possible that financial considerations played a role: the

Yearbook depended on support from donors and received funding from at least one foundation. It is likely, too, that is was technically difficult to edit and produce a book of that scale, and with so many authors. See the Preface to volume 2, and the list of contributors published at the back of that volume (help is acknowledged from the Lucius N. Littauer Fund of the CCAR and from the Cincinnati Cultural Foundation).

32. Preface to volume 2.
33. For example: Nissan Touroff, "Pilosof boded (leyovel hashiv'im shel Santayana," SH 2 (1935): 117–25; Joseph Rader, "Ziyurei hamikra shel Michaelangelo," SH 2 (1935): 171–77; Yohanan Twersky, "Freud ha-za'ir," SH 3 (1938): 163–74; Avraham Regelson, "Elohei hatev'a bashi-rah haamerikayit," SH 3 (1938): 294–305; Isaiah Rabinowitz, "Eugene O'Neill—meshorer hameziut," SH 3 (1938): 318–25.
34. Nahum Sokolow, "Haleumiut ha'ivrit mitokh haenoshiut," SH 2 (1935): 25–47.
35. Ibid., 20–25.
36. Israel Efros, "Vigvamim shotekim" (1932); Ephraim Lissitsky, "Med-urot do'akhot" (1937). Benjamin Silkiner had pioneered the Hebrew "Indian" poem in 1910 with his "Mul ohel timorah." On Silkiner, see Jacob Kabakoff, "B. N. Silkiner and His Circle: The Genesis of the New Hebrew Literature in America," *Judaism* 39, no. 1 (1990): 97–103. Lissitsky and others also wrote "black" poems along similar lines (e.g., Lissitsky's "Beoholei kush" and "Yisrael beshittim," the latter pub-lished in SH 7 [1944]: 283).
37. Hillel Bavli, "The Modern Renaissance of Hebrew Literature," in Louis Finkelstein, ed., *The Jews: Their History, Culture and Religion*, 3rd edn., 2 vols. (Philadelphia, 1966), vol. 2, 918; Kabakoff, *Haluzei hasif-rut*, 17–18; Epstein, *Soferim*, 10; Alter, "Inner Migration," 101:

> It is not surprising that some of the immigrant Hebrew poets should have tried to discover on these shores a new kind of pastoral landscape, producing quasi-epics or balladic lucubrations on Indian and Negro life. Such dalliance with American exotica was of course a self-conscious act of willed acculturation, a symptom of the problem rather than a solution to it.

38. Avraham Zvi Halevy, "Yonim 'al pasei 'illit," SH 4 (1939): 186.
39. Ribalow, *Antologiah*, 8–11.
40. Ibid., 7.
41. See, e.g., Naftali Gross, "Hasifrut haidit beamerikah," SH 3 (1938): 385:

> The monotonal symphony of the older generation has fissioned into a medley of melodies . . . realism, expressionism, symbolism. . . . Their poems and stories are individualistic expressions of men's souls in the contemporary city: moods, images, tender yearnings . . . intimacies of the heart, intricacies of experience, and despair.

42. Ruth Wisse, "*Di Yunge:* Immigrants or Exiles?" *Prooftexts* 1, no. 1 (1981): 45–46.

43. Herman Frank, "Hamazav hakalkali shel hayehudim beamerikah," SH 2 (1935): 319–26; Uriah Zvi Engelman, "Hayehudi beta'asiyah haamerikayit," SH 2 (1935): 330; see also Isaac M. Rubinow, "The Economic and Industrial Situation of American Jewry," *Jewish Social Service Quarterly* 9, no. 1 (1932): 28–37.

44. Ivensky, "Hayehudim vehamahalakh hehadash," SH 3 (1938): 368.

45. Shmuel K. Mirsky, " 'Al hadarshanut vesifrut haderush beamerikah," SH 3 (1938): 393–94.

46. Daniel Persky, "Hukat arzot haberit shel amerikah," SH 3 (1938): 404–15.

47. Ginsburg, "Ner neshamah (idiliah amerikayit)," SH 4 (1939): 20–37.

48. Ibid., 37.

49. Reuven Wallenrod, "Behug hamishpahah," SH 4 (1939): 38–77.

50. Judah Pilch, "Hakolelim hayehudim beamerikah," SH 3 (1938): 396–403; Herman Frank, "Hakehillah hamit'havah," SH 4 (1939): 379–87; idem, "Tenu'at hamerkazim bearzot haberit," SH 5 (1940): 363–70; Mikhl Ivensky, "Hamisdarim hayehudim beamerikah," SH 4 (1939): 388–404.

51. Zvi Scharfstein, "'Esrim vehamesh shenot hinukh 'ivri beamerikah," SH 2 (1935): 296–311; idem, "Sifrei limud uzeramim hevratiim," SH 4 (1939): 260–75; Shmuel Blumenfeld, "Mishnat Dewey vehahinukh ha'ivri," SH 5 (1940): 291–300.

52. Uriah Zvi Engelman, "Leheker hamishpahah hayehudit beamerikah," SH 3 (1938): 369–80; idem, "Simanei ziknah beyahadut amerikah," SH 5 (1940): 341–52.

53. Eisig (Yitzhak) Silberschlag, "Biyemei Isabella," SH 4 (1939): 151–76; continued in SH 5 (1940): 76–102.

54. Yohanan Twersky, "Herzl," SH 4 (1939): 106–44.

55. Gabriel Preil, "Washington ma'aleh zikhronot," SH 4 (1939): 180.

56. Ibid.

57. Ibid.

58. See, e.g., Preil's "Shirei vermont," SH 5 (1940): 109–10.

59. E.g., Israel Efros's poem of the American Gold Rush, excerpts published in SH 5 (1940) as "Leerez hazahav," 27–35; and published in full as *Zahav* (1942).

60. See the opening statement of purpose by Shmuel Mirsky, in the new Orthodox journal, *Talpiot* 1, no. 1 (1943): 1.

61. Ribalow, "Kohelet," SH 5 (1940): 161, 168 (emphasis in the original).

62. Hillel Bavli, "Mul hamifraz," SH 5 (1940): 36–38; idem, "Demuyot beharim," SH 6 (1942): 338–44.

63. Meir Waxman, "Rashi, mefaresh hamikra," SH 5 (1940): 115–38; Mirsky, "Rashi uveit midrasho," SH 5 (1940): 139–50.

64. Nissan Touroff, "Hokhmat haparzuf," SH 5 (1940): 186–209.

65. Aharon Zeitlin, "Nakam veshilem," SH 5 (1940): 69–72.

66. S. Rosenfeld, "Hurban hayahadut befolin," SH 5 (1940): 311–24.

67. Dov (Bernard) Weinryb, "Meah shanah shel hagirah yehudit leameri-kah," SH 5 (1940): 327–40; Israel Naamani, "Arẓot haberit uve'ayat hapelitim hayehudim," SH 5 (1940): 371–78.
68. A. S. Shvarts, "Kan," SH 6 (1942): 382.
69. A. Hefterman, "Hegeulah beor haagadah," SH 7 (1944): 172–81.
70. Aryeh Tartakower, "Sakh hakol shel ḥurban," SH 7 (1944): 441–55.
71. Zalman Shneour, "Luḥot genuzim," SH 6 (1942): 253. The poem was published in its entirety only in 1948.
72. Preil, "Azlu milim," SH 6 (1942): 384.
73. Ibid.
74. Touroff, "Hapsikhologiah shel milḥamah," SH 6 (1942): 7–31.
75. Abraham Joshua Heschel, "Yirat shamayim," SH 6 (1942): 61–72.
76. Efros, "Begermaniah ha'atikah," SH 7 (1944): 208–9.
77. Efros, " 'Am," SH 7 (1944): 210.
78. These included several anthologies; a joint collection on Hebrew and Yiddish literature (in Hebrew translation): Aḥisefer (New York, 1943); a short-lived quarterly, Mabu'a; and two jubilee volumes for Hadoar. See Getzl Kressel, Leksikon hasifrut ha'ivrit badorot haaḥaronim, 2 vols. (Merhavia, 1967), vol. 2, 855–56; Encyclopedia Judaica vol. 14, cols. 149–50.
79. Efros, "Yoter ḥeresh meḥalom," SH 8/9 (1946): 85.
80. Efros, "Maḥar yakum el," ibid.: 86.
81. Efros, "Uleaḥar hashiv'ah," ibid.: 88.
82. Aharon Zeitlin, " 'Al efer umah shenisrefah," ibid.: 129–30. The titles of his other poems in the volume are: "Shir kelot hakiẓin" (126), "Shir haneḥamah" (127) and "Demut ẓel bevarshah" (128–29).
83. Preil, "Aviv benyu-york," ibid.: 173–74. His poem in the same volume, entitled "What the Heart Sees" ("Maḥazot shebalev") is, on the other hand, much closer to his normal style.
84. Benjamin Ressler, "Ḥayal shav min hamilḥamah," ibid.: 131–42.
85. Jacob Lestchinsky, in ibid.: 523–45.
86. Hefterman, "Ha'ayarah hayehudit beamerikah," ibid.: 546–57.
87. See, e.g., Milton Gordon, Assimilation in American Life: The Role of Race, Religion and National Origins (New York, 1964), 181–82, citing studies by Ruby Jo Reeves Kennedy, "Single or Triple Melting Pot? Intermarriage in New Haven, 1870–1940," American Journal of Sociology 49, no. 4 (1944); Kennedy, "Single or Triple Melting Pot? Intermarriage in New Haven, 1870–1950," American Journal of Sociology 58, no. 1 (1952); and Benjamin Goldman and Alvin Chenkin, The Jewish Population of New Orleans, 1953 (Council of Jewish Federations and Welfare Funds, 1954).
88. Zeitlin, "Himnon lamedinah," SH 10/11 (1949): 9.
89. Ribalow, "Besha'ar habayit hashelishi," SH 10/11 (1949): 13–27.
90. Ibid., 18–20, 26.
91. Ibid., 19.

92. Ibid., 26–27.
93. Lissitsky, "Hitler lifnei kes-hamishpat," SH 10/11 (1949): 156–62.
94. A. S. Shvarts, "Harav vehadayan," ibid.: 212–17.
95. A. R. Malachi, "Roshmei gezerot ta"kh veta"t, ibid.: 425–44.
96. Moshe Prager, "Shirat haavadon leyahadut eiropah," ibid.: 583–616.
97. A piece of trivia that relates to the question of "community" among the American Hebraists is the fact that Zvi Scharfstein's son, Ben-Ami, married the daughter of Israel Efros, and settled in Israel in 1955. Ben-Ami Scharfstein taught philosophy at Tel-Aviv University, where Efros was appointed the first rector in 1954. See *Jerusalem Post*, 12 April 1990.
98. Ozick, "A New Yiddish," 152.
99. Alter, "Inner Migration," 97.
100. Raizin, "Sefat 'ever," 175, 467, 546; Touroff, "Hayaḥid veharabim," 193–214.

Notes to Afterword

1. Stephen J. Whitfield, *Voices of Jacob, Hands of Esau: Jews in American Life and Thought* (Hamden, 1984), 4.
2. Ibid., 10.
3. Ibid., 11–12.

Index